A Bullet Well Placed

A Bullet Well Placed

One Hunter's Adventures around the World

by

Johnny Chilton

SAFARI PRESS INC.

The trademark Safari Press ® is registered with the U.S. Patent and Trademark Office and in other countries.

Chilton, John L.

First edition

Safari Press Inc.

2005, Long Beach, California

ISBN 1-57157-322-4

Library of Congress Catalog Card Number: 2004097119

10 9 8 7 6 5 4 3 2 1

Printed in the USA

Readers wishing to receive the Safari Press catalog, featuring many fine books on big-game hunting, wingshooting, and sporting firearms, should write to Safari Press Inc., P.O. Box 3095, Long Beach, CA 90803, USA. Tel: (714) 894-9080 or visit our Web site at www.safaripress.com.

This book is dedicated to my wife, Alexandra, who has always encouraged my pursuits of writing and hunting. Without her encouragement, this book would not have been possible.

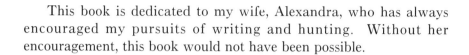

I wish to thank all of the professional hunters and guides whom I have had the pleasure to hunt with over the years. You are truly an impressive group, and you have earned my deepest respect. I extend a special round of thanks to African professional hunters John Fletcher and Gerard Miller. Both wielded significant influence in forming my outlook on hunting and were patient in the process. Thanks also to Craig Boddington and John Wooters, who years ago took the time to offer advice and words of encouragement to a novice writer. I hope in this work that I have not let them down.

Table of Contents

Prologue

In 1975 my dad, John P. Chilton, fulfilled a dream, when he went on his first African safari. Most important for me, he took me with him. He was forty-one at the time (my age at the time of writing this book), and I was all of fifteen. The hunting was, of course, fantastic and unlike anything we had experienced at home in the United States. The diversity and abundance of game, the hunting skills and tactics of our professional hunter and his native trackers, and the added element of hunting the world's most dangerous animals, animals that would gladly hunt you back made that safari a dream come true. But it was Africa itself that had the most profound effect on me. Having arrived in Kenya a typical suburban American youth, I found myself suddenly immersed in a primitive culture, chiefly the Masai of East Africa, whose way of life was as foreign to mine as fire is to ice. At the time, places like China, Africa, and Bangladesh were just pictures in a social studies book to me, or film clips on the evening news. But if this trip came as a shock, it was a much-needed shock, drawing me out of my sheltered cocoon and waking me to the rest of the world. My world.

Africa brought out the philosopher in me. It made me think, it made me ponder, it made me question. Things I had taken for granted before my trip now led me to ask, *Why is it done that way? Does it make sense? How is this handled in other cultures?* And most important, *Where does fact end and bias begin?* Africa altered the way I learned, in that I no longer digested information without question. Now I wanted to chew on each thought, inspect it, make up my own mind before I sealed it away in my brain.

Dad and I shared a journal on this trip. My entries were mostly hard facts: dates, times, names, and the like, and thus I have been forced to flush out much of the trip from memory. It is surprising, looking back, what I thought important and what I thought not. It seemed to me important, for instance, to record the exact distance and shot placement of every bullet, and yet I left out altogether my visit to a striptease, which had to be a highlight at age fifteen. Nor do I mention anywhere Africa's impact on my thoughts about God and life. Such is youth. Thus, much of my recollection of that first safari is the product of long-term memory and not the sharp crystal focus of immediate observation; nevertheless, I believe my account and descriptions to be accurate.

Kenya, East Africa
June–July, 1975

It was midmorning when we finally departed Nairobi in the Land Cruiser, quickly leaving the buildings and residences behind and embarking upon the endless plains that are East Africa. Soon zebra, ostrich, and giraffe appeared out the windows, and ivory-colored gazelle named after some fellow called Grant. Here and there skinny natives wrapped in faded red cloth pushed at herds of even skinnier cattle to search for grass on the parched earth. Dad and I shook our heads in disbelief. It was all new to us, and I pestered Fletcher with a hundred questions.

Fletcher was John Fletcher, a deeply tanned and eager-eyed professional hunter in the employ of Ker, Downey, and Selby, a topnotch outfit. It was he who presided over this crew and in whose care we would entrust ourselves for the next thirty days. Age forty or so, Fletcher was entertaining with his British accent and foreign manner. He was a good-looking fellow despite a nose slightly squashed in the center—was it from boxing or rugby? He had a head of thick, wavy blond hair and the toned muscles to make a man half his age jealous. He was all English gentleman and polite as a little old lady at a tea party, yet I pity the fellow who would spit in his cup.

Around noon that first day, we stopped in one of the small villages that were scattered across this dusty landscape like lonely craters in a vast desert. While Fletcher was busying himself with fuel and last-minute supplies, I noticed a native mother sitting on the hard, dry ground in the shade of a tall tree. Several tots were playing in the dirt around her, including a boy of five or so who was completely naked. His tiny body was gray with dust, and he was skinny as a jack handle— except for a potbelly, which protruded like a balloon. What came next I could never have guessed. The little devil started urinating on his mother's feet, and he was laughing as if it were the funniest thing in the world. His mother picked up a stick with the intention of whacking him, but he grabbed it from her and began to hit her instead, all the while laughing. I thought, *What kind of a world is this, in which a child pees on his mother's feet, then beats her with a stick?*

Several hours later, we pulled into a towering island of flat-topped acacias that hid a sprawling camp inside. The shady canopy brought relief to what was now the heat of the day and served as a ceiling of sorts above the scattering of large green tents. A muddied, slow-moving river ran alongside. As we came to a stop, the black staff swarmed out to greet us, all smiles and handshakes. There were tent boys, trackers, skinners, a driver, a mechanic, a cook, and one of just about every other occupation you could think of for keeping this tented city in operation.

"Jambo!" they said, one after the other, shaking our hands. Greetings!

"Jambo," we answered.

Nearly everyone in camp was from a different tribe, and each tribe had its own identifying marks—either in the piercing of ears or scars or some other bodily disfigurement. Maketi, the skinner, was a wee fellow. He spoke no English but smiled and nodded his head anxiously in our presence. It was his smile that took me aback. His two front teeth, in accordance with tribal custom, had been filed to sharp points that resembled—of all things—the fangs of a vampire. If that weren't enough, there were pebble-size welts, in a distinct pattern, adorning Maketi's small face. The odd design circled under each eye, making a *V* at the temple, then connected above the eyebrows. One or two others had similar bumps on their faces, but in different configurations.

"The scars are made as an infant," Fletcher later explained. "Hooked thorns are inserted into the flesh between two parallel cuts in the skin. Once the wounds heal the thorns are removed, leaving those welts."

At first glance, it appeared to me as if the bottom halves of the mechanic's ears were missing. He was a tall, somber fellow in a blue, garage-style jumpsuit. The droopy lobes, I soon realized, had been twisted up and over the top half of each ear. Perhaps he had grown tired of their dangling, or perhaps it was a tribal custom, but either way, it gave him the appearance of a wrestler with cauliflower ears. Others sported large holes in the top halves of their ears, in which they stored everything from plugs of wood to spent rifle casings. One fellow carried the cork from a wine bottle.

The two trackers were Sangau and Mumaku, both masters of their craft. Sangau, the head tracker, who had been with Fletcher for many years, was a quiet, ever-smiling fellow with a long, friendly face and watery dark eyes. Mumaku was round faced and muscled like a sprinter—there was not an ounce of fat anywhere on him. He wore a serious expression until you caught his eye, and then he would grin, showing a conspicuous gap between his two front teeth. The job of these two was to stand in the back of the truck and scout for game, and to tap on the roof when they saw something—which was always before I saw it.

After getting our gear settled in the tent and our rifles unpacked, we left in the truck with the intention of shooting a wildebeest for bait. The only problem was that I did not know what a wildebeest was, and I was too embarrassed to ask. When we finally got set up to shoot, there were several different animals in sight, and I ended up shooting at an unsuspecting antelope, hoping it was the wildebeest. Fortunately I missed, so no harm was done. Dad then made quite a good shot, hitting the wildebeest at three hundred yards. His marksmanship gave me the chance to examine that funny-looking animal up close.

The wildebeest is oxlike in appearance, with a long tail, humped back, flat black face, and question mark–shaped horns. It has a gait equally comical, often kicking or pitching to the side for no apparent reason. As we took photos of our first African kill, Fletcher shared with us the natives' explanation for the wildebeest's odd features: *"The Masai say that when God was done making all the animals, he had several parts left over. From these, he made the wildebeest."*

We spent the rest of that afternoon hanging the wildebeest for lion bait and looking over herd after herd of animals, the names of many of which were new to our ears. We got back to camp after dark and ate a quick dinner before turning in. I hit the sack at 9:00 P.M. dead tired but

The blue wildebeest—one of God's leftovers.

woke at 3:00 A.M. because of jet lag; I could not return to sleep. Just before sunrise, as I lay thinking on my cot, there came from outside a deep groaning sound followed by three short grunts. Soon after, the tent boy came through the dark with a hissing lamp; he unzipped the front flap and carried in hot tea and coffee on a tray. As Dad and I got dressed, we heard the strange sound repeated several times.

"A male lion," Fletcher explained at breakfast. "The Masai claim he is saying: 'Whose land is this? . . . Mine, mine, mine.'"

We went out after breakfast for another wildebeest, and this time I redeemed myself. There were four of the funny-looking creatures standing in a row, all broadside and all studying us with those quizzical dark faces. Perhaps they had heard of my poor shooting the day before and figured themselves to be safe at 250 yards. Perhaps they had seen few hunting parties in their life. Whatever the case, their ease allowed me to take my time, get steady on the shooting stick, and send the bullet where I wanted it. The bull bucked and ran, kicking up dust, but the shoulder shot proved lethal; no follow-up was needed. Fletcher propped the fellow upright for pictures, making it look like it was a live pet resting in front of me, with legs tucked underneath and the earth cleared around it—a far cry from the "hanging dead deer" photos of home.

Farther on, Dad took two Grant gazelles with shots that appeared effortless and graceful—if the word "graceful" can be used to describe shooting an animal. Yes—they were graceful. Each buck collapsed immediately at the well-placed shot and lay as if asleep. The size of a Hill Country deer, the Grant is an ivory-colored animal with dark horns that stretch quite high for its size. The pointy, ribbed horns serve for prodding the coveted females, which the male is reluctant to leave behind lest another suitor take its place. A dark stripe across the eyes makes them appear even larger than they are.

At the campfire that night, I helped myself with Dad's permission to a bottle of Tusker lager. It was sour but cold and bubbly, which felt wonderful in the throat after the dry heat of the day. The only soft drink was Coke. Earlier I had tried a bottle of tonic water, which was not too terrible once I got past the first pucker. According to Fletcher, tonic water had been a lifesaver for the Indian coolies that built the railroads. The sour drink contains quinine, a natural prophylactic against malaria.

Early the next morning Dad took a second wildebeest for lion bait, making another great shot. Then I proceeded to make a fool of myself. I missed two zebras, a wildebeest, one gazelle, and a warthog.

Masai—once the most feared warriors on the continent.

I was really upset with my performance. It was particularly embarrassing because I had wanted to shoot well in front of Fletcher. As our professional hunter, he was a hero of sorts to me, and someone I wanted very much to emulate. But the harder I tried, the worse I shot. Then, somewhere between the zebras and the wildebeest, the riflescope struck me between the eyes on the recoil and my shooting really went to hell.

Fletcher finally said, "Johnny, I think you are flinching."

"I think the gun is off," I said, unsure what "flinching" meant but sure that it could have nothing to do with me. That was all that was said at the time.

Back in the truck, we encountered a young zebra with a broken front leg. Fletcher wasn't sure how it had happened, but the leg was clearly beyond repair: The bone was severed, with the lower part dangling by a shred of hide. He asked Dad to finish it off, which was easier said than done. Despite its handicap, the zebra gave us quite a chase by truck, around trees and termite mounds, before we could get near.

Then we hung Dad's wildebeest for lion bait, a fascinating process in itself. To spread its scent, we dragged the wildebeest behind the vehicle until Fletcher had selected a suitable bait tree. In the blink of an eye Sangau had scaled the tree barefoot, with the end of a rope clenched in his teeth. He passed the rope over a thick limb and lowered it to Mumaku, who tied it to the hind legs of the bait animal. Then, with the other end fastened to the front of the truck, Fletcher put the vehicle into reverse until the bait was hanging at the right height. Next Sangau secured the rope from above. Finally, Fletcher and his trackers fashioned a blind from a large bush, hollowing out the inside, filling in the chinks with cut branches and bundles of grass, clearing the ground of all noisemaking twigs and leaves, and installing two little peepholes from which to shoot. It was startling how fast a harmless-looking bush could be transformed into a lethal blind—all with the intention of getting the hunter within shooting range of the lion.

The next day arrived. Here's Dad's story: *Today was the most exciting day of my life. Early this morning we crept into the lion blind. It was quite dark. At dawn the bait came into view, and we could see that a lion had eaten part of the wildebeest. But it was nowhere in sight. A ten-minute wait brought out a jackal, which tried to nip a piece of the shredded meat hanging from the bait. Suddenly, His Majesty the King came running out from his resting place to chase off the offending jackal.*

Giraffe.

This lion was magnificent and huge. It walked around the bait, toward us without stopping, then behind the bait and tree, where it paused. I had a clear shot, and it flinched when I fired. It ran to its left, where John fired, knocking it down. In an instant it was up again and disappeared into the thick brush. Sangau heard it moaning, so we confidently went for the truck half a mile away to let it die and stiffen up. However, when we returned with the truck—no lion and only little blood. It was only wounded enough to be mad, and in thick brush! This lion was certainly in its element, not ours.

We found a discouraging sight. My bullet had grazed the bark of the tree that the lion had walked behind. At sixty-five yards I had missed my shot by nearly a foot. That's what comes with firing while your heart is pumping at two hundred beats per minute and you can't breathe. My bullet had given it only a flesh wound. John, Sangau, and I set off on its trail with only a slight blood spoor to follow. Sangau removed his sandals; he was absolutely silent in his bare feet. Fletcher's words repeated over and over in my mind: "When you follow a wounded lion into the bush, one of you is going to get hurt."

When the grass got shoulder high, John sent me back to the truck. Feeling at fault for the mess I had caused, I vowed not to let him send me back again—if I had the chance. They returned to the truck after *five or ten minutes, and we resumed driving. When we came to a stop, I told him, "John, I really want to go with you."*

John shook his head. "Look—when I go in after a wounded lion, the most dangerous thing in the bush is not *the lion. The most dangerous thing in the bush is the nervous hunter behind me with his finger on the trigger."*

"I understand. I am calm. I made a mistake on my first shot, but I will not screw up again. I really want to go in after it with you."

Fletcher thought about it for a moment. Then he looked me in the eye and said, "OK."

"But remember this: If the lion manages to get at me, he likely will knock me down and be standing or lying on top of me. I will give him something to chew on, like my arm—to keep him away from my head. Whatever you do, don't shoot down at him. The bullet could go through the lion and hit me. Sit down and shoot up at the bastard."

I nodded in agreement and carefully checked my rifle and spare cartridges.

This time, John, Sangau, and I headed into the tall grass and brush, then down into a dry creek bed. Sangau, armed only with a machete, followed the lion's trail with his X-ray eyes. I was ready. This time there was no turning back. We tracked the animal down into the dry creek bed and up on both banks. When we came to thick spots, where visibility was poor, we threw rocks, hoping to get a growl or some other response in return. But all was silent. Several times John thought he had the big cat spotted, but the rock throwing produced nothing.

Finally we decided to circle in front of the cat, where we knew it had not crossed, and suddenly we . . . smelled it. It was that close! We surrounded the brush and threw stones, but still there was no response. At last, checking back at the creek bed, John found the lion's tracks on top of ours! It had sneaked by us very quietly.

We again circled, this time farther down. This was the fourth circle we had made, and by now an hour had gone by. But there was no sign of the cat. If it hadn't changed course, it had to be up creek. This time, John and I waited on the creek bank while Sangau walked back to make a lot of noise, hoping to drive the cat toward us. But before he could start the drive, he spotted the cat. It growled. Sure enough, the lion came for us, moving quickly in the open of the creek bottom.

I was the first to spot it, at twenty-five yards. It was trotting directly at me, and moving well. You would never have known it was wounded. I fired into the chest, and the heavy .458 bullet knocked it back on its haunches. Just then John got a clear shot from the left, and the .500 bellowed and knocked the lion over. The lion then did something very strange: It started spinning around and around on the spot, like the tiger in the story of Little Black Sambo that ran round and round till it turned into butter. It was moving so fast it was a blur. John fired once more and I fired twice before the lion was quiet.

It is 450 pounds, ten years old, and in its prime. The tree shooter redeems himself!

Everyone in camp was ecstatic, and we examined every tooth and claw while Dad reenacted the drama for the eager audience. Several Masai warriors paid homage by posing for photos over the big cat, their spears raised and ready. To me, the most amazing thing about the lion once the hide had been removed was the massive amount of muscle that covered its thick frame and powerful legs. Dark muscles bulged everywhere. It helped explain the phenomenal strength that the big felines possess.

Dad's lion was a great success and would probably be the highlight of the trip for him, but for me things weren't going well. My shooting the following morning showed no improvement. I made a poor shot on a Grant gazelle, and the animal ran off wounded. We had to climb a steep, rocky slope to find it, and we could not be quiet with all the rocks crunching underfoot. Just as we would get within range, the

An exceptionally wide-horned impala. Lake Manyara.

gazelle would dash off and we had to start all over again. When we finally caught up with it, it was looking at us head on. I sat down, wanting to get as steady as possible, aimed, fired, and missed.

We followed the herd down the pebbly slope and got as close as we could, which was just under three hundred yards. When the gazelle took off again and disappeared in the brush, I figured it was gone for good. It was moving well, and we would never find it in the thick bush— and if we did, it would be difficult to get off a shot. But just then curiosity got the better of the ram. It stepped back out to have another look at us. Now, standing, I finally made a good shot, using the shooting stick as a rest. (The shooting stick, it should be noted, is a wonderful device. Fashioned from three wooden poles with a tightly wound strip of inner tube at one end, it is carried collapsed and like a spear until you are ready to shoot, at which point it is snapped open like a photographer's tripod, making quite a steady rest.) The ram sprinted ten yards and fell over, dead. Fletcher slapped me on the back.

"Good shot, that," Fletcher said as we walked back to the truck. His praise made me smile. "I wonder why your gun shoots well sometimes, but not others?" I just shrugged.

Dad then continued his fine shooting with a great shot on a warthog. We had spotted it on the plains and expected a long-range shot, but the warthog took cover in a creek bed. The stubborn pig held until we were within thirty yards, then flushed like a pheasant at top speed, whipping up little dust clouds in his wake. Dad rolled him on the run with one snap shot.

[In 1999, when Dad donated the majority of his animal trophies to a museum in Wyoming, he asked me if there were any that I would like to have. Among them all, it was this warthog that I chose. My parents had hung him over the bar and called him "Charley." He was quite the conversation piece. People *ooh*-ed and *ahh*-ed over the lions, leopards, and buffalo, but it was the warthog that always tweaked their curiosity. They would point to the warthog and say, "What is that?"]

Dad talks about what happened the next day: *Crossing the plains below the Nguruman Escarpment, we came upon several buffalo. We gave chase on foot, crouching over. I used John's .375 to place a shot just behind the front shoulder of a large buffalo quartering away. The bullet broke ribs on both sides and passed through both the heart and lungs, lodging under the skin on the far side. Incredibly, the buffalo ran off! We pursued and fired at its rear on the run with the .458—just creasing it. We caught up with the animal some three hundred yards on, lying down. Finished it with the .458.*

The buffalo that wouldn't die. Luckily, it was on the plains below the Nguruman Escarpment, instead of deep in the bush, when Dad tackled it.

Masai appeared out of nowhere as Sangau and Mumaku butchered the buffalo for transport back to camp. How they found us, I have no idea. Maybe they heard the gunshots. I thought we were deep in the bush, miles from the nearest native. Immediately a small fire was built and fist-size chunks of meat were tossed on. They used no grill or stick: The meat was tossed directly into the flames. After letting it sizzle for a minute, the Masai grabbed the chunks out, charred black on one side—red, raw, and bloody on the other—and devoured them just like that, with the blood and juices running down their chins and chests. The Masai get to eat meat so rarely, according to Fletcher, that they are ravenous for it and gorge on huge quantities when it is available. The warriors returned for chunk after chunk until their bellies were noticeably swollen. One native, who was sitting cross-legged on the ground, steadfastly pounded on a buffalo leg bone with a rock, and I wondered what he was up to. Eventually he cracked the large bone open and with a knife scooped the clear, jellylike marrow into his mouth.

Not one ounce of meat, organs, bones, or hide went to waste. (The Masai warriors' colorful, paint-decorated shields are made from buffalo hide. That the shields will turn spears and arrows, as well as the claws and fangs of angry lions, is a testament to the toughness of the leather.) It was hard to believe how quickly a one-ton buffalo could be stripped down to nothing as the natives chopped, sliced, and hefted slabs of meat to carry home. More natives arrived, smiling and waving greetings. Soon there was nothing left but a bloodstain on the ground.

Unfortunately, my own poor shooting continued on the following day. When I shot at an impala and missed, John took my gun and said, "Tell you what, Johnny, let's check this gun of yours." He placed the loaded rifle on the shooting stick and then pointed at a tree not twenty paces away. "I want you to shoot that dark knot there . . . in the middle of the tree."

"Right here?" I asked, thinking I had the wrong tree. "It's so close!"

"That's OK. Just shoot the dark knot."

I settled the butt of the gun against my shoulder, then braced myself for the recoil. The problem was that I was now afraid of the gun, holding my cheek well off the stock, worried that the scope would smack me again as it had the other day—a little mishap that had ended in a headache and a half moon–shaped cut between the eyes. I took a deep

Sangau and John Fletcher constructing a leopard blind.

breath, then tensed my whole body against the impending blow. I might even have closed my eyes. I had become that afraid.

When I finally did pull the trigger, I jerked so hard that I yanked the gun right off the rest. The gun went *click*. Unbeknownst to me, John had purposely left the chamber empty. I looked to Fletcher, but he just raised his brow. He let me state the obvious.

"Gosh, I guess I'm flinching!"

Around lunchtime, a Masai warrior strolled into camp with an injured hand. He was a tall, lanky fellow, like the friends that came with him, and he was joking and laughing about the injury. When I saw the hand, I got that brief twinge in the stomach you get when you see some grotesque injury involving a human being, such as a compound fracture, or when one glimpses a surgical procedure on television.

It seems that throwing and catching a spear is a regular sport for Masai, like throwing and catching a baseball is for us. This fellow's injury was the result of spear-catching gone bad. The spear had entered the palm, sliced through the meat between thumb and index finger, then exited the back of the hand. The hand had now swollen to double its size, was horribly infected, and there was yellow puss oozing from the festering edges of the deep crevice. What worried Fletcher most were the black streaks of blood poisoning starting up the wrist. Fletcher instructed the young warrior to return to camp each of the next few days for a daily course of antibiotic. He went on to tell him that if he did not come, he would surely lose the hand, and maybe also his life.

The Masai warriors then sauntered out of camp, still laughing, hitting each other with thin sticks. They used their robes, bound around their arms, as shields, leaving their naked bodies exposed. When the sticks connected against flesh, they did so with a loud *whack* that brought an instant welt but no other sound or cry. There was only more laughing. Seeing them was a small glimpse into the Masai's harsh and stoic way of life.

"Tough folks, those Masai," Fletcher remarked with a shake of his head. "They've got the pain threshold of a buffalo! They can drink water that would kill you and me."

"You think he'll be back tomorrow?" I asked.

"Maybe. Maybe not."

We never saw him again.

Fletcher went on to explain a man's rite of passage and the Masai customs associated with it. It is a huge event—arguably the single most important event in a Masai man's life. In an elaborate ceremony, at age seventeen, the would-be warrior is presented in front of the tribe, where he is to stand motionless while the witchdoctor performs a circumcision on him. There are no anesthetics, no painkillers of any kind. It is the young man's solemn duty to remain stone-faced throughout the entire procedure. To wince—to make an utterance of any sort—will mark the youth for life as the one who winced or gasped at his manhood ceremony.

"Most never make it to seventeen," Fletcher reflected. "Malaria, lions, infection. If they survive that long, you can figure they are pretty tough."

And I used to cry when I got a shot of penicillin! It made me think.

We spent the next couple of days looking for buffalo for Dad. We tracked several herds, which is tiring work, especially in the heat of the day. I don't know how many miles we walked, but it was a lot; in addition, at times we were stalking in, around, and through thornbushes. The most amazing part of it all was getting to watch the two trackers in action. They could look at the ground where a hundred buffalo had passed and pick out the track of a particular bull and follow it. They could tell you within an hour how old the track was. They could tell you where the animal had stopped to check its back trail. So impressive was their skill that it wouldn't have surprised me if they could tell you the buffalo's birthday.

Most stalks ended with the herd's winding us or sighting us, or else the herd would prove to be composed of small bulls that did not measure up. But there was one episode that ended in more excitement than I had bargained for. After four hours of tracking a particularly large herd, we found the animals deep in the bush. Cresting a small hill in the forest, we came upon them and saw their black bodies advancing steadily to our left in a wide, shallow valley that was more trees than it was brush, making for better visibility than we'd had up to that point. They were grazing on the go, stopping for a bite of grass, then moving on as they chewed, then stopping again for another bite. At this point, the herd was unaware of us—a win for us, whether we fired a shot or not. Crouched behind a thin tree, John studied the advancing herd with his binocular, looking for the biggest bull.

Just then, all hell broke loose.

The herd began to stampede, and with a clamor beyond anything I had expected. It sounded like a fleet of jet engines taking off. It was the sound of thunder, unending. My heart jumped into my throat. One minute we were creeping and whispering in total silence—the next we were up and running, and John was shouting at the top of his lungs. He came sprinting directly at me, yelling, "Beat it! Beat it!" I turned

Hanging the leopard bait.

to run and was looking for the best tree to climb, thinking my young life was over. *Surely we can't outrun a herd of buffalo!*

Unexpectedly, Fletcher snatched the shooting stick from Sangau, then turned and dashed back to his original position. He threw the stick in place and commanded Dad to get ready to shoot. Fletcher had his binocular up, surveying the stampeding herd—dust everywhere, limbs and branches cracking and breaking, nothing but the buffaloes' dark, trundling backs and an occasional sweep of horn visible amid the clouds of dust. A couple of young stragglers went by, and then not a buffalo remained in sight, though for some time we could still hear them crashing away in the distance. The dust that hung in the air was the only reminder that a herd had surrounded us.

"Nothing worth shooting, I'm afraid." Fletcher now turned to me. "Why did you run off like that?"

"You said, 'Beat it!' and I did!"

Fletcher began to laugh. Then he explained, and Dad now laughed, too.

"I said, *'Miti!'*—the shooting stick. I was asking for the shooting stick."

I felt stupid but had to join in the laugh.

Back at camp for lunch, we took photos of several Masai—both men and women—as they wondered through camp. Most allowed us to take their picture, and they were pleased to keep the instant Polaroid snapshots we gave them.

An interesting thing about the natives is that they do not seem to mind the flies that swarm their faces, though a number are missing an eye because of fly glaucoma or syphilis. The flies, thirty or forty at a time, migrate to the corners of their eyes and mouths. The Masai occasionally wink an eye or twitch a cheek at the annoyance, but they rarely raise a hand to wave them away. When they do raise a hand, it's like shooing pets. They do not slap at the flies, as we do. Consequently, the flies here are tame. They slap easily. It is nothing for me to kill twenty flies in an hour.

A couple of Masai warriors strike a pose over Dad's lion.

Dad: *After tracking buffalo all morning with no luck, just lots of tsetse fly bites, we went to the northern part of the concession, 30 miles from camp. Driving along, we came upon a herd of some fifty buffalo on an open plain. They were lined up on the horizon—quite a sight—and stared down their noses at us, an opposing army ready for battle. John picked out the biggest, and once I had located it, I shot it in the chest with John's .375. The animal thundered off with the rest of the herd, as if the bullet had missed completely.*

We followed in the vehicle. As we came over the rise in the plain, we saw the herd churning dust in the distance, with one buffalo falling behind. It was mine. It finally came to a stop and stood there staring at us, alone, blood spewing from its nostrils at each breath, its shoulder covered in bright-red lung blood. But it would not die. I fired again, then again, but it remained standing, huffing at us. More blood spewed from its nostrils. Unbelievably, it staggered toward us, too sick to reach us but full of anger to the end. I reloaded and aimed at the neck. It took a spine shot to put the buffalo down, and the experience gave me a new appreciation for the inconceivable hardiness of the beast.

On our way home, the tracker spotted a lesser kudu in the hills. I jumped out and popped it through the grass and brush—only its head was showing. The lesser kudu is a fairly rare antelope with beautiful white markings on its hide. The horns curl above the head like corkscrews. This is the only one we've seen.

Before dinner I went to the river, where giant fig trees towered up on either bank. From the base of the huge trunks, exposed roots ran out across the ground like overgrown serpents, weaving this way and that, and vines as thick as cucumbers dangled from the upper limbs. It was the perfect place to try out my new Bowie knife. I hacked at the massive roots and chopped down vines until my arms tired. Then I whacked off a vine at the water's edge and played Tarzan, swinging out over the chocolate-brown river and nearly making the opposite bank. Next I fashioned a crude trapeze from a section of vine, using a strip of cloth from my green fatigues, which I had recently turned into cutoff shorts. About the time I got to swinging pretty high, Fletcher happened by and just sort of shook his head.

Then he stopped and said, "I shan't be landing in that water, if I were you. All kinds of nasties in it."

At night in bed I prayed for my shooting to improve. Now that the culprit had been identified—flinching—it seemed it should be an easy thing to control. But it wasn't. If anything, the problem grew worse, and I made another mess of my shooting in the morning. We spotted

Dad with a dandy gerenuk, a fairly rare and graceful long-necked antelope that routinely stands on hind legs to reach browse high overhead.

three male Grant gazelles from the truck, the largest quite a nice one. Sangau and I got out and crept as close as we could. I sat down and fired at the big Grant but missed. We got back in the truck, and I fired at him when I wasn't supposed to. Then we got out—Sangau, John, and I—and followed after. I found some blood and then saw the Grant, but I made a pitiful offhand shot, hitting the gazelle in the stomach. It ran off, guts hanging out. I fired again and broke its hind leg. It continued to run, leaving lots of blood, then collapsed and struggled to get up. We circled around and I shot it in the neck, finally putting an end to the pitiful drama for which I was responsible.

No one said a thing. No one had to. John was disappointed. Sangau was disappointed. I was disgusted. I was ready to hang my rifle up. That was no way to shoot an animal.

Dad's journal for the next day: *Went to the Nguruman Escarpment and saw lots of game in the park, including three of the Big Five:*

rhino, buffalo, and lions. Spent the afternoon hunting for oryx. No luck, but found a trophy gerenuk that we chased on foot. My first shot was at two hundred yards, behind brush, and a miss. Took two more running shots, then a long stalk crouched over. Suddenly, John threw up the shooting stick and said, "You have four seconds." Shot the gerenuk on the shoulder at 258 yards. The small antelope dropped dead. Did a bit of running on this stalk and so was out of breath for the shot, but lucked out.

Dad undertook to improve my shooting and to eliminate the flinching. Sitting cross-legged on the ground, I was handed the gun to shoot at a box target fifty yards away, with my not knowing whether the rifle was loaded or not. It was a humiliating experience, waiting for the *click* or the *boom*, unsure which was forthcoming, getting fooled by it, and grumbling in anger when I did. But it was a necessary exercise, one that was critical in focusing my attention on the trigger pull and not the recoil. Several times I got frustrated and wanted to quit, but Dad wouldn't let me. He just kept handing me the rifle and saying, "Try it again." Most amazing of all, it worked. After a few blunders, bullet holes began to appear in the box. It earned a smile from him and soon had us feeling good about my prospects.

Once the shooting lesson was over and we were back in our tent, Maketi arrived with a grin that flashed his vampire teeth. The little skinner had asked to sharpen Dad's knife and was now returning it, sharp enough to shave with. In fact, Dad did shave the neckline below his beard, paying homage to the skinner's handiwork.

While we were driving along in the afternoon, two black rhino trundled out of the bush in front of us. It was quite a sight, as these were the first rhino we had seen. The big gray brutes plowed ahead of us, moving with surprising speed and agility. It also made me realize that, had we encountered them on foot and had they chosen to charge toward us instead of away, there would have been very little we could have done.

"Would you like one?" Fletcher asked my dad.

"How much is the license?"

"Three thousand dollars."

Dad smiled. "I think I'll pass." (It didn't sound like a bargain at the time, but it was. Now they are of course fully protected.)

A few days later, on the return to camp from the escarpment, we spotted three impala on a rocky slope. The male, which looked to be a fine ram, stood at attention below his two females. It kept an eye on us but did not move as we maneuvered closer. After a short stalk, I got a chance to see my humbling target practice pay off. With immense concentration not to jerk the trigger, I squeezed the metal device as slowly as I could—about as slowly as sap slides down a tree in winter—and held the cross hairs steady. I made a good shot. At 150 yards, I got the ram right where I had aimed, on the shoulder. The congratulatory slap on the back from Fletcher was worth a million bucks.

On occasion, while out in pursuit of game, we encountered Masai warriors strolling across the landscape. Because the women do all the work and the children tend the livestock, and because they are not allowed to wage war or hunt for big game, there is little for the warriors to do—so they roam the country. This afternoon was no different. Fletcher stopped to consult with a couple of roaming warriors, who as a rule are a wealth of knowledge about game in the area.

Asking a Masai the whereabouts of a gerenuk or eland or zebra is no different from stopping a city dweller on the street to ask the location of the nearest drugstore. Each Masai has a map of the land in his head complete with the beasts that inhabit it, and he can tell you that you will find a herd of eight zebra two hills over, and also to watch out for a lame hyena across the first creek you come to toward the rising sun. And, by the way, there is a very fine oryx half a day's stroll in yonder direction. Of course game animals are not static—they move, and the information is always in need of update. But it is the closest thing you can get to a formal game census.

I enjoyed stopping to converse with the Masai, as much for learning about their culture as for gaining any wildlife information they might have possessed. The Masai are a fascinating people, and their customs intrigue me—especially the warriors. Once Masai enter manhood and the warrior class, their hair is grown long and braided into fanciful designs. They clasp it in front above the eyes and down the back. Their braided hair and upper bodies are coated with a red ochre paste, giving them a surreal appearance. Pierced ears, adorned with heavy beads, dangle almost to the shoulders. The ear is pierced, not in the middle of the lobe as is done at home, but *above* the lobe, at the base of the canal, so there is that much more flesh to stretch. When they turn their heads, their ears jiggle and jangle like rearview mirror ornaments.

Each warrior carries a spear, a weapon that is his pride and joy, and he is never seen without it. The handle in the center is made of wood, but the ends are metal. The blade is long and flat, honed razor-sharp the length of each side. The spear is made primarily for throwing, but it can also be held forth in defense against a charging animal, which is most likely to be a lion. Astoundingly, the latter is a requirement in a young warrior's initiation. A lion is tracked up, and the warriors, surrounding it, attempt to direct its charge at the rookie. With the spear held forth like a lance, the blunt end braced against the ground, the rookie awaits the lion's charge. If everything goes as planned, the charging lion will impale itself of its own weight, and the Masai have a new warrior. If not, there's always another rookie.

Every man carries a hardened gourd club or two for bashing rabbits and other small game. Fastened to a crude belt about his narrow waist are a machete and knife in red leather sheaths. The Masai, who shun modern civilization in all its aspects, have been entirely successful in letting it pass them by. They live and dress as their ancestors did thousands of years ago. Their one concession to modern times, however, is in their choice of footgear: They wear tire tread sandals on their feet. The sandals are cut from old tires, tread-side down, with straps fashioned from strips of inner tube. Despite the sandals, the bottoms of their feet are as tough as dried leather: Thick crusts of skin rise up at the sides, with visible cracks in the hard crust where the skin turns black and smooth on the top of the foot. The black skin of their calves is coated in dust and marred by scratches from thorns. Every warrior

A likely spear wound accounted for this bull's unprovoked charge. The irate bull was eventually stopped at a hair-raising eighteen paces. Dad, John Fletcher, and Sangau.

carries scars somewhere on his body that attest to the rugged life the Masai lead.

The Masai are a nomadic people. They can walk twenty miles in a day and think nothing of it. Before the British arrived, they were a fierce and feared fighting tribe, waging constant war on neighboring tribes, conquering land as they came upon it on a continual quest to feed their expanding herds of cattle. Were it not for current law, they would have left this overgrazed patch of earth years ago, declaring war on greener neighbors, north, south, or west.

The women wrap themselves in red or blue robes, their breasts, one or the other or both, hanging in the open. Their heads are shaved completely bald, the shiny black pate a sharp contrast to the red head of the warrior. Their ears dangle as do the men's, but one difference is the beaded jewelry that adorns their heads and necks. Many sport a wide, flattened necklace—more like a collar—decorated with colorful embroidered beads. Some of the young women are pretty, but they do not age gracefully. When they get old, their breasts become flat and hang like pancakes, and their smiles show missing teeth like the black keys on a piano. Many are the matrons who carry the eerie, hollow socket of a missing eye. The women crowd the car window to see us and talk to us and cough and sneeze in our faces. They do not cover their mouths. They ask Fletcher in Swahili about us and repeat their strange language as if repetition will make it sink in. We smile and say, "Hello. How are you?"

All Masai carry the same smell. It is the smell of cattle, smoke, and sweat, all rolled into one—with a sweetish scent that I could not place. It was not a pleasant smell, but it was not entirely offensive either, like the body odor of some of the staff. Or a bus driver back home who has forgotten his deodorant. It made me wonder how we smell to them.

The next day dawned bright and sunny, and my good luck continued with another good shot. Early in the day we glimpsed several impala feeding on a hilltop. We got out of the truck and climbed toward them, moving as quietly as we could among the loose rocks, and soon found the largest male, which happened to be facing away from us. Then it heard us, or sensed us. It turned slightly, its head cocked around to look at us. But it was still unalarmed. I took aim and shot it right in the shoulder, and the copper-colored antelope collapsed in its tracks. Even stern-faced Mumaku was smiling now.

After lunch, while Dad rested in his tent and Fletcher looked after camp business, I went out with Giobani, the headman, to look for guinea fowl and crested francolin—or as Fletcher calls them, "the little

Everyone pitches in to help PH John Sutton out of a sticky situation.

chaps," being the smaller of the two varieties of francolin. At one point Giobani spotted a big flock of guineas and we gave chase. Soon we were sprinting at top speed in the knee-high grass, with me right on the headman's heels. It was pure exhilaration dashing through the grass like that, and I could see the guineas hustling ahead of us. All of a sudden Giobani shrieked and leapt into the air, tucking his legs up into his body like an acrobat in flight. I glanced down to see a large snake coiled in the grass. Because I was running so fast and was upon the snake at such close range, there was no time to do anything other than what Giobani had done. So I too jumped as high as I could, jerking my feet up, and sailed over the snake, hoping against hope that it would not strike. It didn't.

I landed on my feet, then turned back to blast the menace with the shotgun. Had it been a rifle in my hands that would have been tricky, if not impossible. Imagine trying to find a snake in the scope, in thick grass, at close quarters. But a shotgun is the perfect snake gun, and I felt comfortable in the task: I had dispatched several rattlesnakes back home at the ranch.

I returned quickly before the snake could move off or disappear, but not so quickly as to blunder into it. But it had not moved. The snake was coiled right where it had been. It was a cobra, about as thick around as my arm. But it was already dead. Who knows what had killed it. If it had been alive, there is no doubt it would have bitten one of us dead as we sailed overhead. Not even a trained Olympian can hurtle over a full-grown cobra raised up and ready to strike.

A couple of days later, in the heat of the afternoon, we spotted a herd of impala lounging in the shade of several flat-topped acacias; we passed them by as if they were the furthest things from our minds. The herd was typical in makeup—all female with one male escort. The other, unfortunate males remain in a nearby but separate herd, jealously plotting to beat the old boy out of his position. It is pure Darwin in practice.

Once past the stationary herd, we slowed the car and got out. Fletcher and I circled, using trees for cover, and the impala trotted fifty yards farther off, only slightly suspicious. When we were as close as he thought we could get, Fletcher gave me the signal; I sat down and took my time, concentrating so as not to flinch. I didn't, and the 175-yard shot was perfect. The big ram dropped straight down, and Sangau came running up to dress it and carry it back to the truck.

In the evening we went to a water hole to hunt sand grouse, a fast-flying, brown-speckled bird shaped rather like a large dove. There weren't many, but it was a fun shoot. In the end, I got one and Dad got four—and the cook grilled them for dinner. The food on this trip was excellent and well prepared, which is surprising when you stop to consider what the locals eat. The Masai's daily staple is blood and milk, mixed together! I laughed at first, thinking Fletcher was joking, but he was not.

He went on to describe the process of how a suitable gourd is found and hollowed out to hold the nutritious mixture. It's rinsed, not with water—too precious a commodity in much of this land—but with cattle urine. Next the blood is collected. Using the tip of a knife or the close-in shot of an arrow, an artery is pierced in the neck of the chosen cow, and the spurting blood is directed into the gourd. When a sufficient quantity has been secured, a mud patch is applied to the wound, and the cow is none the worse for its blood donation. Then they squirt milk from the udder into the gourd, where it is left to congeal and ferment into a custardy, yogurtlike concoction. Seconds anyone?

Living off the milk and blood of their cattle, Masai can survive where other tribes would starve. Their scrawny cattle scour the plains, finding grass where none can be seen and allowing the Masai to prosper. The Masai never kill a cow to eat the meat. Only if it is old and near death, or killed by some catastrophe, is a cow eaten, because cattle are their currency. Eating cattle to them would be like setting money on fire to us. It is seen as pure waste. Wives are bought with cattle. Because of that, daughters are preferable to sons, as they can be sold for a hefty dowry. Daughters are the social security system for the elderly. When selling a daughter, it is rarely done for a number of cattle all at once. Rather, the father will try to stretch the income as far as he can, negotiating, say, ten cows and ten goats today, and five cows a year for the next ten years.

Everything in Masai culture is bartered in cattle or goats. Consequently, a Masai has absolutely no use for cash money. Given money, a Masai will keep it only until he can trade it for more cattle from a non-Masai, and the trade must be with a non-Masai: No Masai in his right mind would take money for his cattle. Livestock is the only status symbol, the lone measure of wealth in the Masai community. The man with the most cattle is the wealthiest. The more cattle he has, the more wives he can buy; the more wives he has, the more children he can sire; the more children he sires, the more shepherds he has to tend his herds. Only through additional cattle, wives, and children can a man increase the size of his enterprise.

As we started out early the next morning, we ran into a pride of lions in the dark. Although we were in the truck and clearly a much bigger creature than they, the big cats held their ground, in no hurry to give way. We got within ten yards of them and still they lay there, glancing only occasionally into the headlights, as if trying to say, "Try to imagine how little I care." Not wanting to provoke a charge, we finally reversed and went around them. The Masai were right about what the male lion was saying in the morning; this was *their* land.

That afternoon we had a difficult hunt after a couple of oryx. We spotted the bachelor bulls out on a small plain, and there was no easy way to get close to them. Fletcher and I stalked and crawled for two hours, trying to get into position for a shot. We had to crawl under and around wait-a-bit bushes, which make you do precisely that when the claw-shaped thorns get hold of you. I got tangled and scratched, and it was hard to be quiet moving about in the briars. I would just about get one branch unhooked from my clothes and anatomy only to have another reach out and grab me. It was unbelievably slow going, but we had the wind on the old bulls and they held. Finally we got within shooting distance, but I was in a bad position, shooting off a swaying branch. Every time the wind blew the branch would swing, and I couldn't get steady. After a while the oryx spooked and ran off, and we never saw them again.

I was disappointed, as the oryx is an interesting animal. There is a slight resemblance to the bovine anatomy, but the sandy-hided animal is crowned with impressive horns. The dark horns jut from the scalp like lances, three feet or more in length.

Following two uneventful days of hunting—inasmuch as any day on safari in Africa can really be called uneventful—we moved to a new camp in a dry, rocky area. After getting our gear situated in our tents, we went out in late afternoon for a wildebeest and *punda* (zebra), with Mumaku scouting in the back. A wildebeest was the first to appear, and I shot it in the ribs, hitting the lungs, for what was surely a fatal shot. Nevertheless, I made a follow-up shot through the shoulder at two hundred paces, and it went right down. I was glad to have my shooting back on track. Actually, I was elated, now on the high of the roller coaster. In hunting, there is nothing better than a bullet well placed.

A short while later Dad took a zebra at 350 yards. He has always been a good shot.

This area is appropriately named Rumbo for the frequent earth tremors that it produces. Camp in fact was situated between Mount Kilimanjaro and the Chyulus, both of which are volcanic mountains, and much of the terrain has a volcanic feel to it. The land is dry and desolate, the hills covered in rough volcanic rock; it resembles nothing so much as a moonscape. The sharp rocks are particularly hard on shoes, easily shredding leather and rubber.

The next day we experienced some thirty tremors! While we were chasing after a gerenuk, the land began to tremble, and I actually had trouble keeping on my feet. It felt like I was jogging drunk, or trying to run up the aisle of a bouncing bus. During lunch the low rumble returned, and the utensils and plates began to rattle and slide off the wooden chop box. The worst tremor hit while I was resting in the tent. The cot shook as if I were riding on a bumpy train. It was an eerie feeling but not frightening, since there was nothing that could fall on us. Maybe a tree, but that was unlikely.

Later that afternoon, while traveling near our former hunting ground, we came upon the same two oryx that we had made an unsuccessful stalk after the other day. Fortunately they were in a slightly different position, so we did not have to repeat our nightmare crawl through the wait-a-bit bushes. This time we concealed our forms behind a convenient collection of boulders out on the plain. Crouched over, we made a quick, silent dash toward the unsuspecting oryx, then crawled up into the *V* that two boulders made at the top. I was squashed in the bottom of the *V*, having landed there in a hurry. Nevertheless, I settled the gun, aimed, and . . . flinched! The bullet smacked the dirt way off to the right.

"Come on, Johnny," Fletcher chastised. "You can do better than that."

We left the rocks for the open plain, stalked closer, and I sat quickly as the oryx galloped off. One oryx stopped at the edge of the brush to have a look back at us. It was now broadside and three hundred yards away. With the cross hairs on its shoulder, I held my breath and squeezed. The bullet took the oryx low in the shoulder, and I'm not sure which of us was more surprised. The bull ran ten yards and pitched to the ground. It was a beauty. The long horns are pointy as a fencing sword, dark stripes mark its face, and furry tufts of hair on the tips of each ear give rise to the name of this variety, the fringe-eared oryx.

On the return to camp, just before dark, we went sand grouse hunting in the swamps. It was mucky in spots, making for slow going and retrieving, but once we were set up it proved the best wingshooting we'd had to date. Dad was in a bad spot and shot four. I got eleven, surprised to outshoot him.

Around the campfire that night, Fletcher told a funny story about two clients who had come on safari but who never left camp. A couple of older gentlemen, they wanted only to play cards and drink gin all day. In the morning he would greet them and tell them of the day's plan.

"Today we will have a look for zebra and wildebeest. Need to hang some baits," he would say.

But the old fellows would shake their heads. "No, we are going to stay in and play cards today. You go out and shoot us something." So he went out and shot a zebra and a wildebeest and hung them for baits. But the next day it was the same. And the next. Fletcher ended up shooting their whole safari, and they were just as happy as they could be. He reckoned all they wanted was to get out of the house for a spell, and a safari was a convenient way to do it. I couldn't imagine spending that kind of money and not getting out to hunt—even more surprising, *not wanting* to hunt. Here they were in the heart of the best hunting on the planet.

Dad: *Early in the morning, we came across the spoor of several buffalo and started tracking them. One big track in particular had Fletcher's interest. Just at daybreak, we set off down the valley and followed tracks for forty-five minutes, at which point we lost them. It took thirty minutes to find them again, and we continued for another hour, with Sangau leading, John next, then me. We worked our way around the mottes of brush that were sculpted like little islands in a dry sea.*

Suddenly, there was an explosion of brush ahead of us. At twenty-seven paces, a bull buffalo got up from where it was lying under a thornbush and charged straight for us. John raised his .500 double to his shoulder and fired. His bullet took the buffalo in the eye, knocking the charging bull briefly to its knees. While the buffalo was down, I shot it in the chest with the .458. Unbelievably, the bull jumped up and came for us once more. John hit it again, in the neck, which luckily turned its charge to our left. I hit it in the left shoulder as it charged into a thicket. Then I stepped to the left, thinking to get a shot as it exited the other side, but it never came out. John followed with another shot in the neck, and I came around for the coup de grâce. *The buffalo had dropped eighteen paces from us!*

When the hunters returned to the vehicle, I was eager to hear their tale, and even more eager to witness the buffalo that had instigated it. The dramatic scene was instant-replayed for me, and I shook my head in awe. The now-still buffalo was massive, thick all over, and it brought a shiver up my spine to think of looking up to see such a beast charging at me. It made me glance nervously at the surrounding trees.

There happened to be a tree that abounds in this area, one that is very aptly named the thorntree. Not only are the thorns exceedingly large but they are so numerous as to be ridiculous. I couldn't imagine attempting to climb one—why, hugging a cactus would be less painful! But I guess that with an angry buffalo hot on my tail I would. It helped to soothe my disappointment at not being present for the charge, and I realized that Fletcher had been right to leave me at the car.

Not until we had rolled the bull over and inspected it thoroughly did we find the cause for the unprovoked charge. Under a hind leg, near the testicles, was a large, festered wound. Fletcher guessed that a Masai spear was to blame, given the uniform slice to the flesh. A goring by one of its comrades would have left a jagged gash.

On the return to camp, we stopped at an abandoned Masai village and got out for a look around. Encircling the village, or *boma,* was a giant jumble of thorntree and wait-a-bit branches piled high, the purpose of which is to keep lions, leopards, and other predators out. At night, the cattle and goats are herded safely inside the barrier—which had to be a tight fit, based on the numbers of stock we have seen. Inside the *boma* each family lives in a mud and dung hut called a *manyatta*. The huts are built by the women to about shoulder height, and they are shaped like a loaf of bread. Inside one *manyatta* I found the remains of their sleeping arrangements (there wasn't room for much else): a couple of stick-thatched cots built six inches off the ground.

Back at the car, Fletcher pointed to my sock. There was a brown stain the size of an oatmeal cookie, except that the cookie was moving. On closer inspection it proved to be a colony of seed ticks, each the size of a pinhead. How they got on me so quickly, and all at once, I haven't a clue. John fished out a can of Raid and gave the colony a squirt. I shuddered to think of the outcome had the nasty parasites made it to my crotch.

While driving the next afternoon, I made the comment that we probably wouldn't see anything, only because we hadn't seen anything all morning. Not five seconds later, Sangau was banging on the top, having spotted three Thomson gazelles—"Tommies," for short. We coasted behind a boulder and cut the motor. Sangau and I got out and sneaked up to a large rock, using it as cover. The rock also made for a perfect rest, and we waited for the largest of the small gazelles to turn broadside. But it wouldn't turn. It just kept walking away. Sangau whistled. Nothing. He whistled again. Nothing. Finally the Tommie turned at 150 yards, and I shot it well, breaking both shoulders. The Tommie is a smaller, miniature version of the Grant, with similar hide color and markings, but the horn spread is narrower relative to its smaller horns.

A bizarre twist came later that day when we spotted a waterbuck. The waterbuck is a large, stoutly built antelope with ribbed horns that rise above its head like half-moons facing each other. I got out and quietly rested my rifle on a rock, just as I had done with the Tommie, putting the cross hairs on the unsuspecting animal, only seventy-five yards away. It was so big and so close it filled the scope. The gun went *bang,* and eagerly I looked up to claim my prize . . . only I hadn't killed it. In fact, I had completely missed. The waterbuck wandered off in an unhurried trot and disappeared in the brush. I had flinched.

But how was that possible? How could I hit the tiny Tommie at 150 yards, yet miss the massive waterbuck at half the distance? It didn't make sense. Thinking it over, though, I realized that the antelope's size was exactly why I had missed. In fact, it had everything to do with my flinching. Because the Tommie was small, I *knew* that I had to hold extremely steady to hit it—and I did; whereas the waterbuck looked so big in the scope that I thought, *How can I miss?* and jerked the trigger.

A Bullet Well Placed

Dad: *We came upon four cow waterbucks in the open and stopped, looking for a male holding in the brush. After a minute with the binocular, John spotted the bull looking through the brush at us. All I could see was the head and neck, and it was quite some distance away. Fletcher said that was as close and as good a shot as we were going to get, so I held steady and fired, aiming for the animal's neck. It dropped dead at 275 yards.*

The following day a native informed us that buffalo were eating his corn, and he showed us where they were. We crawled up to within fifty yards of the herd; five buffalo were now clearly in sight, lying down. John handed me the .375 and pointed to the biggest one, which was easy to see—it was some eight inches taller at the shoulder than the rest. The native said that the hunter on the last safari had thrown down his gun and run when he saw this buffalo.

As I eased into a sitting position, the buffalo jumped up and stood looking right at me. I put the cross hairs just under its chin and pulled the trigger. The herd ran off in a cloud of dust, and we went running up, confidently, only to find that my buffalo had run off, too. It didn't even seem to be hit. We followed the herd for 500 yards before we found a drop of blood, and it was the size of a pinhead. We followed what became a light blood trail for a mile before spotting the buffalo in a thicket. John climbed a tree on a termite mound and shot the buffalo through the shoulder with the .375. Then the buffalo came for us! Fletcher couldn't see it at that point, and I shot it with John's .500. That knocked the big bull down. I shot it again, and it stayed down. Then I went up with the .458 and gave it a final shot in the neck.

I was quite disappointed with the results of my first shot—how little effect it had had on the buffalo. With a little help from Sangau's knife, we were able to explore the wound. My first bullet had entered the neck three inches under the chin, two inches right of center, and fifteen inches up from the base of the chest. The bullet had penetrated some ten inches and broken up. Moral: The .375 is just too small a caliber for buffalo.

We saw five or six elephants in the swamp. Hidden by tall reeds, each lifted a trunk like a submarine periscope, trying to get our scent. Later, while stalking an oryx, we saw a striped hyena, a fairly rare animal. All day long we saw monkeys and baboons. A crocodile track appeared near the leopard bait, but there was no sign of any leopard. Three different lions have fed on our leopard bait—of course, after I have shot one! We did see one female leopard, which we let go.

Today, we felt the worst earth tremor yet. It lasted about forty seconds.

The baboons that inhabit the riverbeds are legal game and plentiful, but Fletcher is loath to shoot them. "It's an awful sight," he explained. "They screech and pick at the wound—just as a human would. It's the one animal I won't shoot." His sentiments would remain with me.

It is amazing how quickly our month on safari has passed. The first week seemed like it would last forever. Now that it is our twenty-eighth day, I wonder *Where did it go?* But today I got the biggest treat of all. Driving across the open plains, we spotted an old buffalo bull. And when I say old, I mean *old.* It was ancient. The aged bull was gaunt, stiffened with age, and traveling as if the placement of each hoof were the cause of great pain. Its skin was gray where the hair had been rubbed from its bony hide, and its face and sides were scarred from a lifetime of battles.

"We are going to get you a buffalo," Fletcher whispered to me.

"Really?" I asked, thinking he was kidding. He nodded, already looping the binocular strap over his head.

We drove behind a lone hill, then got out and began the short climb to the top. As we went, I wondered if the buffalo had heard us and had perhaps skedaddled to safer country; it was difficult to be quiet amid the rocks. As we peered over a small boulder at the peak, though, the old bull came into view, 130 yards away on the plain below. In its emaciated condition it looked all horns. These were knotty at the boss but rubbed smooth on the up-sweeping ends. I was to use Fletcher's .375, which was now set up on top of the rock. Dad, beside me, had his rifle at the ready. When the bull stopped and turned broadside, Fletcher patted my shoulder.

"OK, Johnny, whenever you're ready. Just squeeze the trigger slowly."

I was worried about the hefty recoil of the big gun, a gun I had never fired, but I was more worried about screwing up the shot. I knew that letting me shoot a buffalo, one of the Big Five of Africa's most dangerous game, was quite a gift. So I wasn't about to screw it up, not if I could help it. I held my breath and squeezed slowly—the cross hairs on the old bull's shoulder—squeezed until my eyes blurred from concentration, squeezed until the bang came as a complete surprise—the way it should. I looked excitedly below for the buffalo's reaction. *Had it fallen? Was it running away?*

Surprisingly, the old bull was standing right where it had been. For a second, I thought I had missed. It made no reaction at all. But then the buffalo humped its back and began to take several halting steps. It wasn't the reaction I had expected, but my shot had been good! In fact, it had been perfect. The truth was that although the old bull did not have the strength to run, it was not about to give up. What resolve it had left from a lifetime of cheating death, an adversary it had fought at every turn, at every step, every day of its life, was summoned now; this bull was determined—absolutely steadfast in its resolve—not to give up the ghost. It was one tough old bull. Dad then put one in its neck, but the buffalo ignored the .458 bullet as if it were no more than a mosquito bite. The bull turned away, in a slow, deliberate manner, and as it did, Dad shot it in the hindquarters, knocking the ancient beast to the ground. It didn't take another shot.

(I don't know the measurements of that old bull, though I guess I could easily take them. Now, twenty-seven years later, the mounted head sits in my study. On subsequent safaris I shot larger buffalo—seven in total—but this one remains my favorite. It is not large by record book standards, but the old fellow looms forever large in my heart. And I would have it no other way. In hunting, it is not what you shoot but *how* you shoot it that matters most. The only record book a hunter needs is the one that resides in his head, the one that tells him he hunted fairly and sportingly. Those "records," those memories, are what return to the hunter each time he beholds the trophy on the wall.)

The next day we stayed out all day. At one point several gerenuk appeared near the top of a hill, and we climbed up after them. They were quite far, however, by the time we got them in sight. Fletcher was determined in his pursuit, though, and we kept after them. I managed to get a very nice one, despite shooting that was less than perfect; in my own defense I might say that the gerenuk's sleek greyhoundlike frame and thin giraffelike neck offered little by way of a target. My first shot was at three hundred yards, so I can't be too upset with myself for missing. My second shot was twenty-five yards longer than that! Although I didn't get to see one do it, these rare, rusty-colored antelope often stand on hind legs to reach edible browse with their conspicuously tiny mouths. A trophy at any size, the one I took happens to have very fine horns, and it made my day.

Dad: *The daily earth tremors have lessened in number, down to about a dozen a day, but they have increased in intensity. The one last night really shook the bed. Maybe it is just as well that we are leaving soon.*

Around the campfire that night, Fletcher relayed the story of an elephant hunt gone bad, gone so bad in fact that it turned into a near-deadly fiasco before it was all over. "After making a poor shot of his elephant, this particular client completely panicked. He seized my double from the tracker and fired both barrels, doing absolutely nothing but angering the elephant even more—it's surprising what some people will do when they are scared. Anyway, it just so happened that these were the only "solids" I had on me, which left me with "softs," and we were hunting in tall reeds where you couldn't see the elephant until it was right on top of you. When the elephant came for us, the client's wife began to scream, and the whole thing grew into a real ball's up.

"I dragged the clients through the tall reeds, trying to evade the angry elephant, but every time the elephant got close the wife would scream and the elephant would charge, and we would have to dash out of the way. I continued to shoot the old bull in the head, but the softs failed to penetrate the thick honeycomb of bone to the brain. Running out of options, I then shot for the elephant's eyes, trying to reach the brain that way. I was no more successful in the attempt, but I did succeed in blinding it, which would have given us the advantage if it weren't for the wife, who continued to scream every time the elephant got close. Now the blinded elephant was searching for us by scent, mad as hell, the end of its trunk up in the air and swiveling about. It nearly got us once or twice, too. Finally, I managed to get the clients back to the vehicle. I returned the next morning armed with solids, and my tracker and I followed it up and put the poor thing out of its misery."

A day later. Dad: *Today we had good driven bird shooting of guinea fowl and francolin. Professional hunter John Sutton and his client Noni Kellog joined us. The boys, as beaters, spread out in the bush ahead of us and began making noise, whooping and hollering and banging sticks. Pretty soon the guineas and francolin came running our way. When they got close, we stood, making ourselves suddenly visible, and the birds began to flush over us. At the first shots they all lifted into the air, and it was quite a sight watching the big guineas sailing overhead. There were hundreds in this flock, and some flew high out of range above us, an unusual spectacle to witness.*

We came upon three sand grouse eggs in the sand, very pretty and spotted. The protective mother did not fly until John was two feet from her. With so many predators about, it's hard to imagine a ground nest being successful.

In the distance (about fifty miles to the south), we can see the twin peaks of Mount Kilimanjaro rising, like ghosts out of the mist, some 19,000 feet. Our elevation here is about 2,500 feet.

And there our journals (and my memory) end.

Tanzania, East Africa
July–August 1982

We started off on quite a successful day (and safari), once I got the first botch out of the way. I missed an impala through the trees on our way to sight in the guns at first light. Minutes later we stopped on a dirt track in the forest, and Kipper, our head tracker, trotted off to a suitable *miombo* tree and whacked off a square of bark with his panga, exposing the white flesh underneath. My jacket laid across the hood offered a perfect rest, and with little difficulty I placed a shot from both the .375 Kleingunther and the .300 Weatherby right in the sweet spot. So there was no excuse. It was all up to me.

"Super," said Gerard, unruffled by my earlier miss and already climbing behind the wheel of the open Range Rover, eager to be on the hunt. This lively fellow, some ten years my senior, was to be my professional hunter for the next four weeks, and I sure hated to start off on the wrong foot. I didn't want him to think me a complete novice. For my part, I'd had a good feeling about the man the instant I met him. Thick dark hair swept above dark eyes, and straight white teeth filled his grin. We were first introduced two days before in the bar of the New Arusha hotel. At the time Gerard was fairly reserved, letting his partner, George Angelides, do most of the talking, but there was a sparkle in his eyes. It was as if he knew the adventures that awaited us—as if it were a great secret that he was bursting to tell. That familiar sparkle now came into his eyes. "We'll just have a look around for some lion bait . . . zebra, wildebeest, or hartebeest. Maybe later we'll take a hippo. A lion can't resist a good hippo."

But on our way, we passed another herd of impala lurking in the woods, and Gerard said, "There's a very big one just there. Get your gun!" We got out and stalked as close as possible, which wasn't very. The herd was jittery, and I had to shoot fast. I missed again. I was 0 for 2 now on impala and not feeling very proud of it. Luckily for me, we were only in the first few minutes of a very long game, and I have always enjoyed being the underdog.

A Bullet Well Placed

We pursued the rather large herd, which at first ran from us. Many of the copper-colored antelope leaped over invisible objects in front of them and left a thin film of dust in their path, while others dashed in and around the intervening brush. Then, luckily, the herd slowed to a stop and turned heads to watch us, and just then the big boy wandered out in front. Even I could tell that it was a monster. I had taken three nice impala in Kenya, so I had a reference—unlike some of the game we would be hunting here, which I had never even heard of, much less seen a specimen. The way this big ram dipped its head and thrust its chin forward on the run reminded me of a whitetail buck pushing its head through a gap in a barbed wire fence. It was a beautiful sight, with the seemingly endless horns swept back and upward and over its spine. Those horns were indeed tremendous. The way the ram tossed its head, you could tell it thought so, too.

I held the cross hairs steady and squeezed the trigger. *Make it count,* I told myself. *Make it count.* The impala dropped straight down at the shot, and we ran up to see my first trophy taken in Tanzania—which was quite a trophy, to say the least. All we could do was shake our heads at the magnificent horns.

"I tell you, Johnny. I don't like to do this, but in this case I will." Gerard retrieved a tape measure from the car and laid it along the horn, starting at the base and holding it at the top of the dark ridges, being careful not to press the tape into the indentations of the horn so as to make the measurement appear bigger than it was. "It's 29¾!" he said, standing and shaking his head. "Johnny, you have just shot what is probably the world's record southern impala. The dividing line is quite near here for southern and northern. We'll have to check. Regardless, it's the bloody biggest impala I've ever seen. Well done." We shook hands again.

Taking a world record trophy is, I must admit, 99 percent luck. More than anything, it is a matter of being in the right place at the right time. Still, it is a noteworthy achievement and a twist of fate for the hunter to revel in, as long as he doesn't get a big head.

I felt some disappointment, admittedly, at the two missed shots, yet in all fairness I couldn't be too hard on myself: I was still groggy after all the traveling of the day before. The drive from Arusha to camp had been a grueling, eighteen-hour ride over bumpy and dusty dirt roads. Amazingly, the drive to this central part of the country known as the Rungwa Game Reserve, where we will spend our first two weeks of safari, took longer than it did to fly from London to Africa—but, looking on the bright side, it was a great way for the

What a whopper! This record impala was the result of being in the right place at the right time. (Note the charred ground where head-high grass had stood earlier in the season.)

two of us to get acquainted. I'm sure a professional hunter likes to get to know the person he will be guiding in the bush, a person who in a tense situation may be standing behind him with a loaded gun. And it was good for me because I got to know Gerard's hunting philosophy, his code of conduct, his expectations, his grievances. Hunting with a guide is a team endeavor. How well would a football team play in which the players had only just met? It is the same hunting as a team. It takes time to get to know each other. The process can be pleasant or it can be unpleasant, but it is a process that must run its course.

What I learned was this. Gerard Miller is a third generation East African, born and raised—Africa is the only home he has ever known. Of British descent, his parents were *both* professional hunters—so he literally grew up in the bush and in the hunting business. Despite their insistence that he complete his schooling first, Gerard couldn't wait to begin his life as a professional hunter, and at age fifteen he ran away from home to apprentice under George Angelides (with whom Dad is hunting this trip). Gerard received his East African professional hunter's license at age eighteen, one of the youngest ever to earn that coveted diploma, which at the time required a full three years of apprenticeship. When white professional hunters were booted from

Tanzania in 1973, Gerard moved his hunting operations to Zambia. With the recent change in the law, however, he has just returned to Tanzania, excited to be hunting his home country again.

"Excited" is an understatement. Whatever reserve Gerard had shown at our introduction in town evaporated the instant we left the city. It was evident that Gerard was keen to hunt, eager to be on safari. The man, I would learn, is an absolute dynamo in his element, which is the African bush. He is fast moving, fast talking, and fast thinking— as energetic as a New York trial attorney trying the case of his career. Only that case is your hunt—that's how important it is to him. He is going to do his best—better than his best—to get you the trophies you deserve. That's how he looks at it. That's how he makes you feel. You aren't just another bloody American here to blast away at the animals. It's as if you were the first client he has ever guided, and the success or failure of your safari will reflect on him personally for the rest of his life. It goes without saying, then, that Gerard was a dream professional hunter to work with.

Midmorning, while driving across the relatively flat terrain of this forested land, we came upon a small herd of Lichtenstein hartebeest. Like its cousin the wildebeest, the hartebeest is not the prettiest animal on the continent. But I had never shot one, and we were in need of bait.

There is good news and bad news in hunting a forested area like Rungwa. The bad news is that there are lots of twigs and sticks and thick shoots of dead grass poking up to sabotage your bullets. The good news is that the animals feel safer than they do out in the open of the pans, and they tend not to run as far when they spot you. So we were able to get within a hundred yards of this herd, and I took the largest male as it stopped to look back at us. Kipper was glad to see a good shot, and he extended his black hand.

"Gude," he said, smiling. "*M'zuri*." And so I learned another Swahili word.

"How do you say 'Thank you?'" I asked Gerard.

"*Asante*," he said.

"*Asante*." Now even tall, silent Roman, our number two tracker, grinned. Both Kipper and Roman were from the Mwanyamwrzi tribe in the Singida region of Tanzania. The last member was Gatsun, the government professional hunter whose job it was, besides being on the payroll, to see that we followed regulations (and that he got a big tip). He was smiling, too, and so I felt very good about our prospects. We had a fine team in the making. We were here to hunt, but we were here to have fun, too. This was fun.

On the return to camp for lunch, we spotted a band of greater kudu on the left and a sable bull antelope on the right. It's not supposed to happen like that, two trophies showing up at the same time, but that's what they did. Since I had neither, it was a tough choice, but the kudu was the more desirable animal of the two. Gerard crouched forward, and I followed closely behind, trying my best to be quiet. Here, as in much of Rungwa, last season's grass had been burned to a stubble. In its place, green grass shoots had sprouted all across the charred ground, a wonderful attractant to the wildlife. As long as I was careful not to step on a clump of burned "stubs," the stalking was reasonably silent.

We had the wind on them, too, so I was rather optimistic of our success. Now hunkered behind a tree, I braced the rifle against the hard trunk, ready for the shot, my heart hammering in my chest. Gerard quickly glassed the advancing herd. The kudu were walking in a slow procession toward us. They had yet to see or hear us, so we had a little time. The ball was in our court. Regardless of what happened next, whether fate would allow me to collect this noble beast or not, we had been blessed with a magnificent sight. I had heard and read about the majestic kudu—the gray ghost of Africa—and here were a proud male and several females strolling through the forest, the sun

Typical native dwelling made of mud bricks and surrounded by thornbush to hinder nocturnal predators.

dappling down through the sparsely leafed trees, throwing patches of light and shadow on their surprisingly well camouflaged forms.

Gerard glassed the male again as he neared, then shook his head.

"I think we can do better. We'll let this chap age a bit."

He turned back and we made our retreat without the kudu ever being the wiser, which was half the fun.

The rest of that warm afternoon was spent hanging the hartebeest for lion bait and the impala for leopard. The hanging of baits for Gerard is a very deliberate venture, and the man is quite choosy in the selection of his sites. Like an architect envisioning a building that has yet to see its first brick, Gerard will take a hundred factors into consideration, evaluating each one, before making his final selection: the direction of the sun and wind, the location of the eventual blind, the shooting distances involved, an approach guaranteeing stealth for the hunters and adequate cover for the cat—but not so much as to screw up the client's shot. He will scout the area so that he knows every nook and cranny, every patch of brush, every hole in the ground, so that he has an idea where the wounded lion or leopard will head even before it does. He would prefer to have some sign of the cat, but in its absence he will settle for the most liony- or leopardy-looking country he can find.

For leopard, the bait carcass is dragged behind the vehicle up and down the banks of the river, or around a rocky hill, to spread the scent before it is hung in the tree. Roman, with a branch, will sweep the ground at the base of the tree, so that any tracks can be scrutinized later; Kipper, high in the tree, will clear twigs or limbs that might interfere with the client's shot. Before he departs, Gerard will take a step back and look his work over, the way a maître d' looks over a dining table set for an important guest.

"Yes, I think that will do nicely," he says at each bait.

First thing next morning, before the sun had even fully left the horizon, a male sable appeared just inside the forest's edge. The sable is a beautiful animal and one that was new to me. A mature male is jet black with white markings on its face and ribbed horns that arc above its head like two samurai swords poised for battle. It is horselike in appearance, in that it reminds one in a way of the noble Pegasus. If a present-day animal were to sprout wings and fly, the sable would be the one. With little difficulty we got within 120 paces of the dark antelope, and I took it with the .375. It will make a splendid addition to the trophy room.

Later that morning we came across two old buffalo bulls in a grassy depression in the open of a small plain. The buffalo in Rungwa are not typically as big of horn as their northern Masailand cousins, and these two gents were no exception—both were downright poor, in fact, in the horn department. But the deciding factor was bait. "A buffalo makes such wonderful lion bait," Gerard concluded.

Excitedly, with rifles loaded and extra shells on our belts, we slipped into the depths of a dry creek bed, a structure that served as perfect cover, and stalked to within 150 yards of the old bulls, which was as close as the winding creek would take us. Even hidden in the creek and soundless in our approach, we had put nothing over on the old bulls. We ascended the steep bank to find them staring head on at us. At Gerard's direction, I braced the barrel against a slim sapling and aimed at the buffalo's chest, at the midpoint between nose and brisket, hoping to hit the neck if my bullet went high, the heart if low. Unfortunately there was a tree in my line of sight, and I had to aim a bit off center. I was shooting a Winchester Silverpoint, planning to save my solids for Masailand, where the second half of our safari would take place. I squeezed the trigger, and at the loud report both buffalo turned and ran. Incredibly, the old bull showed no discernible indication that it had been hit. It absorbed the bullet like a spit-wad from a kid's soda straw; my world shook, and I lost faith in the caliber I held in my hands. I had expected to see a stumble at least. Maybe a falter. But there was nothing.

Then we were up and out of the creek and running after the bulls—Gerard and I, with Gatsun on our tail—and soon we caught up to the two bulls, now stopped and skulking in the shade of a tree. Though winded from the run, Gerard and I quickly shouldered our weapons, but the bulls' position was such that a shot could easily hit the wrong one. Spying our movement, the bulls started out from the shade. The instant my bull was in the clear, Gerard and I fired simultaneously, hitting it well but with little effect, and the bulls ran once more.

"Give me your gun," Gerard said, sitting down hastily. He fired at the running bull, wanting to make a sure hit with the assistance of the scope before the buffalo got into the thick stuff, which was of course where they were headed. But again the shot had zero effect, and the big bulls trundled on. We sprinted after them once more, and Gerard paused to fire the open-sighted .460, hitting the bull in the lungs and stopping it. I gave it another shoulder shot with the .375, which did little more than cause it to twitch. It was hurting now, though—we could see that—and it began to wobble, then staggered, and finally went down on its side.

A Bullet Well Placed

"You want a piece of me?" A Cape buffalo is all muscle and brawn, but, most important, it has the brains to use it, giving it every advantage in thick vegetation.

As we neared, Gerard said, "Shoot it again, Johnny. In the chest, between the front legs."

I did as instructed, and a stream of blood gushed from the hole in its chest like beer from the bunghole of a keg. Then Gerard let Gatsun shoot the buffalo in the shoulder with the .460, and we allowed the now-dead buffalo to lie for a good while, just to make sure. And it was dead. It was dead, dead, dead. Anyone who had witnessed the amount of lead we had just poured into the old brute would have known that, would have been crazy not to bet a million dollars on it. Unfortunately, it would have been a losing bet. As we approached the bull and Gerard went to touch the eye, the bull's head suddenly jerked up, and the black bulk came half to its feet. The three of us jumped back as if a grenade had gone off—our hearts stopped in our throats. Both guns flew to the shoulder—but it was only the last of the life in it, and neither of us had to fire a shot. The big head tipped back as the bull uttered an earsplitting death groan, and the old buffalo rolled hard to the ground, raising the dust around him.

It staggers the mind to think what it took to bring that bull down! A total of eight bullets! Five from the .375 and three from the .460.

Nor, for the record, were any of those shots poorly placed. The buffalo is simply a tough, tough beast. It is the hardiest of animals and never to be underestimated. The buffalo is forever ready to offer the hunter a new lesson in hunting dangerous game. The cost of that lesson, if the hunter is not careful, is death.

This bull, as we knew, was big in body but small in horn. But that was OK with me. The fun in buffalo hunting has little to do with horn size and everything to do with the excitement of stalking and shooting an old bull. Big horns are simply a bonus. If I could choose one African animal to hunt over and over, it would without a doubt be the buffalo.

We hung the sable in a suitable tree for leopard and set out the buffalo in a different location for lion bait. The buffalo was too large to hang, so we chained it to the base of a tree and covered it with branches to keep the buzzards from spotting it. There was nothing, however, to be done about the hyenas. They would find it in good time, and they would stay with the carcass until there was nothing left. The good news for us was that it would take even a large pack a good while to finish off a whole buffalo, and the ever-diminishing bait might still attract and hold a male lion despite the presence of scavengers.

Back in the woodlands, a family of bushpigs caught Kipper's eye, and he banged on the top of the car. We sneaked through the trees, and I took the shaggy boar as it quartered away. Surprisingly, the boar spun and came running right at me! At first I thought it was a charge, and that the bushpig—for its size—was the most aggressive animal I had ever encountered. But then I realized the truth: the boar didn't know where the danger had come from and was simply trying to get away. I shot it again, and the dazed pig spun a complete circle, then came at me again to within forty yards. My third and final shot in the shoulder put it down. I was happy to make the running shots, glad to be shooting well.

On the drive back to camp, while crossing the charred earth of an earlier burn, we blew a tire on one of the burned stumps that booby-trapped the ground. The fires, which are set intentionally at the start of the season, are beneficial in clearing the dead, head-high grass and bringing new green growth, and though they do not bother the mature *miombo* trees in the least, they at times leave charred, pointed stobs that litter the forest floor. The hole in a tire made by a stob is more than a patch can fix. The tire is ruined. So Gerard cussed the stob for being a stob and himself for not seeing it. There were two spares in the bed of the truck for just such a case, and we were quickly on our way.

A Bullet Well Placed

Early the next morning we encountered the same waterbuck that we had passed up twice before. Through binoculars, we studied this stout antelope whose coat is made up of coarse, bristly hair that is salt-and-pepper-colored except for a conspicuous white ring on its rear—a feature that, although probably not nature's intention, serves as a convenient target on its departure. Most important, we studied the long, curving horns that arch slightly forward. After a minute or two, Gerard decided that this male was the best we would see, so we crept to a respectable distance and I took it, facing us, with the Weatherby. The thick-trunked animal dropped in its tracks, and everyone gathered in congratulations.

Then it was time for pictures, a process that took longer than the hunt, for Gerard approaches the taking of trophy pictures with the same deliberation and precision that he does the hanging of baits. The animal is placed in an upright position, its legs tucked underneath, and all blood is wiped from the wound, nose, and mouth. A flopping tongue is unacceptable. Gerard then directs the area cleared of all interfering grass and twigs, and the sunlight is checked on his subject for the best possible angle. It makes for great pictures, obviously, but it is also an act of respect paid to the game. It is a serious business and a ritual that follows the taking of every trophy.

Later in the day as we climbed out of a ravine, we encountered a roan antelope, a fairly rare yet highly sought after trophy named for its rusty brown color; it was standing broadside on a slight rise in the forest. A close cousin of the sable, the roan is larger in body but smaller in horn. The lone bull remained broadside and was no spookier than the sable had been. Although I made a good shot with the .300, the large antelope ran as if unhit. I worked the bolt and fired once more, but the second bullet deflected in the long grass. A third shot up the rear brought the trophy down, and instead of reloading, I finished it with a shot from Gerard's 7mm.

"I tell you, Johnny, I don't like that .300. I've had trouble with the caliber before. It may be a good choice in the open, but in brush country it's completely useless. The bullet is too easily deflected."

So it was decided that I would use the .375 exclusively for plains game, even the small ones. There is simply too much interference—twigs and such—for the speedy .300. Additionally, the .375 is a better gun to have in your hands if in the course of the hunt you happen upon an irritable buffalo or lion that is having a bad day and wants to make yours even worse. The Kleingunther shoots exceptionally well, placing holes in the paper at 100 yards that you can cover with a nickel, so I was fine with the decision. My only complaint was with the design of the safety. The thumb catch, at the rear of the bolt, slides up and down, not front to back, and requires removing the shooting hand to disengage it—a poor arrangement on a caliber made for taking dangerous game.

From a tall tree in a small clearing, we hung the roan and waterbuck together as one lion bait. The baits were hung some 3 feet from the ground, high enough to be out of reach of any marauding hyenas but low enough for a lion to feed on.

"Why don't we split them into two baits?" I asked. "Seems we'd double our odds."

"That's true," Gerard said. "But a couple of male *simbas* would finish this waterbuck in one night, and there would be nothing left to keep them in the area. A hungry cat can eat a tremendous amount of meat."

Once the task was completed, we loaded into the truck and, except for another flat, made the return to camp without incident. Before dinner I reveled in a hot shower, which in the bush is a short affair, requiring one to use the water in the overhead bucket sparingly so as not to run out before all the soap and shampoo are off. Dressed in freshly laundered and ironed attire, I joined Dad in a chair in the dark by the fire. I lifted my beer to him.

"Thanks," I said. "Thanks for a truly wonderful graduation present. I can't tell you how much fun I'm having."

He smiled, and we clinked bottles. "Me, too," he said. We scooted our chairs closer to the crackling fire to absorb the radiating warmth against the evening chill.

Sitting and staring into the dancing flames, we told each other about our day. Dad had collected a buffalo with an impressive horn spread of 45 inches, and we relived the hunt through his telling of it. Then we wondered over the hunting adventures that subsequent days were sure to bring. We were both aglow inside, as relaxed as if in a state of meditation, at peace with the world and those around us. There was nowhere else on earth that we would rather be, there was nothing we would rather be doing than sitting around that very campfire in the middle of Africa. That, of course, is what it was all about. That is why we hunt. If there is a better father-son activity than hunting, I don't know what it is. Hunting is the one thing that will always be our bond. Even when angry with each other, our squabbles go on hold when it comes time to hunt.

The following morning, while we were driving through a fairly thick patch, Roman spotted a warthog lying in the brush. We made a stalk, but the pig was difficult to see. It was sitting tight. Even as we neared, only a stone's throw away, the trophy tusker stayed put. When it failed to get up, Gerard instructed me to aim for its middle. I did, hitting it high in the back, and it jumped up and ran. Quickly reloading, I put one in its flank, which did little to slow it down. My third shot, at its running backside, ended the escape. The pointy tushes were quite long and symmetrical from the lip.

We spent the remainder of the day checking baits, but unfortunately no cats of either variety had come to feed. In the process we covered a lot of country and saw a tremendous number of trophy-size animals, including a 52-inch kudu, a 45-inch sable, a 29-inch roan, and a 32-inch waterbuck that would catch anyone's attention. It was clear that this Rungwa area abounds in trophy quality.

While stopped at one of the baits, I got to talking with Gatsun, the government-appointed professional hunter, and inquired how he came by his weapons, a .458 and .375 that together would not have fetched a hundred dollars at the most liberal of pawn shops. He explained that TAWICO (Tanzania Wildlife Corporation), the government-owned company that directs all hunting operations in the country and that is his employer, loaned him the rifles. Ammunition is provided, however, only if available.

The king at rest.

"Last year," he informed me, "I hunted the whole season with only one shell."

This year the government still had no .375 ammunition to give him, so that gun sits useless in his tent. Earlier in the season, though, a client had left him two .458 shells to add to his precious collection. So now he has a total of three shells, which he proudly displayed in his palm.

When the next day's check of the lion baits turned up empty, Gerard decided it was time to switch to plan B.

"It is time to take a hippo, my friend. We will show these finicky lions a thing or two."

Our goal was to find a hippo out of the water, a more sporting hunt for sure, but a near impossible task during the light of day because hippos feed mostly at night. Gerard did not want to wait, though, so we went to a pool at a bend in the river that he knew held hippo. Even as we climbed the bank, we could hear their noisy grunts and snorts, and soon the heads of the big animals came into view. The bank made a great rest, which I would need to pull off the brain shot we were planning. But even though I was calm and ready for the shot, the hippos were not. Sighting us, they snorted and jostled about. They took turns plunging beneath the murky surface with a splash and emerging a minute later, batting water from their tiny ears. While we waited for them to settle, Gerard in whispers pointed out the largest bull. I would just about get it in the sights when it would disappear beneath the roiling surface, only to emerge elsewhere; we played that game for ten or fifteen minutes. But we had nowhere else to go, and there was no hurry. So we waited.

Finally the old boy came up, and I put the cross hairs smack between its eyes and pulled the trigger. It went under at the shot, as did all the hippos. There would be no knowing whether I had got it until tomorrow; if I had, we would find its floating body.

But we didn't make it to the hippo pool the next day, because of the double bit of luck we had checking the roan/waterbuck bait. While we were speeding along in the twilight of early dawn, on our way to the bait, Kipper suddenly tapped the roof. There was some hurried whispering, then Gerard stopped the car and had a look with his binocular. Suddenly he grew quite excited, more excited than I had yet to see him.

"Get your gun! Get your gun!" He was almost pushing me out the door, and then he catapulted quietly out his own. He ran around the car, grabbed me by the arm, pulled me forward, and said in my ear, "Kudu."

A Bullet Well Placed

I scoured the dark trees ahead but saw no sign of kudu in the dim light. The forest was a lifeless expanse of dusky, drab gray. "Just hit it anywhere," he instructed.

"But I don't see it."

"There! Between those two trees." Gerard pointed frantically.

I was growing quickly frustrated, not seeing it. But just then a horn moved, and the gray antelope materialized into view. Its body was hidden behind the *V* of two trees, and in the scope I could not tell what was tree and what was kudu. But Gerard was nudging me to shoot. I aimed offhand in the center of the *V* and fired, but my bullet hit one of the trees. Luckily, the kudu did not run. It merely took a step forward into the clear, and now I had a perfect shot. I snatched a quick breath and squeezed the trigger. The bullet took it on the shoulder, and it went straight down. We ran up, and as we reached the fallen bull Gerard was beside himself. Even Gatsun was jumping up and down, and Kipper was grinning from ear to ear.

"Just look at the horns on this bull!"

This was the first kudu bull I had ever seen up close, but even with my untrained eye I could tell that it was special. The dark horns spiraled up endlessly, making three wide, unbelievably deep turns, like giant corkscrews, and the sharp ends were ivory tipped and pointed directly outward. The kudu was absolutely magnificent. No, it was more than magnificent. It was world class, legendary, one of a kind—all rolled into one. That, of course, was from a trophy hunter's perspective. The first thing a nonhunter would have noticed was that the kudu was old and run down, with the bones poking up in its weathered hide like a hat rack under a tattered sheet. It was so old, in fact, that hardly a trickle of blood ran from the bullet wound in its shoulder. But for us, as hunters, we saw the king of the species lying at our feet and felt lucky, proud, and elated to have collected it. Here was an animal whose remaining time on earth was measured in months or weeks, if not days. Its condition made the hunt perfect by the book, which calls upon the sport hunter to cull the old, surplus males from the herd.

"Kubwa sana!" Kipper said. Very big. The beaming tracker gave me a bear hug, and we all shook hands again and again and marveled at the grand antelope at our feet. Gerard kept shaking his head in disbelief. By the old system, measured around the spiral, the kudu's horns went 62¼ inches. By the new system, straight up the horn, it measured 58 inches.

Gerard's hand clasped the back of my neck. "Last I looked, my friend, the biggest kudu taken in Tanzania went 57 inches. And the world record is something like 61. That is one hell of a trophy, that. You will never, ever, shoot better, kid. Never." (He was right. That kudu turns heads in my trophy room like a girl in a bikini.)

"Well, perhaps you are due *some* of the credit. I didn't do it *completely* on my own." Gerard went to box me on the ear, and I ducked; we made a couple of playful punches at each other, and Kipper and Gatsun laughed at us. It was a day that we would all remember. The kudu was a trophy that would never be forgotten.

Once the patriarch bull was loaded into the truck, we continued the hunt, happening onto our second bit of luck while driving up to the lion bait. As we neared it, two male lions suddenly appeared in the bush ahead. But it was for just an instant. Immediately the two cats turned and trotted off, disappearing in the scrub, and just as quickly we got out and followed them. It was quite exciting, needless to say, following two male lions in the thick stuff, but try as we might I could not get a shot. Not a decent shot, anyway. And I wasn't about to try anything less.

It is one thing to take a potshot at a departing warthog or antelope, and it is something altogether different to attempt that on a five-hundred-pound lion. I wasn't about to be the cause of a wounded lion, nor the cause of someone in our party getting fatally mauled, if I could help it. In the end, all I ever saw were glimpses of their trotting forms ahead, an unacceptable presentation. When the lions had gotten quite ahead of us, Gerard decided that it was best for us to retreat and not push them off the bait. We would return at sundown.

So that was what we did. In the evening, Gerard, Gatsun, and I slunk up to the blind, as quietly as possible on the dry, crunchy ground. My heart was hammering in my chest, and my senses were on full alert. The hardest part of the hunt, though, and I would never have guessed it, was trying to keep still in the blind. It was not a complete blind at this point, just one wall of thatch, and we were forced to hunker in a permanent crouch behind it. Soon my legs began to cramp. After several minutes, I had to move. I eased one knee onto the ground. Relief! But then both legs and an arm fell asleep. We had a long wait until dark, but nothing showed. Perhaps our earlier appearance and pursuit had scared the lions off. When it was time to go, I could hardly stand to walk back to the car. I made a mental note for the next hunt to assume a more comfortable position right from the start.

We were up at 5:00 the next day and off straightaway for the lion bait. As we whisked along the winding track in the dark, I wondered how I would perform against one of Africa's most dangerous animals, how I would hold up when I got the lion in the cross hairs. Although I was sure I would do well, that I would hold steady and put the bullet where it was supposed to go, one can never know for sure on dangerous game until one is put to the test.

An hour and a half later we had reached our approach spot. Everyone climbed out of the car in the pitch dark, and Gerard and I quietly loaded our guns. My eyes were momentarily useless, having stared into the beam of the headlights as we drove. But even when they had finally adjusted, there wasn't much to see. It was that dark. I shouldered the .375 and tested the scope against the inky sky, then followed Gerard down into the depths of a dry creek, where it was even darker. In the dimness we wandered the creek bottom for cover and made our way steadily toward the blind.

It was more than a little unnerving walking into the "lion's den," so to speak, in the dark. We knew there were lions about—for we could now hear them, very near to us, at the bait. There was the unmistakable crunch of bone and the sound of ripping flesh. There was the smack of hungry jowls. All were sounds that grabbed my attention. The only thing we didn't know was how many lions there were, and in what variety.

At that very instant a sound erupted that stopped time.

It was a sound that was as natural and as much of a ritual to the African predawn calm as is the twitter of songbirds starting their day or a groggy hippo grunting and getting ready for bed, but it was a sound for which we were completely unprepared. At least so close to us. A male lion roared. The thundering sound struck with the suddenness of lightning, rattling our eardrums and bringing our procession to an instant halt. It sent a thumb flying to the safety on my gun and started the adrenaline gushing. Whatever songbirds were present could no longer be heard above the knocking in my chest. Never had a stalk gotten my excitement up like this, but never had I hunted lions in the dark. Quite frankly, I think it was the handicap of the dark, not being able to see my quarry, that made for such an intense experience. We humans are visual hunters. Take away our sight, and we are nothing. In addition, I knew how well my adversary, the big cats, could see in the dark.

With ears straining at the predawn night, we heard nothing more of the old man's presence. There was just the one roar. *Where was it now?* We continued on, if anything much more slowly, and stopping now and then to listen for clues as to the feline's location.

These young male lions (probably siblings) are reminiscent of a couple of punk teenagers hanging out on the corner—cocky and full of themselves and up to no good.

Finally we reached the blind near the edge of the creek bank and crept into position.

As we sat in the dark, the sounds returned of the lions on the bait, the shredding of flesh, the crunching of bones, the occasional territorial growl over the antelope buffet we had provided. Once twilight began to arrive, I peeked out. In the dim light I could just make out two lionesses and two cubs. The two cubs were feasting on the waterbuck. Because only the hindquarters were left, they had to stretch on tiptoes to reach it, but then the bait would swing around from their weight and send the cubs tumbling on their backs to the ground. Then they would leap up and try again. The two lionesses, with noticeably full bellies, were playing nearby. They ran into each other, stood on hind legs, and hugged and tugged like a couple of sumo wrestlers in the ring. The male, however, was still spooked from yesterday, or full from feeding, for it was nowhere in sight. But we soon heard it growling, about 150 yards up the creek.

When it got light and still the male had not shown, Gerard decided that we should take the fight to the lion. So leaving the relative safety of the blind, we struck out on foot and swung through the patchy brush, hoping to come upon it, a task that was tremendously exciting and exhilarating, to say the least. It was the kind of endeavor that holds your attention the way a pair of pliers holds a big bass by the lip. My every thought, my every effort, my every sense was focused on that one task. Then it happened. In the midst of our stalk, not five yards ahead of us, a patch of brush exploded with commotion. It happened so fast in fact that there was no time for any of us to act, or even to react. We had made a fatal blunder on the lion's turf. It was checkmate before we had even gotten the game going. With Gerard directly in front of me, there was no way for me to shoot. No time to get around him. The lion would be on him before I could take a step. In fact, as close as we three were, the lion likely would plow us all over like bowling pins, allowing no one a shot. Then it would be a matter of one of us trying to get a lethal shot into it without shooting someone in our party.

As it turned out—very fortunately for us—it was not our lion that had caused the explosion in the brush, and the three of us sighed in unison. The culprit was two bushbucks launching into flight at our approach. Never let anyone tell you that a bushbuck isn't a dangerous animal. There is no doubt that those wicked little antelope took ten years off my life.

We continued the search for a short while, but we saw no sign of the wary lion.

"Time to get your hippo," Gerard announced upon our return to the car.

At the pool we found the hippo, bloated and floating on the opposite bank, just as we had hoped. My aim had been true. Roman worked his way around the water's edge, crossed the river in the shallows, and tied a rope to the monstrous head. All the while the rest of the hippos, crowded in the middle of the small pool and irritated by the morning encroachment, chuffed and snorted and made mock charges.

Gerard handed me the .460.

"In case they decide to act up," he said. It was a boon to the ego to be put in charge, and I took it seriously. The hippos, only five paces away, were really annoyed. I figured that I had about a second and a half to shoot after a charge was begun, and missing the mark was not an option. Someone could get killed. Tugging on the rope, Gerard and Kipper together towed the bloated hippo across the pool, trying to keep it as near shore as possible and away from any contenders. From the fresh, deep wounds on the hip and hind legs, one or two had already taken advantage of the hippo's unusual passivity to show the old boy their true feelings. Perhaps it had been a rival eager to replace him at the top of the pecking order, or perhaps it was an old grudge that had never been settled—whatever the case, someone had been glad to get in a few free licks. Finally, without incident, the bloated hippo reached the shore where I was standing guard. Gerard secured the winch cable around its neck, and Kipper took an ax to the bank to smooth the steep slope. Revving the engine, Gerard pulled the heavy carcass right out. But that was the easy part.

Next came the chore of moving a four-ton animal from where it was to where we wanted it. It was a slow, laborious process, something like towing a yacht from a canoe. We dragged the bull hippo some five kilometers, not quite to the roan/waterbuck bait, for the clutch began to smoke from the strain.

"I'll send you the bloody bill on this clutch, Chilton! Ruining my vehicle we are, all in the name of getting you a lion." Gerard reached over and knocked the bill of my cap, and I just smiled. I was having a great time. Nothing about the trip could have been better. The weather was good, I was shooting nicely, and everyone in the group got along. It was perfect.

Glancing quickly about, Gerard selected the best site in the immediate area, and we left the hippo there. We then went to cut down what was left of the roan and waterbuck bait and dragged the fetid remains to the hippo, in the hope of leading the lions by scent to our new bait. Then we built a blind—a real blind with four sides and a grass-thatched door at the rear. A good blind takes time to construct, and time was the one thing we had grown short of while busy collecting the long list of trophies on my license. But now we made time to do the job right.

Conveniently situated some sixty yards from the bait was an overgrown bush that Kipper and Roman fashioned into our blind. They hollowed out the inside to accommodate the hunters and placed grass thatch in the openings so that, from the lion's side, we would be completely hidden. They crafted two thatch-ringed shooting holes in the front and then swept the ground inside the blind, as well as the path, clear of every stem and twig. We did not want to make a sound. Gerard even had me slip my gun through the shooting hole and test the fit, just to make sure. It was perfect. Everything, in fact, looked perfect. We left feeling ready.

Juma, the tentboy, woke me at 4:30 A.M., and we departed immediately thereafter. After another cool early-morning drive, we were soon stalking through the dark on our way to the blind. At

100-plus yards I could smell the rotting hippo, ensuring us of a good wind (or bad wind, depending on how you looked at it). As Gerard and I crouched into the blind, we turned to see Gatsun on tiptoe peeking over the top. Gerard shot him an angry glance and motioned him down with a hand. Apparently Gatsun had been unable to contain his curiosity to see what lions were on the bait, for ahead of us, in the dark, there they were.

There was no mistaking those familiar sounds of crunching and chomping, purring and growling. Once settled in the blind, we had several long minutes to wait till the sun would cast its precious light on what was still a pitch-black scene. In the meantime we had only our imaginations with which to wonder at the sounds, some familiar, some not so familiar, that continued to erupt around us; we could only hope that the male was one of the cats now feeding. Time never passes so slowly as in the dark of a hunting blind with animals, especially dangerous ones, close about.

When the dim gray of dawn finally appeared, Gerard removed the grass plug in his shooting hole and peeked through. He simply nodded, then leaned close to my left ear.

"He's feeding on the hippo. Shoot him."

With the plug pulled from my shooting hole, I eased the barrel carefully through the round slot and brought my shoulder to the butt of the stock. It was still dark enough that the three-power scope hardly picked up the lion, some sixty yards off. I hesitated to shoot; I couldn't see well enough. Just then a younger male and the two lionesses became alert. Realizing that something was up, the old boy abruptly rose onto its haunches and glanced about, its back to the blind. Gerard pressed a finger between my shoulder blades, indicating where to shoot the lion. Surprisingly, now that the moment had arrived, I was not nervous. I aimed where Gerard indicated, at the base of the mane, and calmly and quickly pulled the trigger. I knew I didn't have much time. The bullet hit right on the money, and the big lion collapsed, its head face down between its paws. Gerard followed up with an insurance shot, though the lion never moved.

As we walked up, Gerard had me shoot the big cat twice more, just to make sure. The lion didn't move, but it did issue a growl or two on its way through death's door.

"Good shooting, my boy!" Gerard extended his hand.

I was ecstatic. My first lion! It was something I had dreamed about. A lion had been the one member of the Big Five that I had most wanted to collect. And now I had done it. In truth, the lion had less mane than I had hoped for, but a thick mane, at least in brush country, is hard to find. Most important, it was *my* lion, and I was thrilled to have it. What made this hunt so successful, what I was more proud of than anything—was that I had made a good shot. I had succeeded in putting the bullet right where I wanted it, and the lion had dropped in its tracks. It is one thing to wound an impala, but quite another to wound a lion. The first brings disappointment, even sorrow; the latter can get someone killed.

We took a roll or two of film with everyone taking turns sitting on the lion's back and lifting its great head, which is much heavier than you think: It requires quite a tug with both hands. An African lion is a truly impressive creature. If you stop to think how quick and strong and lethal a seven-pound housecat is, then multiply that by seventy, you can begin to picture the awesomeness of the animal that is known as the African lion. Now throw in teeth the size of daggers and claws that can shred flesh like a chainsaw, and the result is nothing less than a total killing machine. The big cats are the final check and balance in a system designed to prevent overpopulation, and they have been well endowed with the tools and talents to accomplish their task. A lion's every feature is designed to further that one aim. No Hollywood producer ever thought up a more deadly creation—nor one as cunning and clever, and used to having its way.

Nature's camouflage. There are some twenty lions in this photo. You can't see them all, and neither can their prey.

A Bullet Well Placed

It was no easy chore loading the big animal into the back of the truck. Once that was accomplished, though, we were on our way to camp. When a lion or leopard is collected, the hunting for that day is done, and the cat is whisked to camp to be skinned. For one thing, the cats have thin coats; if they are not skinned quickly, especially in the heat, the hair can slip. For another, this is the highpoint of the hunt and a time for celebration. We have been getting up early and getting back late, and everyone can use a break. And it would be nice to see camp in the light of day, for once.

On the way home, however, we happened onto an oribi that Gerard simply couldn't pass up. The little orange-colored antelope was a dandy, according to Mr. Miller, with pointy horns no longer or bigger around than a .450 cartridge. "Shoot it in the middle," Gerard instructed. "A shoulder shot tears up the cape on these little chaps." So I shot the tiny antelope right where Gerard said. The oribi ran a ways and stopped, just about the time I got the gun reloaded; my second shot dropped it. Much to our amazement, when we approached, the small antelope was still alive. Kipper nabbed it and put a knife into its heart, and still it took some time for the hardy critter to die. Adrenaline is an incredibly powerful drug. Once an animal gets worked up— even a tiny antelope like the oribi—it is quite difficult to kill it. That is why the Bad Boys that compose the Big Five seem so unstoppable. When they are pumped with adrenaline, shooting a charging buffalo, for instance, is a little like trying to stop an oncoming train by throwing rocks at it.

Soon afterward we arrived in camp, honking and yelling, and the men came out banging on pots and pans, chanting our success, and slapping me on the back. The taking of a cat is a huge event in Africa. It is an act of celebration that surely dates to our earliest ancestors, an act that has been celebrated for more years than any civilization has existed on earth—long before Cleopatra, long before Moses—as long, in fact, as there have been men and lions inhabiting the same patch of ground. The celebration continues to this day, even if the cat is taken by a foreigner and with a gun.

They sure know how to make you feel like a hero.

After our success we slept in and took it easy the next day, which gave me a chance to roam around camp. It was fascinating to see the various work areas laid out like so many departments in a business: the kitchen, the laundry, the mechanics shop, the skinning shed. In each, the men were busy at their respective tasks, preparing lunch, washing our clothes, patching a tire, welding a leaky radiator, caping

56

heads and salting hides. And always there was Gerard, commanding, inspecting the progress of this or that, instructing here, chastising there, joking with the men in Swahili. It made me more than a little envious, and I tried to picture myself leading the same sort of life, the life of the white professional hunter. It was a nice dream, but I realized down deep that it was neither my destiny nor my aptitude, even if the thought did tempt the soul.

Out at midday, we continued our good luck with the smaller antelopes. I shot a gray duiker on the second try. (My first bullet hit a branch and missed.) The gray duiker, slightly larger than the oribi, is the color of the surrounding gray earth, except for its legs, which are much darker. It is quick on its feet, making a running shot nearly impossible. We built a fire on the spot and roasted half of the small antelope for lunch.

On our return in the evening we stopped at the hippo pool beside camp, where several spurwing geese had collected at the water's edge. Unlike at the pool where I took my hippo, the hippos here had grown accustomed to camp and our regular comings and goings. They had resigned themselves to the fact that we men were here to stay, and the general agreement was to ignore one another. Thus the large animals paid me little mind as I stalked the geese on the shore of their home. When the geese finally flushed, I managed to knock two out of the air for camp meat.

The local hippos, I should note, were an inherent part of camp life. The big creatures were noisy in their routine grunts and snorts, like so many cattle in a nearby corral, but were they suddenly to disappear, for whatever reason, their disappearance would be as remarkable and conspicuous as if the nightly campfire were to go unlighted. Camp would seem eerily quiet, as if something were not right; they would be missed deeply. Their soothing sounds are as natural to the African night as is the hum of crickets back home on a hot summer's evening. I did find it surprising, however, that we had yet to encounter one of the big fellows out of the water, despite the fact that their nocturnal clock runs exactly opposite to ours. Not until late at night, when we are fast asleep, do they roam the banks in search of grass.

Our last day in Rungwa, like my first, was quite a successful one. We discovered a herd of eland in a thick part of the forest, a part that had not been burned, and, although under the cover of thicker bush, the closest we could get was some 250 yards. The herd bull was an old one, the tips of whose horns were splintered and broomed. But we

This is what lions do. They don't eat veggies. Three minutes ago that was a healthy, happy wildebeest.

had seen few eland, and these weren't going to stick around long. They were becoming fidgety.

"Once eland start to run, they don't stop. They are the long-distance runners of the animal kingdom. You'd best shoot now," Gerard advised, a tone of urgency in his voice. So I put the cross hairs on the hefty antelope's shoulder and squeezed.

To my great surprise, the big bull went right down, proving easier to kill than the tiny oribi of two days before. My surprise only grew as we approached and I came to realize what a giant animal the eland is—an animal every bit the size and girth of a Brahma bull. I had to marvel. The unique thing about Africa (and what makes it such a great place to hunt) is that it hosts such a diversity of wildlife. Africa is home to both the largest *and* the smallest antelope on the planet. In the same day, one can shoot a five-pound dik-dik and a one-ton eland, not to mention any number of animals in between. Nowhere else in the world do you encounter such a range in size. Again, it was no easy task to load this animal into the bed of the truck, even quartered.

Later in the morning, I took a topi at two hundred yards. It ran, wounded, but a snap shot at its backside brought the dark antelope quickly down. After that I flushed and shot a bush partridge, a ground bird that looks every bit like a large bobwhite quail. We arrived in camp at 10:45 A.M., done for the day; Gerard needed the afternoon to prepare for tomorrow's departure to Masailand.

Lunch was grilled shish kebabs of eland, and the meat, despite its origins, was surprisingly tender and tasty—I would never have guessed that it came from a tough old bull. Whether it was a culinary feat by the cook or the natural state of the meat itself, I didn't know, but it was fantastic. Another thing that I find a wonder is that the meat from each antelope species has its own taste, texture, and color. You would think that muscle is muscle and that it would all be identical, but it is not. Most of the game meat is quite good, but the best, in my opinion, is eland and gerenuk. I could eat that meat every day.

A female leopard had been visiting one of Dad's baits, and George asked if I would like to film it while Gerard was busy packing. The exciting thing about this leopard was that she had made a practice of climbing the tree early, and if the pattern repeated, I would have plenty of light with which to film an animal that is normally hard to capture on film. And I would of course take along a gun, in case her boyfriend put in an appearance.

In the end we had a long, quiet wait, but the leopard never showed. The birds raised a ruckus a time or two, and in each case we thought for sure that she was about to climb the tree—more than once Angelides made a knowing nod—but she didn't. The car came to collect us at dark. The time we spent in the blind wasn't a total loss, however. While under attack, I learned how to squash tsetse flies silently and effectively. The natural reaction to their painful bite is to slap the crap out of them—but you can't because you can't make noise in a leopard blind. So you have to grit your teeth against the sting, then quietly and patiently maneuver your hand into position to mash, roll, and crush them. The little devils are practically armor coated—it is like trying to crush a medicine capsule in your fingertips—but you have to crush them. Otherwise the villains just come back and bite you again.

Around the fire in camp that night Gerard approached and held out his fist. He dropped a weighty lead ball into my palm.

"That was in your eland's leg," he said. "A meat poacher, I suspect. Muzzleloader. Been in him for years."

Up at 3:00 A.M., we were off by 4:30 for Arusha. We were one day ahead of our scheduled departure, but we had shot everything in Rungwa we could shoot. Also, Gerard had business to attend to in town. Fourteen hours later (a little quicker than the drive down), we arrived at Mount Meru Game Lodge, a cozy hideaway on the outskirts of town. There we met the Deutsches, fellow Texans from Laredo. My sister Leanne had met Lisa Deutsch on the floor of her college dorm earlier that year. They got to talking about where they were from, and Lisa mentioned Laredo.

"Oh, my gosh," Leanne said. "We have a ranch near Laredo. My brother and dad are big hunting nuts."

"Well, so are we! In fact, we are going to Africa this summer."

"Oh, my gosh, so are we!"

"What country?"

"Tanzania."

"So are we! Who are you hunting with?"

"George Angelides."

"So are we!"

Small world.

And so, though we knew of the Deutsches, Dad and I had yet to meet them. Present this trip were Seymon and his wife, Linda, and three of their four children: Lisa, Debbie, and Mark. They were an excited group, in the habit of all talking at once, but somehow they managed to keep up with each conversation in play, jumping in and out at a dizzying pace. This was Seymon's fifteenth safari, so I paid close attention to what he had to say.

Two days later, Mom and the girls arrived to join us for the second half of our safari. None of them hunted, so they would be joining us strictly as observers. After a quick breakfast at the lodge, we piled

A nice roan. With me is Gatsun, one of the more knowledgeable government PHs.

into two hunting trucks to leave for Masailand, some four hours away, and a camp named Lavasoret. The camp, which resides on the low banks of a shallow stream, is conveniently tucked beneath the shady canopy of a handful of giant fig trees. Vervet monkeys chattered in the treetops and performed all kinds of acrobatic feats. It was an ideal location for a hunting camp, except that it was also an ideal location for the Masai to water their endless herds of goats and cattle. The rowdy animals paraded through camp continuously. Admittedly, this is their land, so I guess one can't complain too much, but the arrangement was not without consequence, as we would find out later.

As we arrived in camp, professional hunter Armando Cordoza came out to greet us. Armando, a partner of George's, is a tall, dark, and handsome Portuguese.

"Call me Mando," he told us.

We got our gear quickly situated, as Dad and I were keen to get out and see this new country, while the girls, tired from travel, elected to stay in camp for the afternoon. Mando and I and his tracker Hasani—a short, stern-faced fellow—went out to look for guinea fowl and other plains game on foot. In the process we ran into a group of six buffalo bulls. But our meeting was brief, and we got no more than a glance at the wily animals. Winding us, the buffalo ran, quickly disappearing in the bush.

We circled downwind, trying to find them in the narrow openings that separated the thick mottes of brush, but instead we came upon a couple of giraffes that threatened to blow our cover. We knew that if the giraffes spooked, the buffalo would be gone for good. It called for the utmost diplomacy. Admittedly, it's not an easy task to get out of sight of a giraffe, but with a little backtracking and circumnavigation we eventually did. After some further searching, we happened onto two old bulls that had remained behind. They were just standing there, broadside, statue-still, listening and checking the wind. They hadn't spotted us yet, but because they had earlier smelled us, they knew something was up. They were holding tight and waiting for us to make the next move.

Mando quickly glassed their horns. Then he nodded his head and motioned for me to rest the .375 on Hasani's shoulder. At 70 yards, it was not a difficult shot. I put the cross hairs on the thick shoulder of the biggest bull, the dark animal nicely framed by the golden grass around it, and squeezed. I hit it right smack on the money with a solid. Immediately the two bulls charged off into the brush. When we reached the spot where they had been standing, we found absolutely

Gerard and Gatsun with the holy grail. This was the largest greater kudu ever taken in Tanzania—until Gerard took a larger one the very next year.

no sign the buffalo had been hit. No blood, no hair—nothing. To me this was quite disappointing, but Mando did not seem the least concerned. We began a stealthy pursuit with Hasani in the lead and barely glancing at the ground. In fact, the serious-faced tracker was striding along as if he were late for an engagement. I thought, *He's not even paying attention.*

Amazingly, Mando read my mind.

"You think he's just walking, don't you?" he whispered. Then some half a kilometer from where we had started Hasani suddenly kneeled and pointed at the ground. There in the dirt was the first blood—a droplet the size of a mediocre tick. I was dumbstruck. The astute tracker had been on the buffalo's trail the whole time! Then we had another long, barren trek in which we never did find another drop of blood. This took us another half a kilometer, at which point Hasani abruptly stopped and held up his hand.

Presently we heard the buffalo moan from a clump of brush, no more than five or six yards away. The motte was thick, offering no visibility whatsoever. Instantly I was filled with that same tenseness you feel when watching the hapless victim in a horror movie go creeping down a hallway of closed doors from behind one of which the killer is waiting to spring. The important thing was not to open a door. Fortunately, my companions knew this rule as well.

Consequently, Mando had us back up a safe distance. He set the butt of his big double at his feet and lit a cigarette.

"He isn't going anywhere," he said wisely. "No reason to get charged."

The buffalo groaned ten or twelve times more and was finished. After a good wait and with great care, we eased our way into the thick, dark motte, where we found the buffalo bull very much dead. But its partner was very much alive and standing by its side! This bull was only a few short paces away and provided a supremely tense moment for us as it decided what to do. Fortunately, it decided not to charge. The black ox simply stood there, staring down its dark nose at us. The bull was hesitant to leave, but finally it did. The brush was so thick in there that had the bull charged, the results would have been disastrous. Naturally, I was quite happy the way it turned out.

The next day we stalked up on a wildebeest in the open of the plains, but the nearest we could get was 250 yards. On the open plains the animals appeared spookier than they had in the remote forests of Rungwa, and it made for excessively long shots. I took a shot off the shooting stick, then again offhand as it ran, but apparently I missed both times. We got back in the car and followed, then got out and tried again on foot. I fired two more times, but it was so far and the shooting stick so unstable that I knew I would miss.

"There was an oryx back where we first saw the wildebeest," Mando said. "Let's go and get it."

I was angry I'd missed the wildebeest and didn't want to give up on it. I was also afraid that it was wounded, but Mando insisted it hadn't been hit. We got only to within two hundred yards of the oryx.

"I don't think I can hit him at that distance. This stick isn't much of a rest."

"Oh, sure you can, Johnny."

The oryx jumped as if it had been hit, but we lost it in the bush. We continued the search to no avail and had just given it up when Mando stopped to take a leak and the oryx suddenly appeared a short distance off. We followed to within close range, and I used Hasani's shoulder for a rest. The oryx went right down, and we had our first leopard bait, not to mention a splendid trophy.

Somewhat surprisingly, we later came upon the same wildebeest, which was now paired with a Grant gazelle. This funny beast did not seem to know its own species! This time I got set up with a good rest and was steady on the Grant, now 220 yards away. One shot and it made a short dash and keeled over. Then Mando said to shoot the wildebeest, which was watching us from a little farther off, and I got it with one shoulder shot, too. I was glad to have my shooting back on track. I can shoot well enough with a good rest, but forget a two-hundred-yard shot off a wiggly stick. Mando could use a lesson from John Fletcher on how to build a shooting stick.

At breakfast, Dad mentioned that he had diarrhea.

"I had it a week ago, but not since then," I told him. But by lunch I had it again, too. So did the rest of the family.

In the afternoon, Leanne went with Mando and me to hang baits. Of the three girls, none of whom would kill an animal although they all ate meat, she was probably the most sensitive about hunting. I wondered how she would do when we ran into a herd of impala and Mando said, "Johnny, get your gun. We could use one more bait." Hunting, after all, was what this trip was about, but she had been off the plane barely twenty-four hours. *Welcome to Africa, Leanne, and we will shoot the first wild animal you see.*

It probably wasn't the best planning on our part, but as long as we were going to hunt in front of her, I didn't want to make a mess of it. A nice, one-shot kill was what I needed. Luckily, I did just that. The only shot offered was a Texas heart shot, and Mando said to take it. The impala buck went straight down and never moved, and with the placement of the bullet being what it was, there was almost no blood. It was perfect.

This antelope made our fourth leopard bait. We hung the impala, the Grant, and the wildebeest in two halves, all in the upper limbs of tall trees, but Mando didn't hang a leopard bait the way Gerard did. I had learned enough by watching Gerard the last couple of weeks that I could point out the problems with each of Mando's baits: wind was bad on this one; silhouette was missing on that one; sun was in the wrong direction here; not enough ground cover for the leopard to approach there. Needless to say, I was not impressed. There was no doubt that one of the four baits might get the job done, but it was sloppy work. They weren't hung with the precision and planning that Gerard poured into the hanging of baits—as if his mother's soul depended upon their success.

I wasn't feeling too good right then, however—having sharp stomach pains—so maybe I was a little more skeptical about Mando and his leopard-baiting skills than he deserved. By the time we got back to camp I felt bad all over, and Dad had a high fever. The culprit turned out to be our drinking water, which the Masai livestock had continually paraded through. Normally that would not have presented a problem, but it was the unfortunate failure of the staff to bring the water to a proper boil that had allowed the microscopic organisms to attack. Mando dispensed Lomotil to help stop the diarrhea. It did stop it, but I still felt ill. We all went to bed early and slept in the next morning. I got twelve hours of sleep and needed every hour of it.

Mom went with Mando and me the following afternoon. I was glad to have her along, not just for her pleasant company but also because Mom is always good luck. It never fails back home—tell her that we are going out "just to look at the game" and that's when the biggest damn buck of the season steps out. And to top it off, it will come to thirty yards and gawk at us as if it had never seen a human being before. I know Mom must be thinking, *How hard is this?*

But somehow the animals know. They know when they are being hunted. And they know when they are not. Just as the zebra knows from the body language of the lion wandering by that it is not hungry, the same zebra knows to skedaddle when it sees the lion suddenly crouch and take an interest. We humans, often unknowingly, give off the same signals.

But there is more to it than just body language, if you ask me. Scientists will tell you that there are five senses—sight, sound, smell, taste, and touch—but, as usual, their observations are based on the human perspective. I will tell you that animals have more than five senses. Birds, for instance, have a sense of direction. Somehow they know how to point south in the winter and north in the summer. Even more amazing, they know how to return to the same location year after year, which is more than just a sense of direction—it is a sense of positioning, for lack of a better word. Similarly, animals—especially prey animals—have a sense of danger. They can feel the stare of hostile eyes upon their flesh; they can sense the deadly intentions of a carnivore's calculating mind. I can't prove that, but I know it, as does any hunter who has spent any time in the wilds. The worst thing you can do is to stare at an animal you are hunting.

Perhaps Mom's good-natured vibes canceled out my predator vibes, for though we did not get overly close to the impala, the herd remained calm at our approach. Fortunately, for Mom's sake, I made another wonderful shot, and the ram dropped in its tracks. The horns measured 26½ inches, and Mando went on and on about it: "Johnny, this is the biggest impala I've ever seen in Masailand!" But Gerard and I had shot one three inches longer in the southern area of Rungwa, where impala are notably smaller, so I wondered if he was just blowing smoke. With Mando everything we shot was the biggest, so that now I was leery of what he said. If everyone in class gets an "A," a good grade loses its meaning.

But if Mando was anything he was charming, and so Mom had a delightful afternoon in the African bush, and she got to see lots of game and hear lots of interesting facts and stories about this wonderful country that she had traveled so far to see. The weather could not have been more perfect, with the sun out but not overly warm, and the afternoon went by quickly. As on other days, however, we did not stay out late. We returned early, while there was still plenty of shooting light left, and soon we found out why.

Mando liked his whiskey, and he liked it early. By dinner he was feeling pretty good. He was polite and entertaining, and the nicest fellow you will ever meet, but he was tipsy. It's hard to run a camp in that condition, especially if one is in it day in and day out. I was more than ready to have Gerard back. He had returned but was hunting with Dad while George was in town. I liked his no-nonsense style, his commitment to the hunt, and his ceaseless striving for perfection in every aspect of the operation. It was no wonder that, upon his arrival,

Getting our lion bait was the easy part; transporting it was a tad trickier.

Gerard expressed annoyance with the livestock parading through camp. The first thing he said was: "A simple fence around camp would solve everything. I don't mind a warrior or two, but George has got us living in the middle of a bloody village!"

We spent the following morning checking and hanging baits, all in pursuit of the spotted cat that so far had eluded us. Once again there was no sign of a leopard, but as we neared one of the baits we came upon three male lions strolling in its direction. They stayed fifty to seventy yards ahead of us, trotting all the way to the bait, where a large, black-maned lion stood and then sauntered off. It was a magnificent sight, a rare trophy to behold. Once the lion was gone, Mando commented that the lion would be easy to follow up and shoot. But since I already had my lion, we radioed Gerard. "They don't come any better," he told Gerard, and in this case I had to agree. Gerard, Dad, and the girls went there at midmorning, but there was no sign of the big fellow. They did see another pride with a nice male but couldn't get a shot. Kipper, however, got chased by a lion on his way back to collect the vehicle. It must not have been very hungry, or we would have been minus one tracker.

Just before lunch, as we navigated a maze of acacia scrub, a lesser kudu jumped up out of a creek bed a hundred yards away. The unusual thing was that I was the one to spot it. It was about the only animal I had spotted first, as our trackers had tremendous eyes. Mando stopped the car, and I jumped out and quickly shot the white-striped animal. I knew it would not stick around. A lesser kudu bull is as wily as an old whitetail buck, and a much better trophy than its larger cousin, the greater kudu—at least in terms of difficulty to collect. Understandably, I was tickled to have it. It was a nice male, too, with good curls to its horns and ivory tips that stood straight up at the end.

Without delay Hasani jumped out of the car, raced over with a sharp knife, and began to slit the kudu's throat beneath the chin.

"No!" I yelled.

Mando said something to him in Swahili, and he settled for poking the antelope in the base of the neck with the tip of the blade. Hasani was following the Muslim dictate to slit the throat of any animal that is to be eaten. The ancient law originated, apparently, to prevent people from eating carrion. If you slit the throat and it bleeds, you can eat it. One would think that a .375 through the heart would bleed it enough, but Hasani was apparently a stout practitioner; he would slice it from ear to ear if permitted. He had done so to an impala or two that we were hanging for bait (small sections were taken for camp meat), and

My first lion. Rungwa, Tanzania.

I had not said anything. But on a trophy that was going to be mounted, I could not allow it.

(Unfortunately, I never got this lesser kudu's head. It was switched with another, probably in Africa and probably by accident. The one I got back from the taxidermist three years later was a different, smaller bull.)

In the afternoon, Mom, the girls, and I climbed a hill to have a look around. We saw some female greater kudu feeding quietly below but no buffalo, our prime target.

The next day we stayed out all day. After coming up empty on a check of the leopard baits, we traveled to the open, flat plains and looked for Thomson gazelles. The Thomson is smaller but somewhat similar in stature and color to our pronghorn antelope, with a notable black stripe on its side. Their heads bounce noticeably as they trot, and they stay about a thousand yards ahead of you. We finally got to within 240 yards of a nice male, however, and I took it with a shoulder shot. The only problem was that the expanding bullet tore a four-inch hole on exit and threatened to ruin the cape.

"Aim farther back," Mando said, as we approached another. I did and took that one at two hundred yards. But when we came up on it, there was an identical large hole in the shoulder. He said, "You can't stop shooting at the shoulder." When we flipped it over, however, we found that the entrance hole was farther back, just where I had aimed. It had been angled away.

"Actually, Johnny, I didn't think you would get that first one. It was a long shot."

Next I shot a Grant at two hundred paces, but I shot it low, creasing the leg. Four more shots were necessary to bring it down, which left me a bit confused. I realized that the shots at the Tommies were part luck, but a Grant is three times their size and I was squeezing off in just the same manner. When I first developed a flinch seven years earlier in Kenya, I did not know I was doing it. But now I know what to watch for and normally can detect the hideous affliction before it creeps up on me.

Out on the wide plains it was difficult to find a shade tree for lunch. We ate cold meat sandwiches on stools around the wooden chop box, where we were awarded a 360-degree view of the flattest land ever made. The horizon was an absolutely flat line in every direction you looked. Zebra, wildebeest, giraffe, and ostrich were visible all around us. As we ate, Mando asked if I wanted an ostrich, and I insisted I didn't. (I can't remember now why not. Maybe it was something John Fletcher had instilled in me; maybe it just didn't seem desirable.)

The next morning we went with the girls to check all of the leopard baits, none of which had been hit, then climbed a big brushy hill to see what we could see. We spotted the flash of a lesser kudu, but there was no sign of buffalo, which was what we had been hoping to find. Dad returned in the afternoon from fly camp with the results of several days' effort: a pair of tusks from the bull elephant he had shot. At sixty-five pounds a side, they were a very respectable trophy.

Dad was worn out from the long treks the hunt had required, though primarily from the fever of the days before. But despite his exhaustion he was eager for me to experience what he had just experienced. So he took me aside almost immediately.

"Gerard would like to take you elephant hunting."

"Thanks, but I'm not interested." I could see he was disappointed.

"This is a unique experience," he continued. "It's not like you think. And the way elephant hunting is being shut down, you may never get another chance."

I had to shake my head. "I feel sorry for the old fellows. The poachers have hammered them so badly." We had seen numerous remains of the poachers' dirty work. Countless carcasses had been left to rot, the big bones cast about like dinosaur bones. It had repelled me completely.

After charging and giving us a good scare, this rhino posed for a fine photo. Ngorongoro Crater.

"Yes, that's true, but you can't do anything about that. There is a good chance that elephant hunting will close forever, and while you have the opportunity, you ought to take advantage of it."

When I shook my head again, nothing more was said about it, and we all went into the dining tent for dinner. There was quite a celebration over Dad's elephant, and rightly so. He had worked hard for it. The girls and I were glad to have him back in camp, and everyone shared stories around the table of their last few days' adventures. The girls are quite intrigued by the nomadic Masai who stroll through camp in their red robes and colorful beads, fascinated by the women's bald heads and the long braided hair of the warriors, caked in red ochre. Word has spread of the girls' Polaroid camera, and the natives come and pester them for photographs. It is something to see the expression on the face of a Masai girl when she watches the instant picture of herself developing in front of her. With a hand clasped in awe to her mouth, she smiles and giggles with her friends.

Dad came to my tent later that evening, just before bed. "Listen, I know what you think of the poachers and all that, but I've talked to Gerard. He is quite keen to take you. I really think you will regret it if you don't go."

While I thought it over, Dad went on:

"It's a very interesting and exciting hunt, unlike anything you have done before. Despite what you might think, it is not like shooting a cow that's out standing in a farmer's field. It is a difficult, challenging hunt, and I think you will be quite surprised to see what it entails."

I thought it over some more, then said, "OK, I'll do it." Later, Gerard came by to shake my hand and to tell me how glad he was that I had changed my mind. Before turning in, I prepared my daypack with gear and ammo for what could turn into several days away from camp.

Although Gerard and I were up early to get his vehicle and supplies ready, it was almost 8:00 A.M. before our hunting party—he and I, a cook, and his two trackers—left for Kibaya. Along the way we stopped to collect a warthog for camp meat. The husky porker had dashed across the dirt road, disappearing into the thick brush that bordered either side, and we got out and followed it up on foot. I figured that the ugly fellow was gone for good, that there was no way we'd find him in this thick cover. But no, the pig was no more than twenty yards away when Gerard pointed it out in the dense brush ahead. All I could see of it, though, was its rear end. I did my best to estimate where the shoulder was and aimed into the tangle of twigs. My estimate proved worthy, and the warthog dropped on the spot. Roman trotted over to collect it, and our group was happy in the knowledge that camp meat had been secured for the next day or so. Without refrigeration, it doesn't last long.

We stopped in the native villages along the way and asked about elephant, hoping that a large tusker might have been sighted. Our presence in each village was a remarkable event. The natives crowded the car to gawk at us, and all spoke at once, laying black hands on the white skin of our arms, which rested in the windows. It seemed as though the whole village turned out to see us, all crowding, reaching, smiling, all wanting to touch us, until the scene took on the appearance of a rock band surrounded by its groupies. I'm sure my blue eyes and blond hair were a fascination. Regardless, the natives are a "touchy" people; they do not have the same personal space boundaries that we do. It is nothing to see two men standing side by side and holding hands, or clasping each other's arms while in friendly conversation.

Once the pleasantries were out of the way, the talk turned serious, the farmers telling stories of wayward elephants that had destroyed their crops and fields. The rumor of a giant elephant got Gerard's attention. The natives called it Massantulu—Tusks that Drag the

Earth. (Need they say more?) The old bull is bigger and taller than any two elephant put together, they claim, taller than any hut. It can not be mistaken. But size alone is not its only identifying mark; the legendary giant is missing its tail, and its tusks are so enormous that they push the earth wherever he goes, leaving an unmistakable trail. Gerard brought them back to this last piece of information time and again, and questioned them in depth. The tusks were estimated at 140 pounds apiece by the elders, who Gerard said knew elephant. It is one thing to hear about a large elephant from natives you don't know and quite another to hear about one from natives you do.

"They've seen him just the other day," Gerard said as we drove off. "But an elephant doesn't get old like that without being bloody clever. It won't be easy to find him."

It was hard to believe that such an elephant could exist—in today's Africa anyway—but it was possible. The legend of Massantulu had spread among several of the villages, so I had little doubt that a large rogue elephant did exist. My fear was that the fellow had grown to Moby Dick proportions in the telling and retelling.

We stopped about 5:30 to set up fly camp near a stream at the base of several tall hills. We had not paused for lunch and were both famished. While the cook did his magic over a small fire, Gerard and I left to scout the area before dark. We climbed a couple of the smaller hills that offered a view above the forest and the advantage of long-range vision, a luxury that was not permitted on the flat ground below, where in the thick growth one could see but a few yards in any given direction. Although we saw nothing of the big creatures themselves, the good news was that we saw much sign of elephant—clumps of dung the size of bowling balls and telltale missing strips of bark peeled from the trees. Then, on the return to camp, at the edge of a small opening, we found the bones of a cow elephant. That did little to help my conscience over our pursuit.

We turned in early, in sleeping bags on the ground, and were soon fast asleep.

Chik-chik! I woke in the middle of the night to the sound of a round being chambered into a gun—a sound that had more effect than a bomb going off. I was instantly awake. Gerard was sitting up in his sleeping bag with his gun shouldered. He put out a hand, motioning the rest of us to keep still. Then I heard twigs snapping and the shuffle of feet as several elephant came into focus just yards from us in the dark. The big forms loomed up like fantastic ghosts. From our perspective on the ground, they looked as big as ships pulling into port, towering above us. Gerard kept his gun raised, ready to shoot, but the elephants soon detected us and they veered off, disappearing as suddenly and quietly as they had appeared.

We spent the next morning traveling to all the water holes in the area, but all we saw were cow and calf tracks and a few small bull tracks. In truth, what we saw were mostly natives and cattle and goats. The women hike to the water holes to fill large clay pots that are transported to their huts on their heads, but it is the cattle and goats that are the most disruptive to our quest. Young boys direct large herds of livestock to the water at first light, obliterating the sign of any elephant that have come to drink during the night. It is a shame, but tracking the old bulls from the water holes is really the only way to hunt them: By dawn the big beasts have vanished, and you are more apt to find a unicorn than an old bull elephant wandering Masailand in the light of day. Before the first rays of daylight ever hit, the wise old bulls are already back in their thick, brushy haunts, miles from the water hole, where they remain until the cover of dark. After checking the banks of the first water hole or two at dawn, we found that cattle had trampled the rest, and our efforts were thwarted.

"To hell with this," Gerard said in frustration, and we packed camp and moved deeper into the bush. We set up camp two hundred

You won't catch anything other than a game park elephant out in the open like this, but then if you did it would take the fun out of it, wouldn't it?

yards downwind from the small water hole where Dad had tracked his bull. The water hole was quite small, surrounded by brush, and out of range of the natives and their endless herds. Because of the proximity of the hunting grounds, however, we were forced to make a "silent" camp. There was no talking, no banging of pots, no hammering of tent pegs. The car door was "clicked" shut. If we wanted something, we had to whisper.

Later we drove to a hill in the area, climbed it, and found that all the water holes within sight were dry. It had been a very dry year, and no rain was expected until November. That was good news for hunting, though, as the lack of water would concentrate the elephant at the few remaining water holes, making them easier to find. Our water hole, in fact, was not much of a water hole. Situated in the dry center of a sandy river basin—where any water had long since disappeared—the water hole was the diameter of a manhole cover and the size and depth of a fuel drum. The elephants, wise in their efforts, had gouged the hole with their tusks, allowing the water to seep in from the lower depths. They drank it empty each night, then dug deeper and let the water seep back during the day. But in a few weeks the water would run out, and the whole area would be out of water until the rainy season.

From the hill, we saw several vultures circling low in the sky. "Bloody poachers, I bet," Gerard said, and we trotted down the hill and into thick brush to have a look. We didn't find any poachers, but we did find a pit they had dug to catch game. The top of the pit was covered with leafy branches so that whatever stepped on it would fall through and be trapped. As we kicked away the branches to foil the trap, a rat dashed out and bounced off the toe of my boot. Then we found the fresh tracks of a male and female leopard, and Gerard guessed that it was perhaps a kill of theirs close by that was attracting the vultures.

Gerard set up the radio and called Lavasoret before heading back to "silent" camp. Dad had taken a very nice leopard, and we gave congratulations over the radio. Back at camp, we turned in early, tired from the long treks. There is nothing like a long trek in the woods to guarantee a good night's sleep.

We awoke in the early dark, dressed in silence, and then crept to the water hole at first light. Sure enough, there were two bull elephants drinking from it. We watched the huge, slow-moving animals for a while, and Gerard whispered, "One is thirty pounds, the other maybe forty." I had told Gerard earlier that I was looking for something approaching fifty or I wasn't going to shoot. Gerard had been fine with that. In fact, I think he respected my decision.

A Grant gazelle taken on the open plains of Masailand.

Once the bulls had had their fill and left we circled the pond, looking for other tracks. Gerard found the tracks of three other bulls, one quite good. We then began what I soon found, but had yet to experience, to be the essence of elephant hunting: the arduous task of tracking elephant through dense brush. It was not the walk in the park I had expected. Done properly, elephant hunting goes something like this: You follow their tracks at a fast clip, despite whatever brush, branches, or thickets stand in your way. There are times when you have no choice but to duck your head and push into the seemingly impenetrable scrub—at others you are required to drop onto all fours and crawl your way through. At times the wait-a-bit grabs you, and you work your way gingerly from branch to branch, pulling the wicked thorns out of your hide and untangling them from your skewered shirt, shorts, socks, and hat; the hooked thorns are particularly nasty to ears, and later you will reach up to find thorns you hadn't even noticed embedded in your head or neck. You are stabbed in so many places simultaneously that, with all that adrenaline flowing, you don't feel most of the thorns anyway. The sun rises and the temperature rises and you begin to sweat, and soon you wish you had brought a canteen. It is only then that you realize that this was what your father had been talking about when he said that elephant hunting was a unique experience, and that it was a difficult hunt.

For the elephants, however, the wait-a-bit thorns and the dense thickets of brush are of no concern. They pass through them as you and I step through a revolving door at a department store. Even more amazing, you would think that an animal of such size and proportion would leave a path of devastation, a tunnel in the brush big enough to drive a Jeep through, but that is not the case. In fact, quite the opposite is true: The elastic bush closes up around the behemoths, revealing nothing of their passing. If it weren't for the big pugmarks of their feet in the dirt and an occasional heaping pile of dung, you would never know that an elephant had passed through that solid wall of brush. It is an amazing thing.

As we encountered dung, Kipper stuck his finger into the green clumps to see how warm they were, to see how close the elephants were. But they weren't close. It was some five hours later, around noon, that I got a lesson in how surprisingly smart elephants are. Gerard suddenly pulled up and shook his head and began to cuss. So did Kipper and Roman. The elephants had smelled us, he explained, and taken off. Wisely, these bulls had traveled with the wind so they could smell any danger on their trail. We never saw them, never even heard them. They didn't allow us to get that close. But we knew that they had run, from the tracks they left. I didn't know that, but Gerard and Kipper did. The elephant's chief defense in thick brush is to run. And an elephant can run at twenty miles an hour for an hour—after which point it is safe. You could never follow it up before dark. The hunt, at least for these three elephant, was over.

Then it was my host's turn to display an amazing talent. We had spent close to five hours wandering this way and that through some of the thickest brush you could imagine, with no landmarks in sight. I had no idea which way camp was. I couldn't have gotten us there if you offered me a million bucks. But when it came time to return to camp, Gerard turned and simply walked in a straight line directly to it. Surprisingly, it took only an hour to get back.

For lunch we ate warthog stew (which was quite good, despite the animal's homely exterior) and whispered back and forth as we spooned in mouthful after mouthful. Since our afternoons were free, as far as elephant hunting was concerned, Gerard decided that we should try to find a leopard. So we traveled out of the elephant area and collected several baits. I took two impala (one with horns of 27 inches—so much for Mando's record!) and a Grant, and we made five baits out of them. At one point we discovered a poacher's blind beside a dry water hole, but it was so old and deteriorated that we didn't bother to stop and burn it. On the radio we heard that Dad was sick with a high fever and was leaving for Arusha tomorrow. I was comforted, though, in the knowledge that he had brought antibiotics for just such an illness. I hoped it would work on whatever was ailing him.

At dawn we tracked two bull elephants from the water hole until 10:00 A.M., when we got right up to them and I didn't even know it. With our group halted, Gerard kept pointing "right there," but try as I might I couldn't see them. Of course, you couldn't see a whole elephant, which I guess is what I was expecting. In the thick vegetation, all you could see was a patch or a piece of it. Additionally, I was expecting gray. But they weren't gray. The elephants were the color of the beige earth at our feet, and so I did not see them until one of the beige termite mounds in the brush in front of me moved! I was flabbergasted that you could get so close to such a large animal and not be able to recognize it instantly. Then I heard them. Their stomachs grumbled, and their ears made soft flapping noises. They were no more than twenty paces away and as of yet completely unaware of our presence.

We waited and watched, constantly assessing the wind, for a shift in its direction would cause total mayhem at this close range. Gerard had warned me about hunting elephant in the thick stuff—that if the elephants discovered us up close, they would likely charge. He went on to say that if a bull charged in such dense cover, there was a good

Mom and Dad taking a short rest after lunch.

chance that I would not see the bull itself until it was too close, that all I would see would be brush coming down on top of me. "If you can't see his head, just shoot at the brush coming down on top of you." It was just that comforting thought that made me have to fight the urge to take several quick steps in retreat. At the least, it made me recheck the grip on the .450 double in my hands.

When time had passed and still we could not get a look at their tusks, Gerard decided to climb a tree to get a better view. We inched our way up a large-trunked tree, until we were perched in the upper limbs, some fifteen or twenty feet off the ground. There were two bulls beneath us, each surrounded by a sea of brush, with only the tops of their backs and heads visible. It took a while to get a good look at their ivory, but eventually we did. One bull carried notably inferior tusks; the other, older and larger, had tusks near forty-five pounds each, according to Gerard's best guess. But my limit was fifty, so we passed, crawled down, and departed without them ever knowing we were there, which was the best part of the hunt. The hunt had been a true success without our ever firing a cap. Like our Indians of old, we had counted coup on a worthy adversary.

On the return hike to camp, we came upon a beautiful lesser kudu bull in the bush. With its head tipped back, it was browsing the leaves of a branch overhead. Gerard guessed its horns at thirty to thirty-one inches straight up, a hell of a big kudu. But I already had mine, and even if I didn't, we couldn't risk a shot. It would spook the elephant in the area. There was a female with it, both eighty yards away, and we watched them until they fed out of sight. They never saw us.

On the radio, we were informed that Dad was still sick, but they didn't tell us to return to Arusha. That was a good sign.

We stayed in camp from 4:30 on, whispering all afternoon and evening so as not to alert the elephant at the water hole. The tsetse flies were as bad here as they had been in Rungwa. As in the leopard blind, I could not slap them because of the noise, and so I was forced just to wave them off and suffer the bites of repeat offenders.

"Mando told me you saw a huge buffalo the other day—49 inches," Gerard whispered.

"What?!"

"Yes, he said you saw one that would go 49."

"Gerard, we saw six bulls and I shot the largest. You saw for yourself how big it was . . . 41 inches."

What hunter and fisherman doesn't have a story of the one that got away, where time and emotion have magnified the details to grand

A lesser kudu, like a mature whitetail, doesn't give you much time to shoot. One jump in the bush and it is gone! This is quite a nice one.

proportions? But when hunting is your business and your word is your bond, there is no room for exaggeration. I knew Gerard well enough by now to know that he would spend every day of the next safari looking for that bull until he found it. The only problem was: That bull did not exist, at least not the one Mando claimed to have seen, and there was no reason to send him on a snipe hunt.

First thing in the morning, Gerard went down alone to check the water hole for tracks. There were none, so we drove off to check the status of our five leopard baits. One of the baits had been hit, but a look at the tracks left at the base of the tree showed our diner to be a female. Being interested solely in a male, we did not bother to build a blind. Mando had told us over the radio the night before that he had a big male leopard feeding at one of his baits. Since we had only a couple of safari days left, Gerard had a decision to make.

"Johnny, we could stay here hunting elephant for a month. But from what I've seen, I think we'd be better off returning to Lavasoret for that leopard of Mando's. You've had a taste of elephant hunting now, but you shouldn't miss out on the rest of your safari because of it."

"Who would be guiding me?"

"Hey, you won't get rid of me that easily, kid."

"Then let's go."

We left for Lavasoret shortly thereafter and arrived in a couple of hours. Our black government hunter in this camp was Ernest, a quiet, nervous fellow who preferred to stay in camp and drink tea. That afternoon he went out with us, for a change, and as we neared one of the leopard baits, we came upon three male lions lying lazily in the bush. When Ernest spied them, he went berserk and started banging on the roof of the car and grabbing for his gun. Gerard glanced over his shoulder to give him his "What in the bloody hell?" look. Ernest's eyes were the size of Ping-Pong balls, and he kept banging until Gerard leaned out the window and told him to knock it off.

The lions never moved. We backed out and went on our way.

"I think he messed his pants just now," Gerard said. "Poor fellow is in the wrong profession."

Once all of the leopard baits had been checked, our chief task was to construct a leopard blind at the bait where Mando had a leopard feeding. Before we could begin, however, there were a few technical hurdles that had to be jumped. Most noticeably, there was no silhouette to the limb above the bait where the leopard would come to feed. Since leopards often come at dusk, a silhouette against the sky is helpful (at times critical) in making out the shape of the leopard, whose spots blend into background leaves and limbs better than any manmade camouflage ever invented. But there was nothing we could do about that, short of cutting down the forest of trees behind it. The wind and sun were also a problem. The wind was blowing straight toward the bait, and the evening sun would be directly in our eyes if we built the blind in the spot Mando had instructed.

So Gerard had the blind built as far off to the side as possible. Kipper and Roman worked quickly to fashion a square frame out of thick poles cut from the branches of nearby *miombo* trees. To this frame thin sticks were lashed, horizontally, to serve as support for the long grass thatch that was then woven into place to make the whole thing look—to the leopard's eye—like a harmless patch of grass. A functioning door was crafted at the rear, and there were two thatch-ringed shooting holes in the front. Once everything was made to Gerard's liking, we departed to let the area rest.

"That blind is a bit far from the bait," he cautioned as we drove off, "but lucky for me I've got quite the marksman for a client." Nothing like putting on the pressure for a shot that I was already nervous not to mess up.

It would have been ideal to let the area rest for another day, but we were running short on time. We drove up to the blind at 4:30 P.M. and rolled out of the car and into the blind. The car drove off, leaving us to sit and wait. The theory is that the leopard, holed up somewhere near the bait, sees the car drive up, then sees the car drive off, and thinks no more of it. Another method is to approach the blind with, say, five members in the party. Two drop off at the blind, and the other three continue on. It generally is successful, inasmuch as leopards can't count.

The one nice thing about this area was that there were no tsetse flies to torture us, and it made the wait that much more endurable. About 6:00 P.M. we heard something approaching the back of the blind. But it was no leopard. Whatever it was, it sounded big. It turned out to be two giraffes, which, curious, walked right up to the blind. Gerard shouldered his gun about the time a big giraffe head appeared in the blind. The giraffes, startled at the sight of us, snorted like horses, then thundered off twenty yards or so and stopped to have a look back. We were startled, too, for the sight of the huge head descending upon us was daunting. The giraffe's nose came within an arm's length of Gerard's gun barrel before the animal realized what we were.

The Three Musketeers—Gerard, Dad, and George with Dad's hard-won bull elephant.

Making the best of a "bad" leopard blind.

How much that little escapade hurt our chances for success we weren't sure, but it didn't help. The giraffes eventually wandered off, and we sat tight. Silence followed. The sun sank, and the light grew dim. The evening insects began their soulful songs. It looked as if we had been skunked again. This was getting to be discouraging, and the leopard was becoming a much more difficult animal to hunt than I had expected. It was now almost dark. A minute later, Gerard pulled the grass plug and peeked at the bait. There was no mistaking the change in his expression, and I knew what it meant.

"He's in the tree. Shoot him." Remarkably, we never heard it climb the tree.

It was a difficult shot in the dim light. I cranked the power on the scope and held the gun as steady as I had ever held a gun in my life. I was not about to wound a leopard. That was not how this safari was going to end.

The leopard had been feasting on the rotten impala instead of the fresh hartebeest, but it had heard us or seen the movement of my gun. It was now standing broadside on the limb and looking right at us. There is no stare quite like the stare of an African cat. It reaches right down inside you. It humbles you and makes you feel unworthy. It puts you in your place—instantly. But we had worked too hard and too long, and I wasn't about to let this leopard get the best of me.

Resigned to the task, I took a deep breath and squeezed the trigger. The rifle banged, the leopard dropped from sight, and we heard a thud. No growl. No grunts. Silence.

"How was your shot?"

"Good," I said. "I felt good about it. Right on the shoulder." He clapped me on the back and grinned.

We waited for the car, which would return at the sound of our shot. It was now dark. Gerard loaded the sawed off shotgun with 00 buck, and we got in and drove up to the tree, seventy yards away. There at the base of the tree, in the grass, was my leopard. He was stone dead. Only he wasn't a he.

"Nice leopard," Gerard said, pulling the spotted cat into the open. But he could read the disappointment in my face. In trophy hunting, as in war, you don't shoot women and children. The battle is between the males of the species. Gerard quickly measured it at 6 feet 9 inches.

"It's a female. But what a female! You would never know it's a female by the looks of it. The biggest female I've ever seen shot was six feet, six inches, and that was taken by my mom." That made me feel a little better, and, as always, hunting is hunting.

One of the more difficult trophies to collect this trip has been, of all things, the diminutive dik-dik. You see one only for an instant, and then it is gone, disappearing in the tall grass like a mouse in your house. Many is the time I'd loaded my gun at the sight of one, but I had yet to fire a single shot. Finally I met with success.

We were out looking for buffalo the following morning when a dik-dik jumped up and dashed across the road. It made the mistake of stopping in some short grass to look back at us. A 12-gauge with number 4 shot did the trick. The large pellets dropped it on the spot yet did little to mar the fragile hide. For the photo I even raised a fist in triumph, as this feisty little antelope had proven my most difficult adversary on the trip.

Later we found a small herd of bachelor buffalo near the brushy edge of a creek. We parked the car a little distance away and began our hurried preparations. Meanwhile the buffalo disappeared down into the dry creek. Ernest started to come with us, but Gerard instructed him to wait in the car. With our rifles loaded—me with the .450 double, Gerard with his .460 Weatherby—we then crept to the edge of the steep bank and stared down into the dry depths of the creek, which was devoid of buffalo or any sign of buffalo. But Gerard held up a knowing hand, and we waited in silence. Truth was, Gerard had timed it perfectly.

Down in the bottom, a buffalo bull emerged from the brush and swaggered out in that heavy, labored walk they have, as if moving their tremendous bulk were a supreme effort. But a buffalo's looks are deceiving, and they can get a hunter killed if he falls for it. That is just one of the many reasons why the buffalo is responsible for killing more hunters than any other African game animal. With that thought in mind, I gave this bull all my respect and then some. The old bull never turned its head, but it got sight of us or wind of us, or its sixth sense kicked in. The old boy somehow knew something was up, and it abruptly turned and began to run up the opposite bank. But Gerard had me hold off.

Just then another, bigger bull appeared in the bottom of the creek and quickly climbed the bank, trailing the first. Its horns made that beautiful, downward-sweeping arc, then curled sharply upward and back in—the profile that is characteristic of a mature trophy bull. The bull turned broadside at the top of the bank, now forty yards away, and Gerard gave me the nod. I placed the open sights of the double on its shoulder and squeezed the front trigger. The buffalo dropped to its knees, raising a cloud of dust. I then made the mistake of squeezing the front trigger again. Nothing happened. The buffalo got to its feet and began to run. I followed it in the sights, pulled the back trigger on a solid, and hit it in the shoulder three inches from where the first bullet had struck, driving the big animal to its knees a second time. The buffalo then rolled onto its side, and Gerard said, "Let's give him a moment to die." We walked back to the truck.

On our return, Gerard took Ernest with us and even let him bring his gun. Gerard led us at an angle to the bull, however, so that if Ernest got excited and started to shoot, he wouldn't shoot through us. It was a good thing, too, because when we came up on the dead bull, the buffalo rolled up onto its belly. I had never believed in reincarnation before, but I do now. I shot the bull twice more with solids, once in the shoulder and once in the neck.

"You didn't need that last shot," Gerard said.

"I know. I just enjoy shooting this gun—now that I have the triggers figured out."

A minute later, Gerard came up from behind Ernest, grabbed him roughly, and yelled, *"M'bogo! M'bogo!"*

Ernest must have jumped three feet. He flew around with his gun, shaking.

"You are quite jumpy, Bwana."

The cook will transform these two vulturine guinea fowl (note the interesting markings of both stripes and spots) into chakula *(food) at fly camp.*

"No," Ernest said, "I was calm." His eyes still looked like Ping-Pong balls.

"I can see that," Gerard said, winking at me. Ernest had zero aptitude for his chosen profession. He was a square peg in a round hole. It was good food and good money, but surely there was a city job that would have suited him better. The man was a heart attack waiting to happen.

Then came the most embarrassing thing of all.

While the boys set about the task of butchering the bull, Gerard asked Ernest and me if we would like to shoot his .460. When he mentioned to Ernest that it was the most powerful production gun made, Ernest shook his head no. So Gerard handed the hefty gun to me.

"Aim at that knot on the tree," he said. The tree was only eight paces away so there was no chance of missing. I pulled the trigger and found that the gun did indeed give the shooter a wicked punch in the shoulder, but that was the price you paid for the bullet doing its work on the other end.

After much prodding by Gerard, Ernest finally agreed to shoot it. I just wish I had a video of it. The bony fellow was trembling from head to toe and kept flinching—even before he had the gun up! He closed his aiming eye a time or two and held his cheek an inch off the stock (bad idea), while Gerard and I nudged each other and tried not to laugh. It took literally two or three minutes for Ernest to fire the gun, and when he did, he missed the knot by a good foot and a half. At eight paces! Professional hunter? Professional joke is more like it. Nevertheless, Ernest's name will go on every safari document as the professional hunter of record.

With all hands on deck, and a lot of pushing, shoving, and pulling, we rolled the big buffalo onto its side and posed for pictures over what would prove to be my last animal taken on that safari. What a way to end it!

We left for Arusha later that morning and soon arrived at the Game Lodge to find that Dad was better but had lost several pounds that he didn't have to lose. He had been running at both ends with a fever of 104 degrees for two days. When he stepped out of the shower, I was shocked to see his ribs suddenly prominent, his shoulder and elbow bones sticking out like those of a concentration camp inmate. It was unsettling how fast the bacteria had done their dirty work. Had we not brought antibiotics with us, I shudder to think how he might have fared.

That evening at dinner, I noticed that Dad's index finger was taped up and he was favoring it as he ate.

"What happened to your finger?"

He just kind of grimaced and grumbled.

The girls were snickering.

"What happened?" I asked again.

He looked at the girls, clearly embarrassed. Finally he said, "Go ahead. Tell him."

After some more laughing, Kay piped up. "We were showing Dad how we could pet the leopard in the cage, and when Dad tried it, the leopard bit him on the finger!"

"The leopard knew he was a hunter!" Leanne added in the leopard's defense. We all had a good laugh—all except Dad.

"Look at the bright side," I said. "You can tell all your hunting friends back home that you were mauled by a leopard."

Truman Clem and Steve Christenson, two friends from the Dallas Safari Club, arrived at the lodge that night. They had just gotten off the plane and were eager to hear how our hunt had gone, ready to get into the bush themselves. We told them our tales and then they turned in early, tired with jet lag.

"And Dad was mauled by a leopard," I added, as they left us.

We left early the next morning for Ngorongoro Crater, which is where we should have taken the girls at first, except it didn't fit

Those smiles are the result of two well-placed shots on the shoulder. My double is a John Rigby .450 Nitro Express.

with our hunt schedule. Dad had not planned to take them there at all. It was only after having gone ourselves at the start of our trip and seeing how wonderful the place was that he decided to cut the safari short and make another trip there. It was a great idea. The girls loved it; it made the trip for them. One of the highlights was getting to witness two separate prides of lion feeding on fresh kills. One kill was a wildebeest, which the small pride reduced to bone and sinew in a matter of minutes, the lions fighting over every shred in a snarling, bloody mess. Why lions killing a wildebeest didn't bother the girls whereas my shooting the wildebeest with a gun would have, I don't understand. They cooed over the lions as though the vicious cats were newborns behind the glass at a maternity ward. *Oh, look at the cute kitties!* My sisters don't tell me I'm cute when I kill something.

Some fourteen miles in diameter, Ngorongoro Crater is actually an extinct volcano that rises oddly out of the plains and is home to an unbelievable diversity of wildlife. Although buffalo and elephant on occasion roam up and down the steep, brushy lip to travel in and out, most of the animals remain in the bottom of the crater year-round. Near the center there is a large lake. From the rim above nearly half the water looks as though it is pink, but it is really just an enormous flock of flamingos.

The drive to and from the crater is beautiful, especially down the steep backside on the return to the flat plains below. The ecosystem changes noticeably with each drop in elevation. Much of the outer rim is rain forest—dense green jungle and tall trees dripping with shaggy moss, all lost in early morning fogs and low-lying clouds—while the plains below are grassy and dry, hot and endless in whatever direction you head.

While down in the crater we were charged by a rhino. It was the driver's fault, however, not the rhino's. The rhino was feeding in the long grass with its head down and didn't see us. The driver should have whistled or honked at a distance—something to let the rhino know we were there. Instead, he drove right up to it. Not surprisingly, the rhino started and came straight for us, gaining speed amazingly quickly. Fortunately, it veered at the last instant, five paces from the front of the truck, once it had us figured out. The rhino then stopped and posed for some wonderful photos.

As in Arusha, the hotel was out of eggs—out of all food, in fact, except bread and tea and coffee. That was bad timing, as Dad was now famished, his appetite trying to make up for lost time. But he had to make do with bread.

Gerard and the elusive dik-dik, which proved one of the more difficult trophies for me to collect on safari.

A Bullet Well Placed

After a couple of days of game viewing there and at Lake Manyara, it was time to leave, and we did so with mixed emotions. It had been a great trip, more than I had bargained for, and I had arrived with high expectations. But it was time to get back to our daily lives. I was about to start a new job in the audit department of Arthur Young in Dallas, where I would begin work toward my CPA. There was more than just jet lag ahead of me. There would be civilization lag. I would be going from primitive to modern in a matter of a couple of days. It would take some getting used to.

Tanzania, East Africa
November 1985

You never know how a given day on safari is going to turn out, and today, our first, was no exception. Emerging from a dense thicket, we entered a large *mbuga* to a haunting sight: ten poachers hiking in single file across the open field. Upon their shoulders they carted the contraband of their dirty work—dozens of elephant tusks tied in bundles. Three of the poachers were toting rifles. With their backs to us, the bandits had yet to see or hear us, and they continued at a leisurely pace.

Gerard pulled out a .44 Magnum revolver. He was dark and thin from six months in the bush, and his eyes flashed their characteristic passion, only now that passion was anger.

"Load your gun," he said in a low voice. Apprehensively, I chambered a round in the .375. Gerard stomped the accelerator, and we lit out across the stubble field as if we were in a race to reach them. Despite the roar of the Land Rover's engine, the poachers heard nothing of our rapid approach, and we quickly narrowed the distance to perhaps a hundred yards. We would have been on top of them in another second had a dry ravine not loomed up and blocked our path.

Gerard slammed on the brakes, and we skidded to the edge of the sharp bank. He blew the horn and fired the .44 in the air. The sudden blasts sent the poachers scattering like cockroaches under a bright light. In their haste, they dropped everything they were carrying—everything except the rifles, that is. Those they are commanded to protect with their lives, as the guns could be used to identify the leaders of the poaching ring, who are the real instigators of the crime.

In an instant, the poachers had vanished in the brush. Gerard shouldered my rifle and fired six or seven shots over their heads, prompting me for shells when the magazine went empty. Still furious and determined to catch them, he put the Land Rover into gear and quickly searched for a crossing on the steep bank of the ravine. Once over it, we spun circles in the brush, shooting up in the air and hollering at the top of our lungs in search of the vanished bandits. I have no idea what Gerard and his men were shouting in Swahili, but no doubt they were cussing the evil vermin all to hell.

A Bullet Well Placed

My biggest worry was that I would be forced to shoot a poacher. We were whipping around the brush so briskly now that when we came upon one or more of the thieves it would be at close range, such close range that the poacher would have only an instant to decide whether to surrender or to fire. If he chose to open fire, I, as the only member of the party now with a gun, would be forced to shoot him in self-defense. I did not want that on my conscience. I was not opposed to arresting the villains and hauling them into town to face whatever penalty their courts decided upon, even to taking time out from my safari to do so, but I was not about to shoot one. This was *their* war on *their* land, and I was merely an observer.

Back home I would have no qualms about shooting a criminal who was breaking into my house or physically hurting someone, but this situation was different. What's more, it brought to light a key point in the hunting debate. Perhaps it is this distinction that the antihunters miss. Taking the life of an animal is what I do as a hunter. It is a natural right—as natural for me as it is for the lion that takes the zebra. It is not wrong. But killing another human being, except in self-defense—is murder. It is as wrong as hunting animals is right. So I was glad that we didn't come across a poacher with a gun. In fact, we never saw a single one of them again.

When we returned to the clearing to assess the poachers' damage and sort through their discarded belongings, we found homemade axes, knives, ropes, sacks of *poda* (mealy meal—their food), and several .458 and .375 casings. And then there were the tusks: forty-four of them in total. Twenty-two elephants massacred! The largest tusks were a mere three feet in length, the smallest one foot long—from nothing more than a toddler.

The whole problem with ivory poachers (poachers of any kind, actually) is that the criminals involved shoot any damn elephant they see (cows and calves are targets, as well as bulls). If not the actual goal of poaching, the result is the annihilation of the population. Poaching, on a grand scale, is nothing short of the total destruction of a population. It means first-come, first-served until there is nothing left.

That is the exact opposite of the strategy employed in sport hunting, in which conservation is the guiding principle. Sport hunters want only the oldest bulls, the selective removal of which has little effect on the herd's population as a whole or its ability to reproduce. The killing of cows and calves, however, has a direct impact. The killing of female animals should be permitted only when the goal is to reduce the population or to rebalance the male/female ratio. A good example is the handling of the white-tailed deer herds in Texas. There, does are routinely harvested, in predetermined numbers, to keep the population and the buck/doe ratio in check.

A short while later, backtracking their trail, we came across two cow elephants recently slaughtered by our escaped native devils. The vultures were circling by the hundreds, making the carcasses easy to find. As usual, nothing had been touched but the tusks. The poachers had chopped the ivory out, defacing the magnificent beasts and leaving the rest to rot. The gory sight was truly depressing, and it left me with a sour taste in my mouth.

Africa's war on poaching, I'm afraid, is doomed, just like America's unsuccessful war on drugs. When both the demand and black market price for a product are high, there will always be those who are willing to accept the risk to deliver it. Even in Zimbabwe, where the punishment for poaching is death, there are natives eager to poach. The only way to stop poaching is to stop the worldwide demand for ivory, to educate people not to buy wildlife products for which the legal status cannot be documented.

Although poaching is a serious crime, do not think me blind to the poachers' plight or the harsh reality of an economy in shambles. When the per capita income of a country is a meager $250 a year, how realistic is it to expect a native *not* to submit to the temptation of easy gains? If my family were starving or destitute, I too would be tempted. But there is more to the poaching issue than simply the natives' temptation to poach. Poaching is an industry in itself. Despite the rhetoric that flies heatedly back and forth on the poaching debate, despite international good intentions, despite the red tape that slows the whole process to a crawl, despite the corruption that has fed on the ivory trade for more than a century, the real dilemma boils down to one very important fact: Poaching is a war of man against beast, and in the end man always wins. It is as simple as that. Sadly, unless there is a drastic change in either ivory demand or the enforcement of the law, the days of the elephant in East Africa are numbered.

With that bit of unpleasantness out of the way, we were finally able to concentrate on the real task at hand, which was enjoying my first day of safari. The first day on safari is always a magical event, and I quickly put the unfortunate diversion out of mind. The sky was cloudy and gray and the breeze cool, and I found myself staring at Gerard as we drove along. He looked amazingly good for a fellow who earlier in the season had been shot point blank in the stomach with a

Removing the poachers' spoils.

.458. Really, it was amazing that he was still alive. My friend Gerard, like a cat, was on his third or fourth life.

Gerard filled me in on the details of his mishap. We had not seen each other since the previous season, when I spent four months with him on safari. My role then was somewhere between assistant and observer, with a little more emphasis on the latter. Nevertheless, I had helped wherever I could and lent a hand in a number of tasks, setting up hunting camps in the Selous, Masailand, and Rungwa, scouting for elephants, hanging baits, and the like. The best thing about the trip was getting a behind-the-scenes look at a safari operation from start to near finish. It was an exceptional experience for a young man. Gerard and I had become quite good friends, and my respect for the demands, know-how, and requisite talents of the hunting profession had grown tenfold in the process.

I had heard he'd been shot, but I did not know the details. What happened was this: Gerard had just picked up a new client at the airstrip and was heading for camp when a tremendous elephant, with at least eighty pounds of tusk per side, suddenly wandered through the *miombo* forest ahead of them. Bringing the vehicle to a stop, they quickly and quietly got out, gathered binoculars and rifles, and in hushed voices planned their approach. At the last instant, Gerard turned to reach into the car and just as he did—*Booooommmm!*—the client's rifle, in the hands of the government game scout, went off. Gerard felt a tug. That was all. He thought nothing of it at first. He immediately straightened and started yelling at the game scout, shouting all sorts of unprintables. In a sharp scolding, Gerard told him that he had ruined their hunt, that because of his reckless behavior they had missed an opportunity to shoot what might have been the largest elephant of the season, because the elephant would surely be long gone with the rifle's report.

About that time Kipper started jumping excitedly up and down and yelling, "Bwana, he's killed you! He's killed you!"

Gerard looked down in surprise to see the blood pumping out of him. The 500-grain bullet had hit him just below the belly button. It had punched through the bronze buffalo belt buckle that had been a gift from a client and entered his abdomen, taking a chunk of the belt buckle with it. The hefty slug had traveled through his belly, then exited his right side, blowing up four of the twelve .460 cartridges he carried on his belt and leaving a wound the diameter of a baseball in his hip. The blood was pouring down his side, quickly filling his shorts.

Although a hundred things flash through your mind when death is imminent, Gerard's primary thought at that point was to reach camp to see his wife and four-year-old son before he died. The American client took the wheel but was so disoriented by the right-hand drive and left-hand shift that he nearly hit a tree or two and was hesitant in his speed. Thinking they would never make it at such a pace, Gerard had him pull over, and he jumped into the driver's seat himself, where he quickly reached rally speed. A minute later he came flying over an embankment to find the creek below packed with a herd of elephants.

Gerard tried to "push" the slow-moving creatures out of the way, up the bank, honking, hollering, but he was too close. A nearby cow turned and charged. The angry, trumpeting beast was right on top of them and so close that all Gerard could do was to grab the .460 from the dashboard rack, point the barrel awkwardly in its direction, and pull the trigger before the cow hit them. The charging elephant collapsed beside the truck, dead from the brain shot.

When they made camp an hour later, Gerard jumped out, hugged his family, and said his good-byes. Only after his wife had surveyed the extent of his wounds did Gerard realize that he might live after all. It was the flesh wound on his hip, where the .460 cartridges had exploded, that was responsible for so much blood—not the wound in his belly. But help was still far away, and Gerard had to endure another thirty-six hours to reach the hospital. When the doctors were done with him and he was all stitched up, ironically, he was sorest of all in the chest, where the butt of the gun had kicked him when he shot the cow elephant. A black bruise covered his ribs for weeks.

It was a close call, to say the least, and Mr. Miller is lucky to be alive. He sustained some minor intestinal damage, but, amazingly, nothing life threatening. A degree or two of difference in the bullet's path would have ended with fatal results. Likewise, had he not turned at the last instant to reach into the truck, the .458 would have hit him "dead" on and left him as such.

Not surprisingly, the hospital didn't keep him long. His next safari, with Garry Weber, a partner in the firm for which Dad worked, was soon to begin. Gerard didn't tell me this, but Garry did. A day or two into the safari, some stitches pulled loose, and Gerard began bleeding from the wounds. By the end of the day's trek his shorts were soaked with blood. Although the bleeding didn't seem to slow Gerard down, Garry grew quite concerned. After another day and more bleeding, Garry put a stop to the safari and insisted that Gerard return to the hospital and get fully healed before they continue. Gerard did, and when he returned they completed a very successful safari. Gerard is a hardy fellow, to say the least.

So I marveled at the man behind the wheel, glad his luck had held, glad to be on safari with him again. We continued deep into the *miombo*

A typical Tanzanian village.

forests and did not see much: three buffalo, several zebra, eland, oribi, and a few elephants. But to me, it was great seeing game, any game. Since I had already collected most of the game available here, I was looking solely for better heads and manes, and to get the one or two animals I had yet to collect—such as the nimble klipspringer, which makes a mockery of a goat's rock-climbing skills.

Later in the afternoon came a real treat, when a couple of African wild dogs appeared in the openings of a sparse brush flat. The calico canines are a rare sight in Rungwa and were quite skittish, making it difficult to get close enough for a shot. Just as I was squeezing off the wary animals spun and ran, and I missed completely. We pursued them into thicker brush, but despite the cover it provided our quarry— which often will persuade an animal to hold up—we were unsuccessful in getting any closer and soon lost them altogether. Then it began to rain. Our chances looked grim, but Gerard was determined in his quest and soon located the dogs again. Now, however, the wild dogs were just patches of fur in the brush, and the scope was blurred with water drops. I knew that if I were to collect one, it would have to be a quick shot. They were acting like our coyotes, which waste no time in making your acquaintance.

"The one on the right," Gerard whispered.

I drew on the mottled patch of fur, but with the intervening brush and the rain and the splotchy scope, I could not tell which way it was facing. But there was no time to wait for a better shot. I made the snap shot that was required and luckily hit it where I had aimed, which turned out to be the rear, then finished it quickly with a shoulder shot as we neared. A wild dog is not the prettiest animal you will ever take, but I considered it quite a trophy. The wild canine is a fierce predator in a pack, taking down animals more than ten times its own size.

We were up early but didn't get out of camp until nearly eight o'clock. At the last minute Gerard decided to inspect the brake pads and replace those that were worn. I knew well his obsession for well-maintained equipment, so I was not at all surprised. Gerard inspects his vehicles the way a sergeant inspects a new private, scrutinizing every square inch for the tiniest flaw. He knows he must rely on his vehicle to get him out and back, and he replaces parts *before* they announce their wear, *before* they cause a breakdown in the bush. If a hose or belt looks worn or frayed it is replaced immediately. If the radiator shows a hairline crack it is removed and repaired on the spot, and arrangements are made on the radio that night to locate a spare. If a rattle or squeak is heard, the culprit is hunted down and taped or

Typical kids in a typical village.

welded or cushioned, for a rattle is a sign that something is not right. It could mask the sound of a real problem with the vehicle and, if loud enough, announce to game our approach. At the very least it is an annoyance.

Once out and about we discovered some elephant tracks crossing the dirt track in the forest. We followed them on foot a ways but Gerard soon decided they were too small and abandoned the effort. He later proved to be right when we unexpectedly encountered them when we were in the truck. The largest was a small bull with thirty-pound tusks, clearly below consideration. Since I wasn't exactly in the elephant-hunting mood, that suited me just fine.

Continuing in the same direction, we came across a tremendous herd of buffalo—some four hundred in all. It was a magnificent sight to behold, though you couldn't see all of them at once, just clusters here and there in the trees and in the open pan that intervened between a brush thicket beyond. The big black bodies were milling on the fringe of the thicker woods—bulls, cows, and calves all grazing on the move. We loaded our guns, checked our ammo pouches, and Gerard whispered to his trackers. Then we checked the wind to make our approach. But we would need more than a good wind. We would need a dose of good luck, because even with the wind right it would be difficult to get close to a herd of that size without one of eight hundred eyes seeing you.

As we neared, part of the herd indeed got nervous and started to scatter. In one cluster of fifty or so there was an outstanding bull making a trotting escape with the rest. There was no doubt which one it was, the way the horns went out and down and back up. This wasn't the way we had planned it, wasn't what I had expected in the way of a presentation, but even I realized that we had reached the point at which it was now or never. The big bull would soon be mixed up in the scramble, and a second stalk would be impossible with so many animals and the thick scrub for which they were headed.

"Take him in the rear," Gerard instructed. "That big fellow, just there."

I hammered the buffalo in the back end with the .450, then followed up immediately with the second barrel. An advantage of open sights is being able to lock onto your target quickly, and though I had been quick with both shots, I was careful with my aim. The last thing I wanted to do was to wound the buffalo beside him. As it turned out, the shots were well placed, but the bull's adrenaline was already up. It trudged on as if I had done nothing more than deliver a spanking. The bull showed no reaction whatsoever. It was invincible.

I broke the gun and quickly reloaded, and when it stopped and turned briefly broadside to check on its pursuers, I gave it one on the shoulder (a little too far back) then another up the tail as it wheeled and thundered off again. The stout bull appeared an eerie sight through the rising dust, all muscle and brawn, the ultimate in strength and stamina. *God, they are tough animals!* Then came disappointment that the shots had had so little effect. It gave me a touch of that helpless feeling you sometimes get in a dream in which you shoot a dangerous animal—a bear or a lion—and it just keeps coming. The shots have zero consequence, and so you just keep firing, with the bullets rolling out the end of the barrel like harmlessly tossed marbles. The lion keeps approaching, finally landing on you, and you wonder why your gun won't work, why the bullets won't do their job. That's how I was beginning to feel as the big, black buffalo appeared invincible.

We followed after the trundling bull, but the dust and brush did not allow for another shot. Finally my four shots did their work, and the big bull went down, though it was out of sight at the time. When we finally got there it was on its side but still kicking and plenty full of life, so I put a fifth bullet between the shoulder blades as we approached the animal's backside. That brought an end to the hunt, a hunt I had feared would end in thick brush and a charge. Now, for the first time, I got a look at the incredible horns sweeping up from the head and realized what a trophy we had.

Buffalo horns come in all shapes and sizes, and there is something for everyone. Some buffalo hunters look for spread, others at the boss. Those latter hunters like the buffalo's boss to grow together and bulge up like two adjoining ant mounds. I am not a boss man. I do like a certain heaviness of boss, but not so heavy that the boss overwhelms the rest of the horns, making the head look top-heavy, as if the buffalo were wearing a helmet. For me, such a boss detracts from the more desirable aspects of spread and shape of curl. Whatever your preference, one must remember that, as in other things, a trophy is in the eye of the beholder.

This buffalo was right out of my dreams, perfect in every feature. Its horns were dark and full, dropping deeply from the boss into a fine curl, then curving out and up and back in to fine points. The spread measured just shy of forty-five inches, and it was clearly the best buffalo I had ever taken. It was a tremendous buffalo—a picture

The perfect buffalo. Imagine meeting the business end of one of those deep, sweeping points!

book buffalo. So it was quite a day. But the day, little did I know, was far from over.

About noon we came upon the tracks of a large male lion that had crossed the dirt road. I knew it was large because I heard Nyamaiya say, *"Dume kubwa sana."* very big male) Nyamaiya, our head tracker and a Mkamba from Kenya, was an interesting fellow. Having spent three months with the man last season, I had the sincerest regard for him. As a reformed elephant poacher, he was a formidable hunter and tracker, with skills far beyond whatever one might expect from his former profession. The fellow was truly gifted and absolutely dedicated to his craft.

Believe me when I tell you that Nyamaiya reads the ground the way folks back home read the newspaper. He can tell you what passed by and when and how fast it was traveling, differentiating among male, female, and youth of twenty antelope species. There is something about Nyamaiya that is different from the other boys, though I could not exactly put my finger on it. He is quieter, more reserved, and certainly the hardest working fellow you will ever meet. Instead of cigarettes, he dips snuff from a can he keeps in the pocket of his green jumpsuit. He inhales the crumbly stuff into wide, flaring nostrils, then rubs away the ensuing mucus with a rag from his hip pocket. The whites of his eyes are as white as boiled eggs, and he carries two skinning knives on a leather belt slung low on his narrow hips; he uses them on fallen game as expertly as any sushi chef at a Japanese restaurant. Most important, he has stood by Gerard in the closest of calls with dangerous game, so I was very glad to have him on board this safari. If anyone in our group could be awarded the MVP, Nyamaiya was the one.

Everything got hushed after we saw those tracks, and Gerard and his trackers bailed out and began pouring over the landscape, whispering excitedly in Swahili. Bird hunters revel in the magical bond that exists between hunter and bird dog; they love to watch the teamwork between them. Here, I was the hunter and they were the dogs (no derogation intended), and I could only imagine what they were thinking. It was pure magic watching Gerard and his trackers work together. They saw things in the ground that you and I could not. They pointed at the earth and twittered back and forth in Swahili. The surprising thing is that Gerard is a better tracker than his blacks, and that is saying a lot. It is a testament to his dedication and passion for the profession. Gerard is the exception, however; the majority of his peers are dependent on their native trackers to determine the age and condition of the animal being tracked. Later, when I shared my

Tracking this lion on foot made for one of my most exciting hunts. Abdi (government PH), Nyamaiya, Gerard, and David.

impressions with him, Gerard shook his head. "My mother is the best tracker, white or black, that I have ever seen."

After some scouting, the men huddled up to discuss their findings. Nyamaiya and his cousin David believed the tracks to be a day old, but Gerard, their boss, disagreed. He turned to me.

"These tracks were made today," he declared in English. "We will follow up this lion. But remember: The lions in this area are quite cocky, and you must be ready for a charge at any moment." That I knew all too well from last season's stay in Rungwa. Several lions had charged the hunting vehicles, so I knew that following up one on foot was not without risk. It was like a deadly game of tag, with only one winner. The loser was . . . well, dead.

Once the plan was set, I struggled a second over which gun to take. The .450 had the power and the ease of open sights, while the .375 offered a scope for a longer shot. In the end, I took the .375, and Gerard took his own .450. (Secretly, I think he was tired of the punishing kick of the .460!) We checked ammo and gear, went over some last-minute instructions, then set out on what was probably the most exciting stalk of my life. Three years before, I had shot a lion over bait, and it was fun and exciting, but it dimmed in comparison with what I had heard of methods used in the Kalahari, where the big cats were tracked in the sand. That method of hunting a lion had always appealed to me, and now I was getting a chance to try it.

Gerard gave everyone one last quieting gesture with a finger to his lips, and we began following the tracks through the *miombo* forest. The lion's path was fairly straight until it hit a dry creek bed a quarter of a mile away. The big round pugmarks descended the steep bank, then followed the winding, sandy bottom of the creek to the right. As we passed each boulder, bush, or bend in the creek, I wondered if this was it, if this was the spot where the great cat was going to charge out at us. From such close range, when it came it would be a blur. My thumb fidgeted against the safety, and I tried to slow my breath. In turns I wiped sweat from my palms onto the seat of my shorts. My heart was pounding, and I could hear every sound as if it were magnified by ten: every step, every breath, every movement of the men around me. My eyes darted to the shadows, knowing how much lions like to hide there, knowing how readily a four hundred-pound cat could make itself invisible. A full-grown lion can disappear in a patch of golden grass the size of a pillow. Further, I knew not to look for a whole lion. I was looking for the black-tufted tip of a whipping tail, or the fierce, piercing eyes that would signal a charge. That was all I would see, if anything, before the blinding flash of the attack.

Gerard, who was crouched in the lead, abruptly stopped and turned and nodded at me. He pointed at the tracks in the sand at our feet and nodded emphatically. I knew what he meant. The tracks were fresh. The lion was near. We all exchanged knowing glances. Not a word was said. We crept on.

Eventually, the tracks turned to the left and climbed the opposite bank, then turned back to the right and followed the bank of the creek. We hadn't gone much farther along the bank when Nyamaiya suddenly dropped and pointed. There it was! Fifty yards away—lying in the shade of a *miombo* tree. To our amazement, the big cat was looking the other way, a ginger mane framing its large head. Against great odds, we had won the challenge of the stalk. It was a result I had not expected. To get this close to a mature male lion without its seeing, smelling, or hearing us was an impressive feat.

Gerard and I crouched low and sneaked to a small tree that I used to brace the gun for a rest. Still the lion looked the other way. Gerard poked me in the shoulder where he wanted me to shoot the lion. I nodded and took aim, placing the cross hairs just so. It all happened so fast that I had no time to get nervous. The heavy gun bellowed, and

A Bullet Well Placed

I reloaded and quickly fired again. The big lion never got up; it just rolled slowly onto its side. As we approached Gerard and I swapped guns, and with the .450 I put an insurance bullet between the shoulder blades of the big-bodied cat.

When it was all over, I could not believe our luck. This was a superb lion with a ginger, blond, and black mane. The hair was thick and long, and it was as good a lion as I'd seen taken by a hunter. It was big in body as well, measuring 9 feet, 7½ inches nose to tail.

"I will make a half-body mount of him," I said, "to go with the other one we shot, in 1982."

"I'm glad," Gerard said, raking his hands through the thick mane. "That's the only way to do it justice. A super lion."

"And I did it all myself." I was feeling a bit cocky now. Perhaps the cockiness of the Rungwa lions was contagious.

"You did, did you?"

"Well, perhaps you helped a bit."

He laughed, and we took a whole roll of film of the great cat, with everyone getting a turn to pose. Nyamaiya was his same quiet self, but he was smiling and took time to dip a pinch of black snuff before setting off at a fast walk to collect the vehicle.

It was a chore for the five of us to get the lion loaded onto the bed of the truck. We could have used the winch, but that would have been

Gerard's Five Star camp—not a blade of grass nor a twig on the ground, and "fenced" all around.

cheating. There is something about manhandling a full-grown lion. It impresses upon one their immense size and weight: A mature male is all muscle. Then there are its claws and fangs—bigger than you had imagined. It sent a shiver up my spine to think what that beast could have done to us had things turned out differently.

I said to Gerard, "In truth, that was probably the most exciting hunt of my life. That was incredible!"

"That's the way to hunt them," he agreed. "But you don't often get the chance like that. You have to come across the spore at just the right time."

We made a beeline for camp, stopping just long enough for me to collect a couple of guinea fowl for camp meat.

I arrived in camp to the usual celebration for the lion-hunting hero. Everyone came out banging on pots and pans, chanting and slapping me on the back and shaking my hand. Farouk Qreshi was there, an apprentice hunter to Gerard whom I knew well from last year's odyssey. He and I had spent three months together setting up camps, tracking elephants, scouting game for clients, and tackling whatever odd jobs came up. A short, handsome, friendly fellow, Farouk is a third-generation East African who carries the thick Pakistani accent of his heritage. Farouk is also a mechanic (indispensable in the bush) and overall handyman who assists Gerard in the 101 tasks that arise on safari that Gerard cannot attend to while hunting twelve or fourteen hours a day with clients.

"Gude job, Jahnny!" Farouk said, extending his free hand. In the other was a cup of *chai,* of course, for if you knew Farouk, you knew he had a penchant for hot tea. He drank gallons of the stuff. "Sooper lion!" he said.

The whole camp paraded around the back of the truck to study the lion. The men began to prod its paws and whiskers, tail and mane, and admire the enormous teeth. In my experience, nothing excites a camp like a lion—no other animal so fascinates us men. There is just something about a lion that evokes that response. I can't imagine hunting a saber-toothed tiger with a spear, but I bet our cave-dwelling ancestors did. And I bet they shared cheers of excitement just as passionately as we do today over the kill of a lion. The big cats are the ultimate predator. Because we are predators, too, they are our top competitor. They are a most worthy adversary and command our utmost respect.

Africa is home to many worthy adversaries, and that night around the campfire I was attacked by another. After showering and changing,

This is the whole crew—what it takes to run a tented safari in the bush.

I took a seat by the fire wearing only flip-flops on my bare feet. I had a beer in hand and was sitting in the dark, watching the fire dance and crackle, thinking over my adventures, when something bit me on top of the foot. The pain was sharp and instantaneous. I jumped, but my heart sank. I knew it was a snake—what else would attack one so low to the ground and with such force? In that split second—when time seemed to freeze—my mind raced, groping for a different outcome, a different adversary, but there were none I could think of. All I knew for sure was that it hurt like hell, and I bolted upright to see what had attacked me. Sure enough, there was the black ribbon of a snake slithering under the chair. Only it wasn't a snake. It was ants.

They were big, black safari ants, thousands of them. Several of the black villains still clung to my flesh, squeezing my hide with their merciless, big pincher jaws for all they were worth. But I could deal with ants. I was relieved to find that it was not a mamba. I plucked the villains off like big ticks, then called out to Farouk to help battle the seething mass of invaders. I knew what had to be done, having once before dealt with safari ants, although I had never been the victim of their attack. Now I took it personally.

The safari ant is an interesting beast. Periodically, endless hordes rise from their holes to march relentlessly through the bush, knowing no foe living or dead that can stop them. Nor can any terrain deter them. They cross hills, valleys, and even rivers while embarked on their lengthy travels, killing and eating whatever won't get out of their way. But because all you have to do *is* to get out of their way, they are of little risk to humans other than infants or passed-out drunks, which they have been known to kill.

Farouk soon appeared with two shovels. We scooped coals from the fire pit and arranged the glowing embers in a defensive line—a heat shield of sorts—with the goal of diverting the invading pests around camp. It took some time, and we had to enlist the help of several boys, but in the end our mission was successful. I was reminded of a friend who once returned to camp to find it completely overrun—every tent was covered in the black devils. The hunting party had no choice but to abandon camp until the ferocious beasts moved on. Besides safari ants, I can't think of a single animal that can force a hunting party out of camp. Yes, they are a worthy adversary.

We woke early to begin what turned out to be an equally fantastic day. Just after dawn we spotted three klipspringers on a rocky hill. The male disappeared into hiding while the two females remained and pranced on top of a boulder, looking at us nervously. They reminded me of a couple of ballerinas with their big, dark eyes and the way they stood on the tiptoes of their tiny hoofs. Their prissy stance, however, has nothing to do with vanity and everything to do with traction. The klipspringer's specially shaped hoofs allow the small antelope to "fly" over rocky terrain to escape its enemies. When the male failed to appear, Gerard hooted, imitating a rival suitor. After a few minutes the jealous male emerged on a rock high atop the hill. It stood broadside and perfectly silhouetted against a blue sky.

"How far?" I asked, taking the safety off the .375.

"It's 175," he said.

I held my breath and squeezed. The solid took the antelope in the shoulder, making a perfect heart shot. It sprang, fell some ten feet, and then rolled partway down the hill, settling on a large boulder. Luckily, neither of its fine horns was damaged in the spill. And the big solid did little but punch a neat hole through its frame. It will make a great full body mount. On tiptoes, of course.

Later, we came across a small herd of buffalo in the *miombo* forest. Studying them, Gerard noticed a huge bull in their midst. Even I could tell that it was special: The horns swept down and then out and out, and still out! We got reasonably close, but before I could get off a shot the buffalo sighted us and thundered off. We gave chase, and luckily the big boy stopped and turned broadside, offering me its shoulder. I pounded it with the .450, then delivered the second barrel up the backside as it turned and trundled away. A solid would have been the better bullet on that last shot, but I was using softs and there was no time to make a change. Nevertheless, the bull soon slowed and stumbled from the damage.

As we caught up, the buffalo got its second wind and began to run again. I shot it twice more in the rear, then again on the shoulder when it veered to have a look back at us. About the time that I was beginning to feel pretty impotent, the old bull slowed, stopped, and pitched onto its side. I ran up and gave the *coup de grâce* in the spine.

It was truly a grand old buffalo, with horns that measured over 48 inches wide. In all honesty I have to say that my earlier buffalo was prettier, with thicker horns and boss and a better downward sweep to the curl. But there were no arguments here. I happily took them both!

While the boys caped and quartered the bull, Gerard and I threw together a quick lunch of sardine and mustard sandwiches, which happen to be one of his favorites. They are actually quite good, and given the choice, Gerard will opt for a quick lunch in the field every time, leaving more time for hunting and avoiding a backtrack to camp. That is not to say that one won't encounter new animals while on the backtrack. The chances are better, however, with a continual push

This buffalo takes top honors in the spread category: 48 inches.

into new territory, and it allows one to venture farther from camp. Once we got our quarry loaded—quite a job with a buffalo, even quartered—we headed for an area where Gerard had seen some good sable. Sure enough, we found a lone bull. It was a hundred yards away, hidden in some trees. All that was showing was the head and neck. Gerard gave the signal, and I squeezed off the shot. I hit it square in the neck, and down it went. This sable had beautiful horns, making a matched pair for the one I have on the wall at home.

Then, as we were making our way across a large *mbuga*, we spotted a warthog and stopped to collect it for leopard bait. But just as I was about to fire, Gerard said, "Whoa! There's a very large reedbuck at the far end of the pan. Try to get it!"

I looked at the dot on the horizon, then put it in the scope, but it was facing away from us and was far. Really far. My rifle was fitted with only a 3X scope, and the cross hairs at that distance just about blotted out the animal's whole body.

"That's a long way," I said.

"I know. But they are spooky as hell, and if we try to get closer I'm afraid we will scare him."

I took the best rest I could get and aimed at the tip-top of the horns, figuring for quite a drop with the 270-grain bullet. Then I took a deep breath and squeezed the trigger as slowly as I had ever squeezed one. The gun went off and the reedbuck disappeared.

"You got him!" Gerard shouted. "He went straight down. Hell of a shot."

Abdu, the government PH, walked it off at 350 paces. The bullet took the reedbuck in the back of the neck, eighteen inches below where I had aimed. I cuss my misses, so I guess I should celebrate my good shots. That was a good shot, if not damned lucky. Anyway, the reedbuck's horns measured just shy of 14 inches, a superb trophy.

While we were skinning it, two oribi came out to see what we were up to.

"I could hit one with my .44," Gerard announced casually.

"No way, Bwana," I said.

"No, Gerharhd," said Farouk, who had come with us today.

Gerard went to retrieve his pistol, but the oribi didn't care to await the outcome of the bet and departed abruptly. So Gerard fired at a tree eighty yards away, offhand, and hit the knothole he was aiming at.

"Very impressive!" I said.

"Too gude," said Farouk.

"That will teach you fellows to question the master."

An hour later we got another chance to see the pistol put to use when we came upon an old buffalo bull lying in the grass beside the dirt track. It was unusual for a bull to remain prone like that with the truck driving so close to it. Gerard turned off the track and drove right up to the animal in an attempt to get it to move. He even yelled at it, but to no avail. The bull just lay there, studying us with dark, menacing eyes in a black, battle-scarred face. Both horns were broken off at the bottom of the curl, making the beast even uglier than it already was. The old bull was either sick or wounded; there was no doubt about that. In such a condition buffalo are even more dangerous than normal, and normal for buffalo is very dangerous.

This one was like a landmine primed to explode. The old bull would hammer the first unsuspecting native who happened by—it would have hammered us had we been on foot and not seen it first. Except for the bands of marauding ivory poachers (a laudable target for such a buffalo), no humans inhabit this remote area. However, at certain times of the year honey hunters migrate in to set traps and later to collect their treasure. Although I had seen no more than a handful of those barefoot and threadbare collectors, suspended here and there high in the trees were the results of their handiwork:

Gerard and I pose with a super reedbuck taken with a lucky long shot.

An old bull with small tusks, but it was my first elephant and I'm quite proud of it.

hollowed-out logs into which the bees are lured to make their hives. If a honey hunter were unlucky enough to stumble upon a crotchety old bull like this, the bull would surely put a premature end to that humble craftsman's career.

With that in mind, Gerard pulled out his .44 and fired a shot over the buffalo's head. The bull struggled to its feet and came straight for us. Gerard sped off with the bull in hot pursuit, but there was something wrong with the buffalo's rear leg. It was gimp. Leaning half out of the car and aiming the pistol behind, Gerard let the buffalo have one in the chest at close range. Amazingly, it stopped the bull. The bull then turned and limped off, and Gerard shot it two or three more times. After a quick reload we followed it up, and Gerard shot it twice on the shoulder, causing it to falter with each shot. The old bull then dropped to its knees and rolled onto the ground. We circled, and Gerard placed the final shot in the back of the head. I was surprised to see the .44 cartridge work as well as it did. I didn't think it would have enough penetration to do the job, certainly not enough to stop a charge with a shot to the chest. But it did.

None of this is to say that I would recommend hunting African buffalo with a .44. This was one instance in which the cartridge worked, but it was only that—one instance. One of my pet peeves is gunwriters who set out to test some new ammo or caliber, shoot one animal with it, and then proclaim its success. Well, I'm sorry, but one shot does not a true test make. The largest brown bear ever taken was taken with a .22 rifle, but an Alaska guide would no more recommend taking a .22 after the big bruins than he would a baseball bat.

About the time that a friend of mine returned from Australia, where he participated in a wild donkey culling operation, a gunwriter put out an article on the nilgai he had shot with a certain type of ammo. It was the only animal he had ever shot with it, and he was ready to sing the bullet's praises. Well, that might be fine for receiving free ammo or free hunts, but it has nothing to do with helping the readership of a magazine in choosing ammunition. The end to the tale is that my friend shot some sixty donkeys with two different bullets. The first was the brand recommended by the gunwriter, and nearly every donkey ran off and required follow-up shots. The other bullet he used was the Barnes X-Bullet, which knocked the donkeys flat. Sixty donkeys— now that's a test!

Putting this buffalo to good use, we hung three leopard baits and got back to camp after dark. I crawled into bed completely bushed and was asleep in an instant.

Again we were up early and spent the whole of the next day collecting baits and camp meat. First thing out, I took a hartebeest that on first glance decided it didn't want anything to do with us. I hit the departing antelope on the run, then finished it up close in the neck. Because of its size, the male was halved into two leopard baits. Next I shot a zebra with a beautiful hide. The stallions engage in vicious fighting, in constant pursuit of herd dominance, but this fellow had none of the usual battle scars. Moreover, the stripes were jet black and well defined, and they ringed the legs all the way down to the hoofs. This zebra, like the hartebeest, was galloping when I shot it—never an easy task—and it made me that much happier in my success. I was really glad to be shooting well. It seems it always takes me a day or two to get into the groove on safari, but I was now in it.

Next came an eland for camp meat. We discovered a small herd in the cover of the forest and crept close to the big, ginger-colored animals. Taking my time, I hit the big bull solidly in the shoulder, and it ran like hell, the muscles under its tawny hide propelling it along quite well. No matter how many times you see it, it is simply amazing to witness how nimble these giant antelope are. Despite its vast bulk, a bull eland can run and jump with the agility of a Thoroughbred racehorse.

When the old bull finally came to a stop, I was faced with a long shot and could see only part of the animal, its body being shielded by trees. But there was no waiting for a better shot or trying to get closer, for it was likely to bolt. I put one into the thick neck, but the bullet missed the spine and it had zero effect. On the third shot I hit the neck proper, and it dropped, raising a small cloud of dust.

While congratulations went round and the trackers began butchering the fallen eland, I noticed a large hole in the ground next to it. I didn't think much of it until all at once black ants began to boil out and swarm. Making a quick search of the area, Gerard and I found a suitably round rock, which took the two of us to lift, and we plugged the hole. Fortunately it was effective, or the ants would have chased us off the eland. As in most of the world, in Africa might makes right. Not even the mightiest of lions would be a match for the vicious ants. Luckily they gave us no more trouble after that.

Later, while driving across a shallow plain, we spotted a couple of warthogs in the tall grass. I shot the first pig at just under two hundred yards, and it dropped instantly. Its partner ran and I gave it a shot up the rear, but I was low and the bullet hit the gut. We tracked the hardy tusker nearly half a mile through the long grass. A warthog isn't much

A dandy bull eland caught in the open of a large pan.

on size, but its tushes are sharp and it is quick and accustomed to fighting off predators much larger than itself. So it was fairly exciting tracking the porker in the high grass, wondering if it would charge. Given an opportunity, the homely pig could easily dissect a leg.

We searched and searched but couldn't find it. There was no doubt it was in there; the sly fellow was just holding tight. When Gerard came upon it suddenly at his feet, he finished the pig with the .44. At the time I was some distance behind, having backtracked with Nyamaiya and David to look for more sign. We hung both warthogs for leopard bait.

When we got back to camp at dark, everyone was ready to celebrate our success to this point on safari. Gerard and Farouk and I sat around the campfire and drank bottles of Heineken, laughing over stories of old and reliving adventures from previous hunts. Farouk's strong Pakistani accent, combined with his habit of speaking out of the side of his mouth, was comical whether his story was or not, and he had both Gerard and me in stitches. He tried to tell us a story about one of his pets, but Gerard and I were laughing so hard it must have taken him thirty minutes.

"The uther day a dog beet my anteater."

"Your anteater?" Gerard asked.

"Yes, my anteater. A neighbor's dog beet him. So I tuke him to Dr. Shaka, the famous witch dahctor—"

"You took your anteater to a witch doctor?" I asked.

"Yes, the famous Dr. Shaka. He is wery well known. It was just a leettle bite on my doggy's leg, barht I did not wahrnt it to get infected."

"Wait a minute," Gerard interrupted. "I thought you said it was an anteater."

"Yes," Farouk insisted, "an anteater. It is our—"

"Bloody hell, Farouk, what in the devil are you talking about? Is it a dog or is it an anteater? You have completely lost me!"

"It's a dog. An anteater."

"Say it in English, man," Gerard snapped.

"What breed is it?" I asked.

"Anterrier," he said.

"For crying out loud!" Gerard shouted. "You mean a henna terrier?!"

"Yes," said Farouk in frustration, "'na-terrier. Tharht's what I've been tehlling you! So I tuke him to Dr. Shaka and the doctahr gave him a shot and my leettle doggy died right there. He just *kufa*'d right there on the table! I told him, 'You keeled my doggy!' and he said, 'No, Bwahrna, it was the bite that keeled him.' And I told him, 'It was just a leetle bite. It was your shot that keeled him. You keeled my doggy.' But the doctahr just said, 'No, bwahrna, you brought him too late!'"

By then Gerard and I were laughing so hard we had tears in our eyes and I couldn't breathe. Farouk just sat there in his chair grinning out of the side of his mouth and drinking his beer. When our composure returned, Gerard went to the small bar in the dining tent and whipped up a batch of powerful screwdrivers. Returning to the fire, he insisted I join him. A year earlier it would have been nothing to put that on top of four Heinekens, but since I drink little now and my tolerance is down, I was feeling it. A pretty good indication that I was drunk was when I showed them how to do a "Ubangi," named by a workmate of mine after the African tribe with the plates in their lips. With your mouth stretched over the rim of the glass, arms at your sides, you tilt your head back and down the drink without the use of your hands. It was something we did at happy hour after work. It was how a bunch of young, overworked Big Eight accountants relieved stress. Now I jog.

Ouch!

After the night's fling I felt absolutely horrible upon waking and was nauseated most of the morning. Bouncing up and down in the vehicle didn't help, and at one point, as my belly heaved, I swore off alcohol forever. *No more nights like that!* Actually, the night was fine. It's the mornings I don't care to repeat.

In the afternoon, by which time I was feeling much better, we continued the drive, looking primarily for elephant or elephant sign. We saw a few of the big gray animals either at the water holes or wandering through the forest and even followed one herd a short distance, but there were no bulls worth a darn. Additionally, it was hard to get in the elephant-hunting mood with the virtual elephant graveyard around us. Elephant skulls and carcasses littered the land— the remains of the poachers' dirty work.

"Elephant hunting is finished," Gerard commented while we were driving. "I've counted more than 120 elephant carcasses this year in Rungwa. Even more in Masailand!"

"That's why I've never been too keen on hunting elephant."

"Yes, but you saw what it was like when we hunted them in 1982. That was real hunting, boy. You are lucky you got to do that. Soon no one will be allowed to hunt elephant."

I nodded in agreement, sad at the gloomy prediction and feeling a sense of helplessness over the plight of the elephants. It seemed as if there should be something we hunters could do, something we could come up with, to protect the precious animals, but I realized that there

A silver-backed jackal.

wasn't. That's what made me feel so bad. That's what made me curse the politics involved. I knew that while Africa was involved in a struggle of black against white, and tribe against tribe, and as long as corruption ruled, there would never be a solution reached to protect the giant beasts. The elephant had been neglected by a bureaucracy that was busy trying to survive, a bureaucracy that was struggling to feed its starving people.

Up ahead, a black mamba slithered across the road. It wasn't any bigger around than a carrot, but it stretched nearly ten feet in length. Sighting us, the black snake sprang into high gear, moving surprisingly fast for a big snake. It whipped across the charred ground to the trunk of a short tree, which it scaled with alarming ease. The mamba was more dark gray than black, and Gerard shot it with the .44 as it climbed the tree—a challenging shot to say the least. His shot didn't kill the snake, but it stopped it in the lower branches. After he had shot it twice more in the body, we took turns with the big pistol trying to hit it in the head.

We spent the rest of the day following elephant tracks, but none were very promising. After checking two leopard baits early the next morning, we headed toward the Ruaha Park boundary in search of elephant coming out of the park. Gerard had taken only two bulls this season, and both were forty-five-pounders. Just the year before his clients had taken nine.

"The big fellows are all gone," he said. "If we see one of forty or so pounds we had best take it. I know fifty pounds was your minimum, but if you don't take an elephant this trip, I fear you may never get the chance again."

I thought it over, then nodded my head in agreement. "OK," I said.

It must have been fate, for not twenty minutes later we found my bull. We had been up at 5:00 A.M. and off by 6:00. It was now 7:15 as we drove through the *miombo* forest, following meandering dirt tracks. The early sunlight slanted softly through the tall trees. Suddenly, Nyamaiya tapped Gerard on the shoulder, and we came to a stop. A hundred yards ahead, a big-bodied bull was strolling through the forest. We all got out as quietly and quickly as possible. I placed solids in the twin barrels of my .450, as did Gerard. Gerard's face took on his usual expression of intense anticipation, and it was contagious. But everything happened so fast, the elephant bull appeared so suddenly, that my heart hardly had the chance to go berserk. It was like being pushed off the high dive before realizing where I was. There was no time to get worked up. So I was relatively

Note the bullet hole in the horn above the bull's eye. That was meant for between the eyes. Luckily, I got a second chance. David, Gerard, Farouk, and Nyamaiya.

calm, which worked to my advantage. Gerard grabbed me by the arm and led me forward, and we set a fast pace to catch up to the wandering bull. Even strolling, the gray giant moved at quite a clip. We had yet to get a good look at its ivory, but its body was enormous. As we neared, Gerard moved to my right so we were now abreast of each other, rifles ready, stalking quietly.

When we got within fifty yards the old boy heard us or sensed us, and it abruptly whirled around. As it did, its head went back, its ears spread wide, and it stared down its long trunk at us. The old patriarch was truly magnificent. It was a tremendous sight, and its gigantic size filled me with sudden doubts. I was David facing Goliath, and for a second it seemed as if I had embarked upon a very foolhardy venture.

"Shoot him between the eyes, six inches down!"

I threw the heavy gun up and aimed where Gerard had instructed. But in that split second, a hundred thoughts rushed through my head. This was a big moment for a hunter, even one who had mixed feelings about shooting the gray giants. The elephant is, indisputably, the largest land animal on earth. Because of that, it is a culmination, a pinnacle, of big-game hunting. And though I might live to hunt another sixty years, there would never be a bigger animal on earth for me to hunt. For a big-game hunter, this was the end of the line. And now I was graced with an opportunity at the famed brain shot. How many times had I fantasized about brain-shooting an elephant? It is something that every big-game hunter has dreamed of, even one like me, hobbled with qualms. But now that the moment had arrived, any hesitation quickly disappeared, for I was lost in the excitement of it all.

The gun blast filled the forest, and my ears rang. Although I was caught up in the whole thing as if in a dream, I was well aware, however, that the bull had remained standing after the shot, which most definitely was not what it was supposed to do. It was supposed to collapse—the rug pulled out from under its feet. Something had gone seriously wrong. No doubt my bullet had hit a bit low, missing the brain. When the bull turned to run, Gerard shot it on the left shoulder to little effect. It was now moving, and nothing short of a brain shot or a spine shot was going to stop it—at least not immediately. The proper thing to do at this point was for me to shoot it on the shoulder—get the heart and lungs and ensure an eventual kill. But I was so focused on the brain shot, so focused on shooting it in the head, that's what I did. I aimed just behind the left ear canal and pulled the second trigger. The effect was immediate. It was like watching an avalanche in the mountains, except that here it was the whole mountain that was falling down.

The giant went straight down, raising a cloud of dust around it, and rolled onto its right side.

As we approached, I put two insurance shots into the chest, between the front legs. But the elephant was down for good and did not get up. We circled the big animal, and Gerard slapped me on the back.

"Well done," he said.

It was, indeed, an old bull. The pads of its feet, measuring a foot and a half across, were worn down to the point that little if any "print" was made in its tracks. The old bull's feet left only flat, round tracks, like a smooth-seated barstool stamped upside down in the dirt. Because this was such an old bull, it was missing much of the wiry hair from the end of its knobby tail, but Nyamaiya assured me with a gesture that there was enough for a bracelet. I had seen many elephant hair bracelets over the years, in shops and at hunting shows, but had never bought one for fear of supporting the poaching industry. But having shot my own elephant, I would gladly wear a bracelet made from the hairs of its tail. The tusks were right at forty pounds, and I was proud. Unfortunately, the tusks were lost to a taxidermist's fire several years later. When I tell that story and someone offers condolences, I always point to my head and say, "Yes, but the memory of it is still up here, and that's what matters."

We snapped at least two rolls of film, including the obligatory picture of me, the hunter, sitting on top of the toppled giant with my big double in hand. A photo like that can look disrespectful if it's not done right.

The men had their work cut out for them, so Gerard and I left to check all eight leopard baits. Incredibly, not a single one had been hit.

"I can't believe this," Gerard complained. "I am 100 percent on cats this season, and now I can't get a bloody leopard to feed." He turned his dark eyes on me. "It's all because you went on about how easy leopard hunting is."

"Well, it is."

"Quit saying that. You've cursed us!"

"But it is. I mean, you sit and wait and then the leopard comes and you shoot it out of the tree."

"Yes, but we've got eight baits out and not a single one taken. How easy is that?"

"Well, it's not easy if you wound him," I agreed. "Then it's the most dangerous hunt of all. So unless you wound the leopard, it is an easy hunt. That's all I was trying to say."

Daytime is siesta time for hippos. They do their feeding at night.

"Quit saying that," he insisted. "I will put Farouk's witch doctor after you!"

We returned to camp around 10 A.M., where we remained until 4:00, held up by a visit from the local game warden, who was reputed to be a poacher. He came to ask Gerard for ammo: .458 and .375. Why would he possibly want .458 shells, if not for poaching? When asked, the warden explained that he wanted to collect a buffalo for camp meat. *Right!* Gerard tried to put him off, but when it looked like the fellow would cause trouble, Gerard disappeared into his tent and returned with a handful of shells. Here was a fellow who at the snap of his fingers could shut down Gerard's entire hunting operation immediately and permanently, so Gerard had little option. The chain of command in a communist country is rigid and absolute, and there is no recourse. You do as you are told or you are out of business.

"Try these," he told the heavyset fellow. "They are really super!"

When the game warden had left, Gerard said, "Cheeky bastard!"

"You didn't have a choice," I said.

"No, but I gave him the worst shells we had. The .458s are handloaded with 300-grain bullets. They shoot about a foot high. And the .375s are Silver Tips. You saw firsthand on your 1982 trip how poorly they penetrate."

We went out that afternoon on what should have been an easy assignment, once we embarked on it. Our plan was to take an impala—any impala—the size of the horns didn't matter. I was after a cape for mounting the near-world-record impala I had shot in 1982. The original cape had never made it to Dallas. But for whatever reason, my shooting went to hell. We got to within respectable range of a nice male, which stood warily behind a bush, and the bullet shattered in the thick limbs. We never saw that impala again.

Soon we encountered another small herd, and I missed a shot at two hundred yards. We made another stalk, and I finally took a nice ram on the run at eighty-five paces. I knew to lead it, but I did not lead by enough; the bullet took it in the gut. We followed the ram to a creek and waited on the bank while it crossed. Then it turned and sprinted across in front of us, and I shot it at thirty yards and it dropped. Again, though, I didn't lead enough, and the bullet took it in the back. Our goal had been merely a good cape, but this ram had good horns for a southern impala.

Later we came upon another herd of impala, and my shooting improved. The lead male was at a fair distance, pointed away and looking over its rear at us. I wasn't sure how far it was, so I aimed at the neck, allowing for bullet drop. I figured that if it was more than two hundred yards, the bullet would fall and make a Texas heart shot. What I didn't want was to plan the Texas heart shot only to find it was farther than I had thought and hit the animal in the gut. The bullet struck the neck, where I'd aimed, a small target at that distance, and I was happy to have my shooting back to form.

In the afternoon we found a herd of eland that held what, even at a distance, was clearly a good bull. The hard part would be getting close enough. We circled into the brush, trying to keep the wind on them, but they soon sighted us and stampeded into the open of a nearby *mbuga,* where my only opportunity was a running shot as they departed for the next country. Eland are the long-distance champions of the African antelope, and once they spook and run, your hunt is usually over. So it was now or never. I placed the cross hairs on the shoulder of the running bull, then knowingly swung ahead of it, leading its body by a whole two feet, and pulled the trigger with the confidence of a batter who knows that he has just been thrown a home-run ball. I don't know how I knew, I just knew. And I was right. I hit the big animal smack on the shoulder, getting both lungs. The well-placed bullet, however, did not stop the running bull. If anything, it ran faster. The eland kicked into high gear, and I fired again—but without leading

Unfortunately, there are few rags to riches stories for the citizens of Tanzania. It is mostly rags in this impoverished country.

enough; the bullet struck the gut. But the first shot had done its work, and the animal soon went down. Even as we approached, we could see a tremendous set of horns.

"I can tell you right now," Gerard said with a grin, "that this is the biggest eland we've taken this season."

I just nodded.

After putting up what had seemed like a hundred leopard baits, our persistence finally paid off. Two out of the three baits we checked the next morning had been hit—both by male leopards, based on the size of the tracks. An old blind was already in place where the bigger of the two leopards had fed, so that saved some time. Gerard just gave the blind a quick once-over to make sure everything was in order. You can't start clearing branches and making changes when you come to hunt, not if you want the leopard to show.

This left us with a few hours before the afternoon hunt, and as we continued on in the Land Rover, crossing the sporadic pans of the *miombo* forest, Nyamaiya spotted a herd of zebra in the distance. They were quite wild and ran at the sight of us, kicking up a cloud of dust in their wake. One stallion made the mistake of stopping broadside to inspect us while the others fled out of sight. Gerard guessed the distance at three hundred yards plus, so I put the cross hairs a foot over its

Africa is home to both the large and the small. Although one of the small, this steenbok sports quite impressive horns.

back. The bullet took it low in the neck, just in front of the shoulder. No second shot was needed, as the bullet had clipped the jugular, finishing it surprisingly quickly. As with the stallion of a few days before, we found the coat to be in excellent condition.

We spent the long, hot afternoon in the leopard blind. The truck dropped us off at 4:00 P.M., and we remained seated and motionless until 7:00, when the truck came to collect us. Three hours had never passed so slowly. Sitting in a leopard blind is like being sent to the corner when you are a kid, only you can't move, you must be quieter, and it lasts nearly forever. Furthermore, no matter how you sit, whether in a chair or on the ground, your legs or feet will fall asleep. But I was not allowed to move them. If I did, Gerard would shoot me a reproachful look. But there is a greater test yet of one's ability to remain still. From the start, the tsetse flies commence their torture. The fiendish bastards drill your neck, back, and legs, and you can't slap at them. For those who still can't get the picture, imagine being surrounded by several delinquent kids armed with safety pins and having to sit perfectly still and endure them poking you wherever and whenever they want. That's what it was like.

Yes, there are better ways to spend one's time than leopard hunting. In all honesty, I would have been just as glad to spend the time driving around or hiking the hills and taking pictures of game. But Gerard had taken this quest personally. He was on a mission to find me a leopard, and there was no deterring him.

Sitting there, I thought of Mando and the phrase he used to describe the odd, trancelike state the natives adopt when faced with a long wait. At first it had been an eerie sight to see a native standing statue-still on the side of the road, frozen, face blank and staring at nothing, completely unaware of my presence. But I quickly grew accustomed to it, to what apparently is a self-hypnotic trance. Now bored to death, I was jealous of the talent and thought how much more tolerable the wait in the blind would be if, like them, I could simply "shift into neutral," as Mando had termed it. Just shift into neutral until the leopard showed, or it was time to go home.

There are times, admittedly, when the interminable wait for the leopard is broken up: birds chatter (which often heralds the approach of the leopard), a lion roars, a baboon hoots, some unidentified animal screeches, leaving you wondering what it was—but those are sensations for the ears alone. The blind, true to its name, is four sided, and the shooting hole remains plugged until the final moment. You can't even admire the sunset. There is nothing to look at but four grass-thatched walls and the dirt under your fingernails. Reading a book, between tsetse persecutions, is the best way to pass the time. *The Winds of War* came in handy.

The leopard never showed, and we returned to camp tired from the early mornings and late evenings on the hunt.

For supper, the cook whipped up the linguini that I had brought from home, adding exotic spices and a dash of bush magic. It was excellent. It is simply beyond belief what a bush chef can prepare on a bed of hot coals.

We awoke at 5:00 A.M. and left first thing for the blind. The car dropped us off in the dark, and we sat there quietly and hopefully: A good portion of the bait was now missing. But once again we were in for a long, disappointing wait. We sat there until after eight o'clock but saw nothing of the spotted cat. The clever feline had come to feed during the night and had departed before daylight.

"This leopard is a wise one," Gerard said as we drove off, gesturing with a pointed index finger for emphasis, the wheels turning in his head. "I think we should offer this chap a baboon or two." At first I thought Gerard was kidding, but then I saw that he was serious.

"A baboon?" I asked, rather incredulously. *We don't shoot baboons!* My prejudice against shooting baboons had been firmly instilled by John Fletcher on my first safari in Kenya and again by Gerard when I first hunted with him.

"This *chui* is being difficult. A baboon might be just the thing to get him to show himself. A leopard absolutely loves baboon. If we put one or two up right now, there is a good chance he won't be able to resist and will climb the tree before dark."

I wasn't convinced, but on the drive back to camp for breakfast we came upon a large pack of baboons making their way across the charred ground of the forest. A big male followed up the rear, glancing over its shoulder at us. Of all the animals to botch a shot on, this was the one animal I feared wounding more than any other . . . and I did. I hit it in the rear, wounding it. Gerard tried to finish the big male with his 8mm. He anchored it, but the baboon was still alive when we reached it. It took a shot up close with the .44. The whole thing felt more like an assassination than a hunt.

After lunch we went out for a short spin, and Gerard had me shoot another baboon. Without elaborating, it was a pitiful sight if ever I saw one, just as John Fletcher had promised, and I swore off shooting another.

"That was my last baboon. Ever."

Gerard and a couple of knob-nosed ducks.

"Agreed," Gerard said.

We dragged the baboons along the creek to spread their scent, then hung them with the sable bait where the leopard had fed. We then sat in the blind from four o'clock that afternoon until well after dark, hoping that this night would prove different. But no *chui*.

At dinner I refused a shot of whiskey, not wanting another morning like the one after the four Heinekens and the screwdriver.

Farouk jokingly said, "Barht, Bwahrna, we moost saylebrate the zebrah!" We all had a good laugh. Talk about digging deep for a reason to celebrate.

The next morning I shot an impala to replenish one of the baits that had been fed on heavily and was nearly gone. The tracks at the base of the tree indicated a big male, and it offered a spark of hope that perhaps all our hard work would pay off. Continuing on, we came across a spitting cobra in the open. Gerard blasted it in the head with his shotgun before the black snake had a chance to flare its evil-looking hood. The deadly serpent measured seven feet in length. I could not help but look at that snake and ask, "Why?" I know that every animal has its place in nature, but why on earth did God see fit to make certain snakes poisonous to such a ridiculous degree? It seems like overkill.

Once more we spent the afternoon in a leopard blind, but this time it was in a new blind. Gerard had felt there was something wrong with the old blind, that it was spooking our cat, so we built another, forty yards farther back. We changed another thing, too: This time we lay on the ground instead of sitting in chairs, which was a great improvement. It was a lot more comfortable, for one thing. Also, my legs didn't fall asleep, and I didn't have to worry about the chair creaking. And last but not least, the tsetse devils couldn't bite me on the back when I was lying on it! When the leopard finally appeared, it would be a simple matter to rise quietly to shooting position.

Late in the afternoon, the excitement mounted when we heard the leopard growl; we just knew we had it. Then we heard it moving around, making that deep, husky grunt they make, and the birds went bonkers. Gerard kept glancing out of a tiny peephole and making knowing nods of his head, but this leopard was too clever. Somehow it knew something was up, and it refused to climb the tree. By dark all was quiet, and there was no sign of the cat. It was very disappointing, but that was hunting.

We awoke at four o'clock the following morning and went straight to the blind. Once we were inside, it started to drizzle. My rain gear was tucked away in the daypack beside me, but I could not take it out

The magnificent sable antelope.

for the noise it would make. So I made do with getting wet and lay there in the dark and drizzle. Then at dawn it really started to rain. I sat up and put on the rain jacket, then huddled over my crossed bare legs, trying to keep them dry. Gerard, who had forgotten his coat, pulled the ground tarp over his head. There was no leopard, of course, not with all that noise. But we waited until eight o'clock anyway, just to be sure, and departed the blind like a couple of drowned rats.

We returned to camp for breakfast and a strategy session. Gerard's eyes flickered at the dining table, and he announced: "I have the answer: If the leopard won't come to us, then we shall go to the leopard."

Farouk and I looked at each other in curiosity.

"This afternoon we are going into the hills on foot to find that leopard." Gerard drummed his fingers on the table in contemplation. "Yes," he continued, "this leopard has been hunted before, and it is not about to come to the bait in the light of day. We must go to it."

I had never done that—much less heard of it—but it sounded like a most exciting proposition. My mind buzzed with the possibilities. In practice, it proved to be every bit as exciting as it sounded.

After a short consultation, I chose the .450 loaded with softs for this unique adventure, while Gerard opted for a sawed-off shotgun with 00 buck. Between the two of us, we were set for just about any range at which the leopard might appear, though Gerard would shoot only if the leopard charged. After a quick paring of nonessential equipment and now outfitted in our quietest shoes—which for both of us were jogging shoes—we climbed the rocky hill by the bait and began a slow, methodical search for the leopard. Farouk and three boys, functioning as beaters, circled the hill in one direction while Gerard and I circled it in the other.

The hill was home to huge rocks and boulders that formed deep holes, crevices, and caves beneath them. That was deluxe leopard habitat, and soon we found irrefutable evidence of its habitation—proof that we were on the right track. Inside a narrow, flat cave were the skulls of two young hartebeest that the leopard had killed. Its paw prints were everywhere, and we found a fresh wet spot where the big cat had just urinated. We were in its house. The question in our minds now was, How would it react to intruders?

Would it come with claws and fangs to fight, or would it try to slip out a back window? Knowing well that our adversary would not take kindly to our unannounced visit, it was quite intense peering into the black depths of these caves and fissures, wondering if and when the big cat would come charging out at us. Chances were that it would come in a blinding rush, claws and teeth bared, offering at most a split second in which either to shoot and kill it or to wound the cat and feel the wrath of its fury.

Our pace was deliberate, for obvious reasons, and we covered every inch of the hill, every opening in the rocks, whispering at times but mostly using hand signals and facial gestures, which, like a picture, are often worth a thousand words. When our painstaking search had turned up nothing of the cat, we directed our efforts to the adjoining hill. The whole operation took perhaps an hour and a half to accomplish, though it seemed much longer. My forehead was beaded in sweat from the intensity of the endeavor, the concentration, and the strain on the eyes in darting here and there, trying to spot the camouflaged cat before it launched at us. This was hunting up close and personal, as I had never hunted before—at least not for dangerous game.

In the end the wise old cat eluded us in the hills, as it had at the bait, and despite the thorough search, we never caught sight of it. The search in the hills had, of course, been a last-ditch effort. With all the disturbance, it was doubtful the leopard would return anytime soon.

So we gave up on this difficult cat and quickly built a blind at the other bait that had been hit, sitting over it from 4:00 until dark, hoping this leopard would be less shy in its feeding habits. No such luck. Nothing showed. Admittedly there had been a lot of activity and disruption to the area, with the blind building in midday, and one would not normally hunt leopard out of a blind built the same day. But our options for leopard during our remaining days were running short.

"If only you hadn't said, 'Leopard hunting is easy,'" Gerard said in reprimand. "This is all your fault, Chilton."

I just shook my head.

The next day we decided to put leopard hunting aside and try for a kudu. That turned out to be a good decision, not just because I was free of the tormenting wait in the blind but also because we had quite a successful day. While we were driving across an opening in the woodlands, a common duiker darted in front of us. It soon stopped in a small patch of brush, and I crept to within 140 yards of it, where I could just make it out. There was no waiting for a better shot, for with its next step it would be gone. Luckily, one shot in the shoulder and it was mine. And it was a whopper. The horns curved slightly out, forming a *V*. It was a splendid trophy. If our measurements were correct, and if I were to enter it (which I wouldn't), it would be the new No. 1 in the record book!

Later we spotted four buffalo bulls trudging unawares across the opening of a wide *mbuga*. One looked quite good, and so Gerard and

Replacing a tire blown by one of the fire-burned stobs that littered this part of the Rungwa forest.

I, moving quickly, tried to reach them before they disappeared in the surrounding brush. But by the time we got to the opening and spotted them again, the buffalo had spooked and were running like hell for the thick brush beyond. They were running straight away from us, and Gerard gave me the nod. There wasn't time to do anything but fire quickly, and I did. I fired three quick shots at the big boy's ample rear end, emptying the rifle about the time all four buffalo vanished in the brush. The trundling bull showed no reaction, and Gerard and the trackers were skeptical I had hit it. But I knew my aim had been good, and I said so.

As we circled the island of brush, three buffalo came out. Only three. We watched them trot off and disappear. The fourth bull never showed.

"Well, you must have hit him," Gerard said. I was using softs, and though the .375 was capable of doing the job, we both knew the penetration would have been less than ideal on a shot through the length of a buffalo's body.

Hiking the perimeter of the brush, we returned to where the four buffalo had entered the thicket, and there we found some blood. Just a little.

OK, so it was hit. Now the question was, How well was it hit? There was no sound at all from the bull, no death moan—the groaning grunt buffalo are apt to make in their last living seconds. Was it dead? Or was it alive and waiting for us in ambush? Whatever the case, it had remained silent, a clue that in all probability indicated the latter.

Now the fun was about to begin, but not before Gerard went over the plan with us all. That did not take long, but it took some discipline, as the silent call of a wounded buffalo is quite strong, enticing even the smartest of hunters to blunder right in after it. But doing so would show no more forethought than that shown by lemmings eager to jump over the cliff. In other words, it would be a good way to get oneself killed. The plan was no guarantee that we wouldn't, but it at least put the odds back in our favor, which was where they were supposed to be.

So, resisting the urge to rush, we went over the plan, which required a change in weaponry to open-sighted doubles and determined who went first and what the order was. With the .450s now loaded and ready in our sweaty grips, we began the nerve-racking stalk into the thick bush, which initially called for Gerard and me to lead the way, with one hand moving stiff branches aside, the other pushing the barrel of the rifle into the dark undergrowth. It was slow going and miserable

Three young male lions chasing an old bull buffalo. It ended in a stalemate when its horned buddy arrived on the scene.

stuff to be in, but there was no other way. (If I were a recklessly brave man, with no self-concern whatsoever, my only worry at this point would have been in firing the gun at the buffalo at such close range, for surely the muzzle blast would singe the hair on the cape and permanently mar the mount. But I am not a recklessly brave man, and if I'd had hand grenades, I would have used them.)

When there was no immediate sign of the bull and visibility opened up beyond the end of my gun barrel, step number two of the plan came into play. Nyamaiya and David moved ahead of us and began the serious, hunched-down task of tracking. Farouk brought up the rear with my scoped .375, loaded with solids, on the slim chance that the buffalo might make a run for the open and I would be faced with a long shot.

It was downright spooky, creeping through the dense scrub after the wounded bull, wondering how we would find it and when it would charge. Excitement surged from head to toe, priming me as if I had downed a whole pot of coffee. Every nerve ending was awake, my whole body on red alert. My eyes and ears took in sights and sounds that would have gone utterly unnoticed were it not for the lurking black hulk waiting for the chance to kill me. We were literally stalking death, looking to find the Grim Reaper with horns before it found us.

It was frightening, but it was also wonderful in a weird kind of way. It was surprising how this experience of tracking a wounded buffalo could bring out the best and worst of emotions—all at the same time. Fear and exhilaration. Hesitation and eagerness. One minute feeling like the hunter, the next feeling like the hunted. It was perhaps akin to what a race car driver must experience when pushing his car to the edge. But it was more powerful than that. I would argue it is unique.

There is no sensation in the world like tracking a wounded Cape buffalo in the thick stuff, knowing that it is responsible for killing more hunters than any of the other Big Five, knowing that it is eager to make you a statistic. The buffalo in its element is formidable. It is the true king of beasts. It is wise as a general in its tactical decisions, and it has the keen senses to allow it to execute its ambush accordingly. Patience is one of its greatest assets. A buffalo draws you into battle on its own terms. It won't charge out the way a lion will at first sight of you. It waits until you are close, close enough that it is sure that it can reach you, crush you, pound you into the ground. There would come a grunt, then the explosion of hoofs chopping at the earth like a hundred lumberjacks' axes falling in a tree-chopping contest. Only I would be the tree and the buffalo the ax. The old bull wanted to make kindling out of me.

I woke this old boy from a nap. He was sleeping off a full belly from a recent kill.

Knowing that, I was honored that Gerard had let me go with him. My shooting had been a little inconsistent, and no matter how much we might wish it otherwise, a client is more of a liability than an asset when tracking dangerous game. Going into the thick stuff after a wounded buffalo with a novice at your heels is a little like a seasoned cop taking along his accountant kid brother on the biggest drug bust of his career. It's a serious distraction and a good way to get one of you killed. Maybe even both of you.

After ten minutes or so of very slow but steady tracking, we came to a small clearing in the brush. From the tracks, it appeared that the buffalo had made a semicircle around the perimeter, wisely reluctant to enter the open and give up the advantage. The wounded bull had then reentered the brush on the opposite side and continued in the direction of its comrades. Faced again with brush the thickness of a concrete wall, our order changed, and Gerard and I once again took up the lead. Entering this thicket, Gerard paused to climb a termite mound and scout ahead. His body suddenly froze, and a frantic hand behind his back beckoned me to come. I knew what that meant. I joined him at the top of the mound, where I was met with the awesome sight of the buffalo lying in the bush twenty paces away. All I could see was its head. And it was looking straight at us. It was not happy.

Gerard leaned close and whispered. "Shoot him right between the eyes."

I raised the big double and put the V of the open sights right where he had told me, on the gray expanse of forehead between those two dark orbs—a target about the size of a car's license plate. But just as I was squeezing off, the buffalo heaved to its feet to come for us, dropping its head in the process, and the bullet hit high. I watched it hit just above the left eye, in the boss of the massive horns, and I knew instantly it was a losing shot. But there was no taking it back. I had laid my cards on the table.

Because it was high and wide, the bullet missed the brain, which was the intended object of my aim. Consequently the misplaced bullet did nothing to stop the bull's upward momentum, although it was successful in turning the bull to the side in its charge. Gerard immediately fired both barrels into its left shoulder, and the bull continued on. I fired my second barrel as the bull trundled off at an angle, but the bullet just skimmed a haunch. Quickly reloading, we each fired once more at its retreating rear end, which was hastily swallowed by the dense growth, and now we were back to where we had been—searching for a wounded buffalo in thick brush. I cursed myself for the muffed shot at the head, a shot that should have ended this whole episode.

It was right then that I realized that my gun had a serious flaw in its design. The big double had extractors, but not ejectors—meaning that when the gun was broken open, the empty shells protruded but did not automatically eject. They had to be removed by hand, a time-consuming task when split seconds can mean the difference between life and death. Had the buffalo charged instead of running off, I would not have had time to reload before it reached me. I'm sure Gerard would have saved the day, but that is not ideal. Above all, it defeats the object of the pursuit, which is shooting the game yourself. My father's .470 had automatic ejectors, and I made the decision on the spot either to use his on future hunts or to get one of my own. Although I still held the double in my hands, it was no longer my gun, if you know what I mean.

Once more we followed the wounded bull into the thicket. After the shooting I was calmer now, more focused, ready to end this battle that had dragged on for too long. When we finally found it, the buffalo was in thick brush, lying on its side and groaning. I put a bullet into the chest and it stayed put. Even so, we gave a moment, just to make sure, then approached to find a super trophy. The mud-caked bull was old as they come, with beautiful horns and a massive spread.

Gerard went over to the buffalo and after checking that it was indeed dead, placed his finger in the bullet hole in the boss above the buffalo's eye. He glanced over his shoulder, fixing me with a stare.

"What can I say? Thanks for letting me try a brain shot on a buffalo that was so close."

"I wouldn't do that for just anybody," he said.

"I know."

"Normally, I would have shot him myself *because* he was so close. You can get into trouble not taking advantage of an opportunity like that."

"Thanks, Bwana."

"You are welcome, kid."

We wondered at the buffalo's size and studied every inch of it, examining the bullet placement and speculating on which shot did what damage. Then we took several photos and finally turned it over to the trackers and their skillful knives. Overall, it was indeed an exceptional hunt. The buffalo is my favorite of all African game. If I could go on safari and shoot only buffalo, I would do it and be in heaven.

On the drive home, we spotted a really nice kudu bull. Gerard judged the horns at fifty-two to fifty-four inches around the curl, but we could not get a shot. Once it had spooked and gone galloping into the bush, there was no chance for us. The kudu is a beautiful antelope, well proportioned, with white vertical stripes and horns fit for a king, but there is one thing that a kudu should never do—in order to keep from dispelling the majestic image—and that is run. Like the giraffe, the kudu has an awkward, seesawing gate that does not become it.

A few miles later, three young males appeared, standing at the edge of the brush on the bank of a sand river. A second later, I spotted a much larger kudu to their right and was already aiming at it through the scope when Gerard said, "Shoot!" The bullet took the kudu on the shoulder, dropping it on the spot at 125 paces. Like the large bull I had taken three years earlier, this fellow was old and thin and near the end of its days—a perfect specimen for trophy collecting. Although it was shorter in length, its horns were extremely wide and would make quite a contrast to the other.

As we reached the airstrip near camp, a steenbok jumped up and went running across it, then disappeared in the long grass. I got out and followed the tiny antelope, and when it jumped again I took a snap shot offhand as it darted away. I hit both a back and front leg, which brought the little animal to a halt. At 150 yards, I don't consider that poor shooting at an antelope of such small size. In all honesty, it was pure luck that I hit it at all. I fired again and missed. Surprisingly, with such injuries, the little antelope managed to run off.

We tracked it for a quarter of a mile, when again it jumped up and ran, but I could not get a shot. Gerard sent David back to the truck for the shotgun. Continuing on, we finally found the antelope hidden in a patch of grass, and Gerard finished it with buckshot. Each horn was no larger than a crayon, and I knew I would catch grief at home from nonhunting friends who would wonder why I had shot a baby. But in truth this specimen was no baby. It was quite a brute—as big as they come—a real trophy!

On the way to camp, Gerard shot two francolin with the .44. It was impressive shooting, hitting a moving target little larger than a quail with a pistol. They would make for good camp meat, though the .44 bullet was not efficient in that regard, destroying a good portion of the birds. But it had not been efficiency he was after. Since mine was the last safari of the season, Gerard was using up all his ammo. There were complications involved in trying to store it in Tanzania or crossing the border with it into Kenya, and it was easier simply to use it up.

The safari had been quite a success, to say the least. In fact, there was nothing left for me to shoot except roan and leopard. Because I already had a nice roan and because their mounted head takes up so much room, I decided to pass. We saw one of thirty inches or so that Gerard was eager for me to shoot, but I turned it down. *The roan is a highly sought after trophy. Why not leave it for another lucky hunter next season?*

So that left leopard, and another day of collecting and hanging baits.

A couple of hartebeests stopped to stare at us from just shy of 200 yards, and I shot the larger male through the heart. Then I shot an oribi for camp meat at 150 yards as it faced us head on. Later, at the same distance, I shot a male sable. The sable was also facing us, standing on top of an anthill, which was quite a noble sight. I was quite happy with three one-shot kills, glad to be in the groove, placing the bullets where they were supposed to go. By cutting the animals in half, we made four baits out of the two larger antelope and hung them in likely spots.

Several days earlier, the men had taken down my tent and replaced it with a small Eureka model. Gerard did not want to risk getting the large, expensive Tarpos wet should the rain begin again before the end of my safari. Packed and stowed wet, the large tents would mildew and rot. It turned out to be a good idea, because subsequently it really poured. The rain was so loud on the roof of my tent that I could not sleep. It rained from midnight until after 2:00 A.M., and a fair amount of water leaked into my tent. I managed to keep dry, although Gerard and Farouk got soaked.

We were in for disappointing news the next morning, however. None of the baits had been taken. With the recent rains, a good portion of the wildlife had moved on (the leopards with it), migrating to drier areas to avoid the upcoming rainy season. For that reason we hadn't seen much game in the past few days, even though we had collected some excellent trophies. For me, that was what counted. I can go to a game park to see quantity. While hunting, I would much prefer to see quality.

But quantity was not far off in my future. The plan was to leave here for Arusha and then to have Farouk take me to Ngorongoro and the Serengeti for a little game viewing and photography. It would be my first trip to the Serengeti, and I was eager to see the famous park.

We returned to camp about 3:00 P.M. and took the rest of the afternoon off: reading, chatting, resting. It didn't rain; perhaps a leopard would venture out and discover one of our tasty baits.

Farouk Qreshi and his family. Arusha, Tanzania.

Again in the morning we checked all our baits. Again we found nothing, arriving back in camp around eleven o'clock. The truck, sent to Arusha a few days earlier with equipment, refrigerators, tables, tents, and so forth, returned, and Gerard and the boys were busy packing it for a second trip and getting the Volvo ready for the drive to town. Both differentials were out and under repair, parts scattered all around, but these amazing bush mechanics would have it back together in no time.

The sun shone all day for a change, and the temperature was around seventy-five—just perfect. Looking out from my tent I could see a hill covered in trees, *miombo* and others I didn't know, with occasional palm trees poking up at the base. Many of the trees were turning colors: bright rust, deep red, and fiery orange. The remainder were a lively green. Set against a clear blue sky with the odd puffy whites overhead, the view was nothing less than spectacular.

Abdi, Gerard's headman and chief skinner, sought me out and presented me with two elephant hair bracelets. Both were crafted with consummate skill and made to a perfect fit. The old man still called me Bwana John from the previous year's season together, and I called him Mzee—a similar title of respect. We clasped hands, and I thanked the gray-headed gentleman profusely. *"Asante sana,* Mzee!" He just nodded his head with a knowing grin, then turned to leave—

moving a little more slowly than last year—and tramped to the skinning area and the several heads and hides that were still in need of his attention.

We checked all of the new baits the next morning, as well as a couple of the old ones, but no *chui*s had come to feed. Gerard was put out. He was taking it personally; it was a matter of pride and honor with him. He was 100 percent on cats this season, and he did not want to go home with less than perfect success. It was all right with me, though, as leopard was not a high priority. And besides, that's hunting. If you collected a certain animal every time you went searching for it, it would be called "searching" or "collecting" but certainly not hunting. And I'd had a fantastic safari—beyond what I had expected.

Before lunch I shot a hartebeest bull, the partner in fact of the one I had shot the other day for bait. This one, however, was for camp meat. Without a refrigerator meat does not last long, and the men eat a tremendous amount. They know they are headed home, where meat is a luxury, and they are gorging on it, making ready for the off-season when they will return to their farms and huts and families and a diet of *poda*.

The truck left this afternoon bound for Arusha, and we were up early in the morning to pack and follow. With both Land Rovers packed to the hilt, we got on the road by 8:00 A.M. and had clear weather, except for two small rain showers. Lunch was a tin of sardines eaten with the fingers on the drive. The trip was long, dusty, and uneventful, except for one flat tire and the fact that we hit a baby goat that ran into the road. That baby goat cost Gerard a good many shillings. It is always the farmer's most prized animal that you kill. The fellow wailed on and on as if the goat could walk on water, at least until a satisfactory amount of cash had crossed his palm. Then it was a smile and "pleasure doing business with you."

My last bit of excitement was lunch at Farouk's the following day. I have always been somewhat of a picky eater, so it was with fair trepidation that I sat down to the table with Farouk, his wife, three young children, and mother-in-law. Much of the food was unrecognizable, and both his wife and mother-in-law, wrapped in colorful Indian saris and veils, ate with their fingers. Farouk, spoiled to Western ways, used a fork and spoon. The main dish was a bowl filled with a cold, green, soupy mixture that looked like cactus run through a blender. On closer inspection it looked like . . . well, it looked like puke. Because it was the main dish, there was no way I could refuse. So I scooped up a spoonful of the green mess and armed myself with a chunk of a breadlike dish with which to push it down if the taste was as awful as the looks.

"What do you call it?" I asked Farouk.

"Dahl. It's gude, Jahnny. Go ahead."

Now all eyes were on me. His wife and smiling kids were watching; the mother-in-law, too. Unwittingly, I had drawn attention to the one thing that I did not want attention drawn to. There was no turning back. I raised it to my lips and swallowed it down like a kid taking the medicine spoon. It wasn't bad. In fact, it tasted quite good. I eagerly spooned up the rest, even returned for a second helping of what turned out to be a type of lentil. What a pleasant surprise! Little did I know that the real surprise was still forthcoming.

We got through dinner, and I was actually full and pleased and congratulating myself on how well it had gone. Then came dessert, the one course I always enjoy. A plate was passed around stacked with a brown sugar type of cookie, and I nonchalantly stuffed one into my mouth. By then it was too late. I have no idea what spice or flavoring was in it, but it was the most horrible thing I had ever tasted. It brought on a gag reflex, and it was all I could do to choke the mouthful down without anyone noticing. So much for my smug success!

After lunch, Farouk dug out photo albums and showed me pictures of the trophies he had personally collected over the years and those his clients had taken this past season while he was working for Gerard. His children swarmed around him, laughing and giggling and glad their father was home. I was taking him away again, but we would be back in a few days.

We finally got off by 3:00 and made it to the Ngorongoro Crater Lodge by dark. The real treat came in the morning, when we came upon three young male lions toying with two old buffalo bulls and were allowed to watch the story unfold. At one point the bulls became separated, and the young lions surrounded the hind bull and took turns charging in on it. The old bull met each charge with dropped horns, and as it chased each offender off, the other two would rush in from behind, trying for a hamstring. Then the old bull would whirl around at the last instant and brandish its weapons just before they could jump it. At times it was difficult to see the battle, what with all the dust kicked up at the bull's feet. And the lions' movements were blindingly fast. I did, however, manage to capture some of it on film. The harassment continued until the buffalo's loyal cohort returned; together, horns lowered, they chased off the cocky young cats.

In the Serengeti, we awoke to a beautiful, sunny morning. The sky was blue, the air still, and the panorama breathtaking. The endless level of the Serengeti Plains opened in all directions, interrupted only by the occasional flat-topped acacia in the distance, one here and one there, as if the Creator had been sparing in the placement of their seeds. It was here that we came upon the wildebeest, herd after herd of them. In places the drifting herds spread from one end of the horizon to the other, and it was probably the closest I will ever come to experiencing what my forefathers experienced when they witnessed the great herds of bison on the prairie a century and a half ago. I *oohed* and *aahhed* at the vast numbers, but Farouk dismissed my awe, claiming this to be but a fraction of the wildebeest one would see at the peak of the migration. The wildlife were just beginning to return to the park in anticipation of the short rains ahead.

On our return to Arusha, we stopped at a place that I had long been curious to see. Olduvai Gorge—where the Leakey family staked its archaeological fame. On display in the small museum were the fossil remains of extinct animals such as the three-toed horse and the australopithecine, the first hominid to walk the earth. This ancient hominid was what piqued my curiosity the most. It had been one thing to read about them in school, but standing on the soil where such history had been made, staring at the bones in the case, was quite another. It brought about a certain comprehension, a sudden clarity of thought with regard to at least one small part of our human existence on this planet.

Australopithecine was the first (or the first so far identified) in a long progression of continually evolving humanoid species. More to the point, the ancient hominid became extinct, as has every successor. *Homo habilis, Homo erectus*, Neanderthal. Every successor except . . . us. It made me wonder if we Homo sapiens are just one more step in the evolutionary ladder. Are we nothing but a temporary inhabitant? Are we to be replaced by a more advanced race when our function has been served?

Staring out at the steep ravines and the conspicuous layers of rock, the many layers buried like so many secrets, I pondered such questions. It was a humbling experience, like looking at the billions of stars at night. It made me feel small, insignificant, not just in relation to the size of the universe but also in relation to time and the life history of the earth. In the end, it left me with no doubt that we humans are a transient species on this planet, and that can be a difficult thought to swallow. But it needn't be. Each one of us must come to terms with his own mortality, the fact that he or she will die, that no individual life is permanent. So perhaps it shouldn't be a great leap to realize that our race, our species, is no different. Species have come and gone in the past on this ever-evolving planet, and they will continue to do so. Man is just one of many. To think otherwise would be to put blinders on to the true functioning and mechanics of nature.

Olduvai also made me ponder another great intangible: the human soul. If it is true that man has a soul, where in the process did the soul begin? Did Neanderthal have a soul? Did australopithecine? Do monkeys? Just as my first trip to Africa had a tremendous impact on my religion, so too did this trip on how I looked at man, his place on the planet, and beyond—the question of whether man has a soul. It seems ironic that it takes a trip to a primitive land like Africa to reflect on such heady subjects as evolution, the afterlife, and God, but that, at least for me, is where such subjects seem to arise. (Why, the australopithecine I was looking at in the museum case could be my direct ancestor!) These kinds of thoughts do not arise in the confines of a metropolitan jungle like Manhattan, where there is nothing but man, where all one's senses—sight, sound, smell—are overwhelmed by man's masses, man's activities, and man's creations. In all its modern finery, the city is smothered in humanity, handicapping us from thinking beyond man and man's experience. Civilization blinds one to the facts of nature. So it is that it often takes a stint in the wilderness for one to think beyond man and to see the natural order of the world in which we live.

Soon it was pouring buckets and time for us to go, and for a second time in the rain we made the trip up the slippery cutbacks of the Ngorongoro Crater rim. None of the dirt cutbacks had guard rails, and now that all was mud it made for an uneasy feeling when the truck slid or slipped close to the sheer edges. Farouk is not the driver that Gerard is, nor is he as attentive at the wheel. There was one point when the truck slipped sideways and I thought we were going over the edge for sure—I swear a good portion of the tire on the passenger side saw air! But at the last instant the vehicle found traction and Farouk got us through.

When the rain eased, we pulled off to the side of the road and filled the Land Cruiser with diesel from the drums in the bed of the truck. The ride would be bumpy, as the roads to Arusha are a mess. The old roads have not been touched since colonial days. The tarmac reaches only some forty kilometers from Arusha, and the potholes and gaps in the old tarmac can swallow a car, busting a spring or chipping your tooth if you aren't careful.

Once in Arusha I was invited to another lunch at Farouk's, where I wisely declined dessert.

Alaska
September 1989

Flying in a Piper Cub, which is nothing more than a tin can with wings, is a unique experience. Squeezing through the single side hatch, the first thing you discover is that the tin isn't even tin but a kitelike material stretched tight around a flimsy frame. The second thing you find is that there is only one seat (for the pilot, not you), and the cramped quarters will bring to mind go-carts from your childhood that had more room. With your luggage formed into a seat cushion of sorts, you sit crammed behind the pilot, knees wedged to your ears, the pilot literally in your lap, so that if you reached out your arms you could easily take the controls. You have to yell to each other over the loud buzz of the engine to communicate. That is flying in a Piper Cub.

Once in the air, however, I quickly forgot the cramped confines of the plane, captivated by the beauty of the landscape below. The ground was made up of rolling brown tundra and pockets of emerald green water that reflected the bright clouds and the suddenly blue sky. In the distance I could see snow-topped mountains. Very quickly there was no remaining sign of man or man's footprint on this vast frontier: no roads, no buildings, no telephone lines. The land below was as wild and pristine as the day it was made. If it weren't so cold for half the year, it would be a paradise. Then too, of course, there is the little problem with the all-or-nothing sun for big chunks of the year.

Alaska, at this time of year, was a land of water. Ponds and lakes overwhelmed the landscape like puddles on a rain-soaked parking lot. The rivers, like the Newhalen below us, were deep and wide; the pilot shouted that it could not be traversed by foot. Lake Iliamna was just visible on the horizon to the south. Anxiously I watched for signs of both the caribou and brown bear I would be hunting, but I saw neither. It didn't surprise me not to see a bear, but I had expected to see at least a few caribou.

We landed with a bounce on the flat stretch of tundra that served as a runway beside camp. Camp was a couple of wood-framed, canvas-covered cabins and three or four pup tents huddled on the shore of a large pond or small lake, depending on where you are from. Being

My good friend Gary Collins (left) disembarking from a Piper Cub.

from Texas, where water is scarce, I would call it a small lake. As we motored up to camp, everyone came out to greet us and to help cart gear. There was Frank the outfitter and his wife, four clients who had just flown in ahead of me, and the two guides. Guide John, a marine on leave, was a big, strapping fellow who looked a match for any bear.

Quite a storm hit after dark. A fierce wind billowed up, then rain, and all night it sounded as if my small tent would be ripped up by the roots. The wind seemed to blow from several different angles at once, causing the tent to pop and suck, heave and puff all night. Combined with the nonstop rain that hammered the tent walls with the ear-ringing clatter of a machine gun, it made for a difficult night's sleep.

So I was up early. Although the rain had taken a breather, the sky was gray and the wind came in strong gusts. My first impression of the tundra, as I strolled down to the lake, was that the ground had been sprinkled with fluorescent green popcorn. My lasting impression was that it is a smorgasbord of color—the tundra is as alive with colors as a painter's palette: bright reds, greens, browns, brilliant blues, olive, and rust abound.

In late afternoon the sky cleared, somewhat, and John the Marine and I made a short outing in search of caribou. We found a small herd near dark, but they were too far to intercept with the slim light that was left us. At dinner everyone collected in the mess tent, sitting elbow to elbow on wood slab benches that ran the length of the table, hunkered over bowls of steaming caribou chili clutched in cold hands. Tin cups held hot coffee or whiskey or both, and the stories began to flow of past hunts and adventures. Frank and the pilot told of bush planes they had crashed, or that friends had crashed. Most of the latter were stories in which no one had walked away. Then Frank told the story of a brown bear that had broken into the camp's stores one night and lapped up a five-gallon can of green paint. The bear crapped a green streak for days, fairly painting itself in the process. For years they told folks not to shoot the green bear. Then one day someone did and, skinning it, reported the skin beneath the hide to be green.

We awoke to a low fog cover, with no chance of making fly camp, and I was reminded of the bad-weather horror stories that my friend Gary Collins had shared. Fifteen days of his eighteen-day hunt were spent inside the tent waiting out the weather.

"Alaska is the only place in the world that has gale-force winds and fog at the same time!" he told me. "Take lots to read. I read every book in camp twice and was down to reading the ingredients label on the aspirin bottle." From what I had heard and the little I had glimpsed, I was beginning to believe that the sun was about as common to the Alaska tundra as snow to a Texas beach.

But I got lucky. After breakfast the fog cleared, and Frank retrieved his plane, which was tethered in the alders where it received at least some protection from the winds. Soon we were bouncing in the rough air, headed for Pike Creek camp. Minutes later Frank dropped me at the airstrip and there picked up Jerry Peterman, a friend from Dallas, who was returning to main camp. (I should mention that the "airstrip" resembles nothing of what is generally called to mind by that word. Nor could the average fellow make it out, even if he were standing in the middle of it. It is an airstrip only by virtue of the fact that it is a level stretch of ground that has caused no less-than-successful landings, and therefore it is used time and again by Frank when visiting this camp. Given enough headwind, these tiny planes, with their big, squishy tires, can land just about anywhere. But why risk unseen rocks and holes when one spot has proven to be a success?)

Crawling out of the plane, I shook Jerry's hand in congratulations on receiving the news of his caribou and was then introduced to my guide, Jeff Welch, a burly, woolly-haired, bushy-bearded fellow who looked like a mountain man of the first degree. It's often said that folks look like their pets. Well, Jeff looks like his quarry—a big, shaggy brute of a bear. He seemed a good fellow on first impression, though his voice was hoarse and he kept snorting, hawking, and spitting.

"I've been down with a bad cold," he explained, as we hiked the steep slope down to camp.

Camp was tucked in against the alders of a creek bottom flat. A couple of deep-green spruce, a rarity in that barren land, had found refuge in this low, sheltered spot. They were the size of the Christmas tree you might encounter in a really large house, and I could hear water trilling in a stream nearby. Except for two green pup tents, you would never have known that man had set foot here. The spongy tundra lining this bottom was as soft as your grandmother's feather bed and would sleep just as well—if it weren't for the water beneath it.

The last occupant in my tent had sunk into the soggy ground, and the water had pooled to form a tub of sorts in the tent floor. A wooden pallet had been placed over the sink hole, but it was now nearly submerged itself. I baled as much water as I could (it was like scooping the bottom of a sinking canoe), then laid my gear on top of a plastic trash bag to keep it dry. I left my down bag in its stuff sack, so as not to risk getting it wet before nightfall. Water is the enemy in Alaska. The goal is to keep dry. Coming in soaked and

Main camp was composed of wood-floored, tarp-covered structures huddled against the alders.

chilled from a long day's hunt only to find that all your extra gear is equally wet could mean the difference between a pleasant night's sleep and hypothermia.

The game warden dropped into camp that afternoon before the rain returned. His plane buzzed camp, then circled three or four times before attempting to land. He came hiking into camp a few minutes later. I didn't catch his name, but he was fortyish and friendly enough, given his profession. He checked our licenses, then joked a bit, asking me what I did for a living.

"Well, give me an accounting joke," he said. "Every profession's got one."

I thought a moment, then said, "Did you hear about the accountant interviewing for a job who was asked if he knew double-entry bookkeeping?" The warden shook his head and smiled.

"The accountant said, 'Heck, that's nothing. I know *triple-entry* bookkeeping!'

"'Triple-entry bookkeeping? What's that?'

"'That's where I keep one set of books for the IRS showing a loss; a second set for you showing the true profit; and a third set for your wife showing that you're just squeaking by.'"

The game warden laughed, chitchatted some more, then left.

In Alaska it is against the law to hunt the same day you are airborne, and possibly that was what this warden was checking. It is a good law, curbing the abuses of years past, when hunters would "hunt" from the air, looking over the caribou herds for a trophy head or scouting a trophy bear, then would land close by and shoot it. It is the reason we spent the afternoon and evening in camp, chatting and reading, preparing for the hunt the next morning.

For dinner Jeff whipped up some pasta on the Coleman stove inside his tent. Then he grilled up a couple of caribou steaks. The steaks were simmered in butter and onions and some sort of garlic seasoning. He dipped his thick fingers repeatedly into the bag of seasoning and sprinkled its magic until a heavenly aroma filled the tent. The sweet scent rivaled that of any five-star restaurant. And the process itself was entertaining to watch. As he cooks, Jeff tosses dirty utensils—pots, pans, spoons, plates—out the tent door to be collected and cleaned later, shouting the whole while.

Yes, shouting.

We were hunkered less than an arm's length from each other in the confines of the small tent, but as the evening wore on and the mark on the whiskey bottle dropped, Jeff got louder and louder. Eventually his tone took on the pitch and fervor of an inflamed debater, except that I agreed with most everything he said until he was left debating himself, with me nodding my head now and then and saying, "You're right. You're right." Had I not been a like-minded conservative, I can only imagine what course the discussion might have taken, or how worked up he might have become.

Soon it was time to turn in. Because the cooking had been done inside the tent, I smelled of seasoning and fresh-cooked steaks as if I had rolled in the stuff. And our meat store was a hunk of caribou meat stored inside the tent, along with all the other foodstuffs. Yosemite came to mind and the park ranger warnings: *Don't leave food in camp! Tie it high between two trees. Even toothpaste can tempt a bear to rip into your tent!* Those warnings were for black bear, hardly a threat to people. This was brown bear country. A brownie is three times the size of a black bear and relishes fresh meat. I wondered if we weren't setting ourselves up as bait.

"Ever worry about a bear coming into the tent?"

"Nahh, one whiff of us and they're gone. That's only a problem where they ain't hunted."

The wind howled most of the night, each gust forewarning its attack with a *whish* through the spruce trees to the east. It rained off and on—mostly on—all night. To avoid having to get dressed in the dark in the event my tent collapsed, I slept in full attire: boots, coat, and even hat, pulling the sleeping bag around me when the shivers woke me late at night.

The next day, our first hunting day, came and went in a blur. Not much happened; it was just that the clock seemed on fast-forward. We set off at first light and hiked the lee side of the airstrip hill. Along the way, Jeff stopped to point out brownie dung and a hole the bear had dug in search of ground squirrel. Circling the hill, we paused now and again to glass the surrounding valley and hills. The airstrip hill proved quite strategic in its placement—and in the manner in which Jeff employed it. Situated apart from the taller surrounding hills, it rose in the center of the valley floor as if for no other purpose than to serve as a lookout post for us. It was the perfect place from which to glass, providing a magnificent, unobstructed view into the encircling valley and slopes. Moving between stands on all four sides, we could take in a tremendous amount of country with little effort. It was very efficient.

But efficiency is not always what one is after. Where I hunt deer, in South Texas, the most efficient method is to hunt from a tower blind. Yet I routinely shun those boring posts for the far more exciting method of spot and stalk, knowing full well that my chances for success are reduced. In addition, coming from the city, I had been hoping to cover a good bit of ground on foot and maybe work off some of the middle that has collected from too much city life. The exercise was something I had been looking forward to. But primarily I was here to get a bear, and if this was how it was done, then this was how I would do it.

We glassed until 10:30 A.M. or so, then returned to camp, where Jeff whipped up an outstanding onion and cheese omelet. It was astonishing what the man could do over a blue flame. About 2:30, tired of sitting in the tent, I went out on my own, returning to the last place we had glassed from that morning. The wind was blowing like mad, and I hunkered into the damp hill, my back to the gale, and glassed periodically. Jeff doubted a bear would venture out this time of day with such wind, and he was right.

I didn't see a bear, but I saw several caribou on the facing slope. They were miles away, no more than dots to the naked eye. After feeding they bedded for a long while, not happy about the misty, rainy, blowy weather. The temperature wasn't cold, maybe 50 degrees, but the wind was constant and strong enough that I had to lean against it to keep my balance. Then there was the rain, which drove sideways, trying its best to soak me. Despite the elements, with rainproof pants and coat, a hood cinched about my face, I was reasonably warm. Only after extended periods of reclining against the sloped ground did the shivers force me to move around.

Jeff came out about 6:00, and we stayed till dark, he on the camp side of the hill, I on the other, glassing for bear. Nothing of our quarry appeared, so we returned to camp for dinner and a hot toddy of apple cider and Canadian whiskey. I don't care much for the taste of whiskey and don't regularly drink it, but I must admit that the combination was outstanding against the cold. The fiery warmth soon spread down to my toes, and as I watched Jeff man the stove and breathed in the wonderful aromas arising from the pans, I thought how wonderful life is and how happy I was. There was nothing I would rather have been doing, no place I would rather have been. No amount of money could buy or replace the happiness I felt. Life was perfect.

Once I was in bed the wind rested a spell, but it was only to gather its strength to return full force in the night. I awoke to my tent popping, rocking, and lurching, as if any minute it would be torn from its moorings. Miraculously, the ropes and stakes held and the fabric didn't rip, but there was no way I could sleep with such a racket, or with the continuous expectation of at any moment being tentless. I wondered

A Bullet Well Placed

The season's catch so far.

how the wildlife put up with this kind of weather. It was like living in a war zone. It was not the peaceful, romantic picture people have of nature, certainly not the soothing escape portrayed in magazine or television ads.

Despite the harsh weather, luck smiled on us the next morning. We returned to our previous night's positions and fell in with our established routine of glassing. About 10:00 A.M., fed up with the rain and wind, I trudged back to Jeff, who was busy fleshing out the hide of Jerry Peterman's caribou while he monitored his half of the horizon. We agreed that not much would be out in such a storm, so I hiked on down to camp. My gun was soaked, and I was anxious to oil it. I had just wiped away the rust-promoting droplets and was about to recline with a book when I heard what sounded like someone calling my name. But it was hard to tell with all the wind.

Poking my head out the tent, I heard it again. Then I located the source. Jeff was on the steep embankment above camp, waving at me to come.

"Get your gun!"

I did, quickly. I followed the trail up and out of the creek flat as Jeff hurried parallel on the ledge above me. When we met at top, he said, "Saw a good caribou. Hurry." We set off at a jog-trot, with Jeff pausing now and then to glass the creek bottom below. A quarter-mile from camp we came to the edge of a steep draw that dropped to the creek below.

Squatting behind a small rise in the tundra, Jeff peeked below with his binocular.

"Here they come," he said. "It's the one in front, I think."

All this time, I, who was down lower, had seen nothing of our prey. Eagerly I searched for sight of the caribou, but despite my efforts I saw nothing. It flashed through my mind that this was going to be one of those situations when the client can't see the game and the guide is pulling his hair out, telling him to shoot before it gets away.

The problem was that I was looking two hundred or three hundred yards off down the valley. Imagine my surprise when, thirty yards away, a horn suddenly poked into view. Only then did I realize that when Jeff had said "here" he meant *here!* The animals had been hidden from sight in the draw. Now two of the three appeared in the ravine, and given our proximity, I was surprised they did not spot us instantly. They continued to climb at a leisurely pace, and it was something to be that close to a live caribou. What I noticed first was the double shovel splayed above the nose of the one in front—like a Yield sign turned on its side. It was magnificent.

When the big fellow, trailed by a smaller sidekick, was even with us, now twenty-five yards away, Jeff lurched up to verify that the third, still invisible to me, wasn't bigger. It wasn't. Dropping back down, he said, "Shoot the big one!" The caribou startled at his erect form and the sound of his voice and ran the rest of the way up the steep incline. When it reached the shelf, the big bull angled away on the relatively flat terrain, then turned and stopped sixty yards out to see what we were. You couldn't have asked for a prettier shot. And I had a perfect rest. From a sitting position, I put the cross hairs in the middle of its chest and squeezed the trigger. The caribou hunched, then turned, but it did not go down, not even with the weighty .375 bullet placed right where I had wanted it. Now all it offered was a rear-end shot as it staggered slowly away, and I almost took it. But seeing those great antlers waving above its rump brought to mind the story of another hunter this season who had been presented with a similar shot and had accidentally blown off one whole antler, the only double shovel taken so far this year. I had seen those broken horns in camp and did not want to repeat the misfortune. So I held off. The big fellow finally turned broadside, and I dropped it with a shot to the shoulder, not five yards from where the first bullet had taken it.

A Bullet Well Placed

We ran up and admired our trophy, then shouted out our elation. This was quite a caribou, with a huge rack and a beautiful coat. Not only was it a double shovel but it also had fine bez and great tops, with antlers the rich color of a finely made cigar. It was certainly a trophy. Then we took a bunch of pictures, knowing that when it comes to photos, it often takes quantity to get quality, and film is cheap.

Next came the real work. Jeff set to caping and butchering the large animal, and I packed the meat to the embankment above camp. There I laid the meat atop the stout branches of a squat spruce: the fore- and hindquarters, ribs, and backstrap. What with the heavy load and steep slope, and the awkward footing on the spongy tundra, I was breathing hard with each trip. Jeff brought the final load, with the head and cape. I was glad we didn't have far to go.

Having to haul the meat, head, horns, and hide makes for a strong incentive to find an animal close to camp. I asked Jeff if they hauled all the meat like this when they shot one several miles from camp.

He said, quite simply, "We don't shoot caribou several miles from camp." In Alaska, the hunter's back comes into play in the judgment of any trophy.

My gun, fortunately, was shooting beautifully. Strangely, Jeff had never had me test fire it, the first thing an African PH does

Fly camp during a rare sunny moment.

upon a client's arrival to camp. For the African PH, test firing the rifle is a religious ritual. That is understandable, with all the human-wrecking machines running around the African bush. But a big brown bear is a match for at least two of the Big Five and not an animal to be taken lightly. I would equate it with the rhino, which has the same handicap of nearsightedness but is equally deadly if it gets a hold of you.

I put the brown bear one notch above the leopard, though there are those who might disagree. My reasoning is this: The brown bear is less likely to reach you than a wounded leopard and doesn't have the camouflage or the cunning, but the leopard, if it gets to you, is less likely to kill you than the bear. For that reason alone, in my view, the brown bear tips the scales in the dangerous game department. In any case, the brown bear ranks in the top ten of the world's most dangerous game, no matter who is doing the scorekeeping. Were a client of mine about to light into an eight hundred-pound bear, I think I might like to witness a test shot or two beforehand. But perhaps it was like the human scent: He didn't want the noise.

That evening I returned to my spot on the hill, glassing for bear, trying not to get blown off the hill, and hoping to stay dry in the intermittent volleys of rain. It was difficult to believe that the wind could drive the rain so hard, to the point it felt like being pelted with pebbles. This was truly a harsh land. Looking over the endless expanse of earth, my thoughts returned to a German gentleman I had met in the lobby of the motel in Anchorage. He had just returned from moose hunting with several friends but no guide.

There are a lot of places I would consider guiding myself, but Alaska is not one of them. The severity of the weather presents the biggest threat. That and getting lost. My hat is off to anyone who can wing it solo in a foreign land. Unless you truly know the wilderness into which you are setting foot, you can get yourself into trouble—or killed—quick as lightning. Long story short, they might as well have been hunting the Autobahn. The bush pilot dropped them off, and they never saw a moose.

The funny thing about our meeting was that he and I had spotted each other right off. In my experience, it is like that in most places that harbor hunters from around the world. We hunters have a way of spotting each other, even without the camouflage, and striking up a conversation and an instant bond. "Where are you hunting?" "Did you get anything?" "When do you leave?" It is the bond of fraternity brothers. The Fraternal Order of Hunting.

A Bullet Well Placed

A very nice double-shovel bull caribou.

About eight o'clock that evening I met Jeff at the stunted spruce by the airstrip, and we sat on the lee side with our backs against the wind, the rain pelting us with real force. Our binoculars were useless, but we stayed till dark because of something I've forgotten to mention. Just down from this spot on the hill was where my friend Jerry Peterman had shot his caribou. When we approached that morning, Jeff noticed that the gut pile had been partially covered with dirt. We did not move in any closer, not wanting to leave our scent or disturb the area, because he believed it was the work of a bear. "Then again," he had explained, "it could be just a wolverine." So we remained in the wind and rain until it was too dark to see the mound of fresh earth and trudged down the hill to camp in the dark.

At this point, I was soaked from the waist down and so cold that my teeth were chattering. Suddenly I could not stop shivering, from head to toe. Both my pants and boots were made with Gore-Tex, and both had leaked. If we had been miles from camp, or if we had been forced to spend the night out in our clothes, I don't know that I would have fared very well. The surprising thing was how suddenly I had gotten cold. I went from being a little chilled all afternoon and evening to being really cold in a matter of minutes. This was exactly the type of weather that fosters hypothermia, which claims so many lives. You would think that most people who freeze to death do so in subzero

Now the real work begins.

temperatures, but in reality hypothermia claims more lives between 30 and 50 degrees. The problem is being wet. It is the wet that robs the body of heat. And it happens quickly.

In camp I shucked the wet pants, socks, and boots, replacing them with dry ones. Then I huddled around the blue flame of the cookstove in Jeff's tent and downed hot apple cider until I began to warm up. A little whiskey in the cider, and soon we were both shouting and bashing our political opponents.

It was raining heavily in the morning, and we ended up staying in, waiting for the weather to clear. By evening, however, I was ready to get out, even if the weather was miserable. So at 6:00 P.M. I headed up the hill solo. About an hour before dark the rain really cut loose. My rain pants leaked again, but now with wool pants underneath, the leak was not as noticeable. Wool, when wet, remains reasonably warm against the skin, which is exactly what a good hunting garment is supposed to do—and why wool is so popular.

When the rain really started up, the visibility, which had been poor, became nil, and I sought shelter on the lee side, hoping the rain would stop before dark. Bears are mostly nocturnal, according to Jeff, and the best times to find them are at sunup and sundown. But my prospects, at least from the looks of the sky, appeared grim. The offending clouds stretched from one mountain peak to the next, north and south, blowing west. Seeing no relief, I headed down to camp. But when I got there, I found no Jeff. Earlier I had spotted him at the embankment, fleshing my caribou skull. I didn't want him to think me lost, so I went to find him. No dummy either, he had taken refuge beneath a spruce. As we sat beneath the scanty canopy of branches, watching the creek bottom below, every now and then Jeff would stand to glance up the slope at the mound where something had buried the gut pile from Jerry Peterman's caribou.

Figuring that nothing would show in this weather, I suggested we head down and fix some dinner. I'd only had oatmeal and a few snacks all day. Unlike some hunts, during which I have been truly physically miserable, I was quite content sitting on the embankment watching below. I wasn't shivering the way I had been the night before. I was simply hungry, and what shootable light there was, was going fast. I figured the day's hunt was over.

Not a minute later, Jeff stood for one of his over-the-shoulder inspections. Then he dropped and said, "I see it. I think I see the bear."

We sprang into high gear. I shook off my daypack, swung the binocular behind my back (so it wouldn't *clack* against my gun), and started at a good clip up the hill behind Jeff, hiking directly into the storm. The wind was strong, and it carried the rain with incredible force—so hard that the rain stung our faces like a flock of birds pecking, causing us to squint against the painful drops. But if it was hard for us to see in the storm, it was equally hard for the bear—if it was a bear. And that was important, because there was nothing but open tundra between us, nothing behind which we could hide our advancing forms.

During one of several pauses to glass, I finally saw the bear—a dark shape gliding across the tundra just below the skyline, heading toward the buried gut pile. We crept on, hunched over, in single file, until we got within shooting distance of the dark shape on the slope. The bear was at the pile and presumably unearthing its dinner (or breakfast, depending on how you looked at it). As to how far it was, I have no idea. It was getting dark quickly, and my ability to judge distance, which was hard anyway on this open landscape, was going with the light. You might have told me the bear was 15 yards or 115 yards, and I would have believed you. Then we were sitting on the mushy tundra, and Jeff, only a couple of yards to my left, was saying something. His words were lost in the storm. The wind brought only blasts of cold air to my ears. I finally had to shout, "WHAT?"

"*Shoot!*" he yelled back. "Shoot if you've got a shot!"

Jeff had his battered, rust-ridden .300 Winchester up and ready for backup. I threw my gun up on the dark shape, but all I saw through the scope was an unrecognizable brown blob. The water on the lens distorted an already unclear image. Cranking the magnification to 5X gave slight improvement, but still I could not tell whether the bear was facing us or away. The light was fading fast, and the rain stung my eyes.

Although it lasted only a few seconds, this was by far the best part of the hunt. My heart was beating fast, but not uncontrollably. I was ready, through excitement, to take on a freight train and would have welcomed a charge. What I really would have welcomed, though, given the choice, was clear weather and a bit of sunlight. There are wiser things to do than to be unsure in the placement of your shot on dangerous game, and that was what I was faced with. The ball was in my court. I had a decision to make. Do I shoot? Or do I call it off? The one thing I had going for me was that I was sure the bear was either facing us or facing away. Either way, a shot in the center of the body should do the job. It was a go.

Conditions were not getting any better, so I centered the cross hairs on the middle of the blob and squeezed the trigger. It was probably best that it was dark: I could not see the blasting wind messing with my aim. An orange burst of fire filled the lens, and when I threw back up with a fresh cartridge in the chamber, the brown blob was still there, only closer to the ground. I sent along another.

Jeff never fired, for the bear never moved. According to him, it dropped like a ton of bricks. Elation. Good shot, no wounded bear to track down, and done alone.

Now the bad luck. We crept toward the brown hulk, rifles at the ready, not able to make out its features in the failing light until we were ten paces or so from it. Finally, I could see that it was on its belly, facing us. Once abreast of it I put one more in the shoulder for insurance, but it was unnecessary. The first bullet, just over the left eye, had been fatal.

It looked smaller than I had imagined a brown bear to look, and upon rolling it over we discovered why. It was a sow. I tried not to show my disappointment, but it was like a blow to my heart. It took away from the glory of the accomplishment. It was like a soldier in battle rolling over a worthy but less fortunate opponent only to find that it was a woman.

I had been so excited approaching and shooting it that the thought never occurred to me it might be a female. I had asked Jeff days earlier how to tell a sow and a boar apart, and he had said it was difficult. Even if it were the last day and a sow was the only bear we'd seen—I

Jeff Welch with my bear the morning after.

Jeff warms up with some coffee after the job of skinning and caping our catch.

would not shoot it. A surplus of animals and the need to reduce or keep the population in check are, I believe, the only reasons ever to shoot the female of a species. Shooting a sow goes against my principles.

But outwardly I showed elation. In hunting you sometimes have to take it as it comes, and going a week without sighting a bear is not uncommon. Debbie Tolson, a DSC friend hunting here the same week, never saw a one.

It was too dark for pictures, so we headed down to our tents to dry out, start some dinner, and end the day (and hunt) with a hot toddy of apple cider and Canadian Mist. We had reason to celebrate. It had been a very successful hunt.

Hunting, like jogging a marathon, is one of those activities that humble you. It demonstrates your physical and mental limits, yet allows you to appreciate your accomplishments that much more. It teaches you to appreciate the little things in life, like sitting on a bucket in a storm in the middle of nowhere in Alaska. We had shelter, we had food, we had fire, we had hot drinks cupped in our cold hands. What more could a person want? There are nonhunters that will read this and think I am ready for a round room, but they are missing the point. In our modern world we get caught up in materialism, needing this and that, when really it is not a matter of needing but wanting, and the wants never stop. Hunting, whether in harsh weather or in harsh territory, quickly teaches you what is important in life and what you really need to be happy. It is surprisingly little.

The rain poured, and we talked and talked and drank more hot toddies and listened to the wind pound the tent sides, ever more loudly. It sounded as if the tent might go any minute, and Jeff himself got louder and louder as he argued as if to a hostile audience, though I shook my head in agreement. Then, somewhere in the middle of it all, I mentioned that I had been to Africa.

His eyes opened wide, and he about fell off the plastic drum he was sitting on.

"You've been to Africa? . . . You got the Big Five?"

"Big Four. I didn't get a rhino."

"But elephant? You got an elephant?! I didn't know you'd been to Africa. No wonder you can shoot. No wonder you do what I tell you. Most young guys are all over the hills, spreadin' scent everyplace. Won't sit in one spot like I tell 'em, and then I gotta hunt their ass down and chew 'em out." He chunked his plate out the tent flap, ran a thick hand through his shaggy head of hair, and said, "Tell me about it. You gotta tell me everything. Don't leave nothin' out!"

The whiskey bottle made another round, and he kept me up late into the night wanting to hear everything about Africa.

The pleasure was all mine.

Kamchatka, Russia
May 1997

After a four-day delay in Petropavlovsk (PK), we arrived in Korf to a howling wind and dark skies. Descending the steps of the Aeroflot plane, we were met by two rugged-faced Russians in big fur hats and, for the first time in many days, I was beginning to think that this hunt might actually take place. The whole trip up to now had been fraught with delays, setbacks, and more delays. But I couldn't say that I hadn't been warned.

When my good friend Dale Bilhartz phoned to say that he had landed the hunting opportunity of the decade, I was immediately interested. He went on to explain that this was an exploratory hunt and that we would be the first Americans to hunt the remote northern strip of the Kamchatka peninsula, home to the largest brown bears in the world. The hook was a price tag well below those offered by the outfitters running hunts at the southern end of the peninsula. Always a sucker for a deal or an adventure, I had been quick to agree.

So I was glad to see these two men in oversized fur hats, if for no other reason than it made me feel one step closer to the hunting grounds. Shouting above the wind, these two men, who were later introduced as Sergei, the head guide, and Alexander, the government game officer, quickly informed Nicholai, our interpreter, that the weather was too bad to fly to camp. The two Russians then snatched up our heavy bags with no more effort than if they had been toting a couple of sack lunches and led us to a ramshackle hotel where we were to await news on the weather.

On first impression (and honestly, this port town isn't big enough for more than one), Korf appeared even more destitute than PK: The town has not seen a coat of paint in years, and all of the streets are dirt. In all fairness, though, our hotel room on the second floor overlooking the Bering Sea was surprisingly clean and comfortable. The ocean, out our window, appeared dark and dismal under the weight of an equally gloomy sky, and a constant wind whipped whitecaps across its black surface. The streets were empty, as the wind had driven everyone inside. There was nothing for us to do but wait.

A Bullet Well Placed

The news later in the afternoon was the same. The weather was still bad here and toward camp. Sergei dropped in to ask Dale and me about our hunting experience, which was interpreted through Nicholai. The seasoned hunter, built like a boxer with thick shoulders and a slim waist, nodded his head approvingly and studied us with shockingly blue eyes—the color of glacial ice. Alexander was leaner but no less rugged looking, with squinty eyes that had seen their share of raging winds and the worst that nature has to offer. Either of these gents could have stepped out of that picture on a Canadian whiskey label, the one that features a mountain man trapper, rifle in hand, husky dog at his side, and a brace of beaver pelts flung over one shoulder.

Here were two men who were at home in the outdoors, fellows you could implicitly trust to lead you wisely into the woods and—more important—back out again. You could learn things from these two men—things that might save your life, such as how and where to build a fire, how to survive a blizzard, and what to eat if you were starving. They would be equally lost in my world, trying to fill out a tax return or writing an audit report, but their knowledge was the greater in that the situations they faced were often matters of life and death. They had my deepest respect.

In the morning the weather did improve, at least initially, and we embarked on what was probably the most dangerous part of our trip: the Aeroflot helicopter ride to camp. (Little did we know that it would involve being lost in a snowstorm in the mountains.) The basic problem with these flights was maintenance or rather the lack thereof. The Russians had had a hard time keeping their helicopters up, and often only a few out of a fleet were operating, while the rest were cannibalized for parts. Periodically one would drop from the sky, killing everyone on board.

Sergei remained in Korf to meet more hunters arriving the following Saturday, but the rest of us climbed aboard the trademark orange-and-blue helicopter, which was surprisingly spacious inside. The cabin was the size of a small living room; it could easily carry a Jeep and a small platoon of men.

The improvement in the weather didn't last long, however. Once we were in the air the wind picked up and the sky began to thicken as we headed toward the mountain ridge separating the eastern and western shores of the peninsula. Camp was somewhere over that ridge on the western shore. The ground below was solid white, with an occasional patch of tundra showing through. The clouds soon grew heavy, pressing down on top of us while the rising earth pushed up

Dale models a fancy local headdress and fur pullover.

from below, the two threatening to sandwich us in between and not leaving us many options. And then, halfway into the flight, it started to snow. The snow worsened, reaching blizzard proportions near the peak of the ridge. Visibility dropped, and soon we were flying blind in sporadic clouds of fog. There were times when the ground—just a hundred feet below us—would blur in the snow squall and then "white out" to nothing. There was no way in hell the pilots could see where they were going, or the mountain in our path. We just hoped they knew what they were doing.

After crossing over the mountain ridge, the pilots anxiously called Alexander in to the cockpit. With all of the snow and fog, they could not locate camp on the ocean shore below. Alexander soon appeared back in the cabin to peer hastily out the side windows, searching for signs of the camp. The thicker clouds had now swallowed the mountain ridge: There was no going back to Korf. We had to find camp. Before long the descending clouds had pushed us out over the ocean, and the helicopter flew north, the pilots trying to keep the slim shoreline in sight. Exchanging concerned glances, Dale and I now stared out the snowy windows and tried to will the camp into view. I wondered what we would do when the columns of dark clouds descended to sea level because most of the shoreline had no beach to land on, just rocky cliffs that joined the crashing waves below. Thankfully we were spared that fate, for it was only a few minutes later that the red tops of the tents came into view. Everyone breathed a deep sigh, and we landed in camp to end what had been a very tense seventy-minute ride.

"Landed," however, is not the right word. Because of the thaw in the tundra, the pilots were afraid that the landing pads might get sucked into the muddy bog and stick there. So, with the helicopter hovering above the ground, we were told to jump. Our bags were tossed after us.

It was snowing heavily now. While the bags were whisked to our sleeping tent, we were ushered to the dining tent to meet our guides. There were three of them: Boris, Nicholai, and Vassily, as well as a camp manager named Sergei. The cook was also named Nicholai, and the camp assistant was a tiny fellow named Anatoli, who looked part Eskimo. So we had three Nicholais in camp: Nicholai the interpreter, Nicholai the cook, and Nicholai the guide.

Given the isolation of the place and the difficulty in reaching it, camp was remarkably well set up, and that came as a bit of a surprise. Our canvas tent, whose octagonal shape made it look a cross between a teepee and a yurt, was quite roomy and well laid out. The wood stove in its center was a welcome sight. It was surprising that such a plain and simple apparatus could make such a difference to camp life, but the small tin box was endowed with the power to transform the whole of the frigid, frosty outdoors into a toasty and inviting retreat— a little piece of heaven at the end of a cold day. Beds around the perimeter had been handily fashioned from fresh-cut planks laid upon thick logs. Caribou skins spread on top provided excellent insulation and padding for our sleeping bags. We would be quite comfortable here. These Russians knew what they were doing when it came to setting up a hunting camp.

The camp itself was situated on a flat shelf at the base of a mountain, a hundred yards or so from the Sea of Okhotsk. There was little flat land except for the shelf and the pebbly shore, and the shore itself came and went with the tide. The tide went out at midnight, then returned to reach its high at about 7:00 or 8:00 A.M., gobbling up whatever beach there was. All of the mountains were covered with snow, as was much of the ground around camp, and, as in much of Alaska, alders were the primary vegetation on the steep slopes.

On the shore we encountered a natural phenomenon neither of us had seen before. The snow accumulated there into lofty banks at the water's edge, towering in places to fifteen feet. At high tide the waves lapped at the foot of this snow wall, slowly washing away the base and forming shallow snow caves up and down the beach. Over the course of the long winter, fantastic overhangs of snow were created that stood until the weight of the structure caused it to collapse. As a result the beach was littered with blocks of snow—some the size of a car—that floated off with the outgoing tide. Consequently, the sea was awash with ice and floating chunks of snow, giving it the color and consistency of a frozen blue daiquiri.

The bears, waking from hibernation, were famished, and they would peruse these beaches for food: fish, seals, seaweed, plants washed ashore. They eat just about anything when they are in that state. Like most wildlife, the bears are active primarily late in the evening and early in the morning.

The snow cleared in the evening and the hunt was on, though the method employed came as a bit of a surprise. The staff used small boats to cruise the coastline and glass for bear, either on the shore or on the steep mountain slopes that rise above it. Only one boat out of three was in operation that day, and after a short discussion it was decided that Dale would go in the boat with Boris and Nicholai the cook and that I would walk along the shore with Nicholai the interpreter, Vassily, and Sergei. It was now around 9:00 P.M., which, this time of year, was really like late afternoon. After all of the traveling I'd done, I was looking forward to getting to use my legs, taking in the winter scenery as we hoofed it down the beach, and the good feeling that comes from putting miles under one's feet.

We had not gone far, however, before we spotted a dark bear making its way down the side of the mountain. Here the snow bank rose to no more than shoulder height, and it provided the perfect cover for us as we slipped closer. When we next spotted the bear, it was almost to the beach. Just then the bear did something unexpected. It stood on its hind legs and looked about, which was quite a sight, ranking up there in my top ten of wildlife sightings. Dropping then to all fours, it ambled along the shore, straight toward us but still unaware of our presence. Sergei and Vassily were quite eager for me to shoot it, but Nicholai wisely said, "Let's see how big he is." Meanwhile, the guides kept saying, *"Bolshoi, Bolshoi"*—big.

It was good that we waited, because as the bear neared to fifty yards or so it was plain to see that this was a small bear—maybe six feet nose to tail.

But now that we didn't want the bear, what were we supposed to do as it continued toward us? Wave our arms? Shout and yell? Ask it to leave? The guides chose simply to flatten themselves against the snow cliff and remain as still as possible. The only problem with that

Outfitted against the harsh, cold wind, Dale hunted comfortably all day in this native getup. (Notice that the fur is worn hair side in.)

approach was that it did not allow for an exit strategy, nor did it take into account the logical conclusion to the little drama. Suddenly the snow bank, which had served as the perfect cover on our approach, didn't seem like such an attractive feature. Here it towered into an unscalable wall behind us, an effective trap, leaving us no means of retreat. But it was too late to do anything about that now. I felt for the safety with my thumb as I awaited the bear's approach.

The bear, strolling unawares, drew near on the beach until it was perhaps twenty-five yards away, directly between the water and us. Although I had little leisure to think about it just then, I was put out at my guides for placing us in this situation. If they were at all familiar with this area and this method of hunting—not to mention their quarry—surely they had come upon this scenario before. But then I had to remind myself that this was an exploratory hunt. These were the kinds of things one had to expect. We were guinea pigs. But at least this guinea pig had a gun and the confidence to use it. I readied for a charge, if one came. But when the bear sighted us, it swapped ends and ran.

It was apparent that our plan was in need of modification when it came to hunting bears beneath the snow cliffs. We couldn't rely on the bears always running away. Such a strategy would eventually force a charge, one that would end with our having to kill a bear in self-defense, and a bear that likely as not would be below our expectations. That was if we were lucky. The other possibility was that someone might get hurt or killed. Nicholai and I agreed that in the future we would keep an eye out for an opening in the cliffs for use as a retreat. That way if an approaching bear were less than desirable, we had only to pass through the snow cliff and circle back down to shore, allowing the bear to pass unmolested.

A short distance later, I was the first to spot a yellow-furred bear descending the steep slope of the mountain. The terrain was quite steep and the bear took its time, testing the crumbly earth with front paws and working its way determinedly lower, making switchbacks as it went. We tried to judge its size with binoculars, and again the guides wanted me to shoot right away. I wanted to hear what Nicholai had to say. After further glassing, Nicholai reckoned the bear at 7½ feet, nose to tail, and the guides were visibly upset when I passed on it. They complained to Nicholai that it was a grown bear and therefore a trophy, that I was being unreasonable. I couldn't figure why they were in such a hurry for me to shoot a bear the first day out of the box. Maybe they were anxious because there were only three guides, and four more hunters were due to arrive Saturday. Granted, had there not been so many complications and delays getting to camp, I'm sure Dale and I both would have had a bear on the ground by now. But that wasn't the case, and I was not about to shoot a junior bear just to put their minds at ease. Maybe it was something else. Perhaps they were accustomed to non-American hunters who wanted only to collect the species and were unconcerned about size.

We returned at dusk, just after midnight, having seen a total of six bears. *Whether I ever pull the trigger or not,* I thought, *this has been a great hunt. I saw a total of six bears in one day. In Alaska, I hunted six days and saw one bear!*

It is a funny feeling to find the sun still up at midnight. You feel as if your mind has made a mistake when it is telling you it's time for bed. But that's how it was. The nights are unbelievably short, with sunrise around 4:00 A.M., so that there are only three hours or so of dark—and it is really only a twilight, not true darkness. In fact, even at night, in good weather, the mainland was visible across the sea to the west, some forty kilometers away. Because of the late hours and the extremely short nights, we did not try to rise for a morning hunt.

The following afternoon there was still only one boat working, and I was just as happy to walk. The water temperature was in the thirties and there were no life vests—not that one would do you much good. Hypothermia would kill you in a matter of minutes. If you were within fifty feet of shore you *might* make it, although you would be shaking so vigorously from the cold that even if you did manage to get a fire started you would have few teeth left after the fierce jaw chattering. It was the state of the fleet that brought such thoughts to mind. The boats were ancient and battered metal craft, some ten or eleven feet in length. To say their seaworthiness was suspect would be to put it mildly. The sea-rusty motors were literally held together with homemade parts and scraps of wire that had been tied and retied in the regular challenge of getting them started. So I was more than glad to let Dale accept that peril when he was so inclined.

Around 4:30 P.M. my group departed—Nicholai, Sergei, Alexander, and I—and we started north along the shore. The sky was thick and dark and the wind brisk; unlike the day before, there were few bears out. I wasn't sure if it was a result of the weather or our earlier departure, but we didn't see much. The mountains grew taller as we pushed into new territory, eventually passing some rather steep rock cliffs that held an occasional bear at the very tops, where the tundra rounded down to the sheer edges. Those bears were wisely out of range, of both rifle and foot, and Nicholai jokingly nicknamed them "alpinists." Again I was amazed at the steepness of the terrain the Kamchatka bears can negotiate; the burly animals move up and down the rocky inclines with the skill of mountain goats.

Around 6:00 or so we spotted a bear on the snowy slope at the foot of a rockslide, a quarter-mile away. It was decided that the fewest number of people approaching would be best, so Nicholai and Alexander remained behind. Before we left, however, Nicholai explained to Sergei the kind of bear I wanted and that if it was a good one he should give me a thumbs up; if not, a thumbs down. Anxiously, he nodded his rusty-bearded face in agreement. Leaving our daypacks behind, we hiked the shore, using the chest-high snow bank as cover and keeping well hidden. It brought us to within one hundred yards of the bear. It was oblivious of our presence, engaged in pawing at something in the snow. Peeking above the snow bank, Sergei glanced at the bear a whole split second before nearly spraining his thumb in its instant snap skyward.

Now it was my turn to look, but it was a binocular and not the riflescope that I used. First, based on my guide's past performance, I had a suspicion I couldn't take his word for a given, and I wasn't about to pull the trigger without a good look. Second, I just plain wanted to see it. I eased the lenses above the brim of the snow bank. The bear was still digging in the snow, its dark hide a sharp contrast against the bright white of the snow. Taking in the magnificent sight, I tried to recall the hastily memorized "Big Bear facts" that Dale had given me. *Small ears = big bear. Small head in relation to the body = big bear.*

Well, no matter how you sliced it, this was a small bear. It was no more than five feet from nose to tail, and I was hoping to shoot a nine- or ten-footer. Bears, admittedly, are one of the most difficult animals to judge, but a guide must be able to make a good estimate; it's one of the things he is paid to do. This was literally a baby! I motioned to Sergei that I would not shoot it. He huffed, flabbergasted, and stalked off in a pout. Instantly, I was as visibly upset with him as he was with me. It's probably best that a language barrier existed, and that no words were exchanged.

Nicholai, who read our faces, approached and said the first words. "Johnny, that was a very small bear. You were right not to shoot it."

In my view it is bad manners to show disappointment on a hunt or disapproval of your guide, and it goes against hunting etiquette. However, I had explained to them that I would rather return home *without* a bear than shoot a small one. My only guess is that Sergei was ready to have the hunt over, not to mention a bear's gallbladder in his possession—something worth several hundred dollars to him on the Asian black market. Dried and ground, the bladder is believed to possess medicinal and aphrodisiac qualities. Tragically, as a result of poaching, that belief has accounted for the mass slaughter of all types of bear around the world. I didn't know for sure that's what was on Sergei's mind; it was just a guess. Maybe he was just in a hurry to have the first bear down so we would shoot a second and he could collect part of the fee. Whatever the case, this wasn't good. I had lost faith in my guide, and a successful hunt is built around trust and faith.

The feeling was apparently mutual, for then came guide payback. Sergei set off at a fast clip down the beach and never slowed. We hiked for miles. We were clearly hiking and not hunting, and I should have stopped him and asked, "Are we hiking or hunting?" Instead, I let pride rule my steps and I made the bad mistake of physically exhausting myself. Both feet got blistered and I overheated in sweat, not a wise move in cold country where temperatures can plummet in the blink of an eye.

Not surprisingly, we didn't see a single bear, apart from a couple of "alpinists" at the top of high cliffs and out of harm's way. Each was just a brown dot, 1,000 or 1,500 feet above. The thought did cross my mind, however, as to a possible approach using the steep drainages carved into the side of the mountain. A hike up one of those surely would lead to one of the mountain's bowls; then all that would be left was to climb the peak. It would be a tough, half-day ordeal, but it seemed doable. But Nicholai didn't like the idea. He seemed to think that the bears would wind us; also, the alders were as thick as fence posts, making for a miserable climb.

It was past midnight when, upon our return, with Sergei still hoofing it as if in a footrace, we heard the familiar buzz of the boat. Soon the craft came into sight in the distance, and Boris, who had come to look for us, steered into shore to pick us up—saving us at least two more grueling miles on foot. Once in camp I was too exhausted to eat (though I didn't show it in front of Sergei). I had some tea and collapsed in bed, asleep before I had even closed my eyes.

I awoke stiff and sore and in a gloomy mood. I was also homesick, missing my wife and kids, yet realizing how much I needed this break. Life had been hectic with work and kids and the ranch, and this hunting trip had come at the perfect time. But there was something else eating at me, the real cause of the dark cloud I felt overhead. I was still in grief from the terrible news I had received in PK. My good friend Gary Collins had died. Apparently he had been on his way to celebrate his anniversary with his wife, Donna, when he had collapsed with a heart attack. Besides being a good friend, Gary was my liaison with the group of eighteen deer hunters on our ranch. No one but Gary could keep a group that large in check and running smoothly. The big fellow knew more about Texas deer hunting and management than I would ever know, and my stomach ached at the realization that I would never see him again. Everyone always says, "It won't be the same without so-and-so," but in this case I knew it wouldn't.

After another moment or two of reflection, I did my best to push those thoughts aside and focus on the task at hand. Once I'd gotten up and out of the tent, I felt a lot better, both physically and mentally. At my request Anatoli brought a bowl of hot water, and I washed my face and hands with soap and was soon back to myself and ready to tackle the world. In the dining tent Nicholai the cook had laid out enough food for a king's banquet, and I quickly got stuffed on the heavy fare.

Eating, I discovered, is the national hobby here. Food in big quantities is pushed at you constantly. Like the Eskimos, the Russians eat every two or three hours, keeping their bodies stoked to fight the cold. And the foods they eat are packed with calories: butter, cheese,

Launching the boat in a moment of rare calm.

meat, gravy—all washed down with vodka. Caviar filled a giant jar on the table—golden roe the size of peas—and at each meal the fellows spooned a mouthful or two. Boris was as skinny as a flagpole, although he ate more than anyone I have ever known—even my dad, who is just as skinny. Huge quantities of food disappeared in front of the man, and I could not imagine where he put it.

The guides finally got a second boat working after lunch, and in early afternoon I climbed aboard with Nicholai the guide and Sergei. At first I was hesitant to have Sergei come at all, but Nicholai the interpreter assured me that Nicholai the guide knew bears well and would do all the guiding, and that Sergei would come along only to assist. Although the day was still cloudy, the water happened to be calm, which made for an effortless launch and a smooth ride. Admittedly the boat was an easy way to cover a lot of country, and the view of the passing snow-covered mountains was magnificent. The water itself was beautiful, with icy-white chunks floating here and there in the deep blue. Far from shore, an occasional seal was visible using the ice islands as a base from which to establish fishing operations, but also as a means of keeping away from hungry bears.

If asked to name the most dangerous part of this trip, most folks might promptly point to the bears, but in my mind the boat was the clear winner. There were a number of things that could have gone wrong, any number of which would end up with hunters in the water. If the boat hit an ice chunk and sank, we were goners. If a wave flipped the boat, there would have been no further reason for me to be concerned about the solvency of the Social Security system. If the engine quit for good we were at the mercy of the prevailing wind and might never see land again. That, I decided, was the most likely calamity, as the rusty engine was more finicky than a Persian cat at the food bowl and took great coaxing and patience to get started. When it didn't, the procedure went something like this: Nicholai pulled the housing off, fiddled with the carburetor, cleaned the spark plugs, blew the hoses clean, tugged on this and that, retied the wires rigged to hold the various components, and then took a screwdriver to loosen parts. When all else failed, he would curse in Russian and whack the block with a hammer. Those steps were repeated until the stubborn thing revved to life. Then we would go for a while until the engine would again decide to quit and the process would start anew.

Fortunately, the engine presented us with nothing more than the usual breakdowns, and the water stayed calm for the remainder of the day, making for a delightful ride and providing a much needed rest after the previous day's marathon hike. Despite the use of the boat and the extra country it allowed us to cover, we didn't see much—only two bear sightings, in fact: a small boar and later a sow with two cubs that were nearly as big as she. We got into camp a tad before midnight, and I crawled into my down bag more tired because of the time of day than from the activity of it. I drifted off to sleep while waiting for Dale to show. It was 4:00 A.M. when I awoke to the noise of someone pushing through the tent flap. It was, of course, Dale who came stooping through, dead tired but with an exciting tale and the bearskin that went along with it. But this wasn't just any bear. No, he had gotten a great bear—a 9½-footer—not to mention a hunting adventure that had ended in a close charge.

As he collapsed on his wood-plank bunk, wearily pulling off boots and socks in the dim light, Dale shared his adventure. It had begun when they were stopped on the shore for an evening snack and Boris spotted two bears far down the beach. Not long after the two bears appeared, one chased the other into the brush. Boris thought they looked quite big, so the men began the long hike down the beach. Once near where the bears had vanished into the brush, Dale and his guide eased into the tangle of thick alders, working their way up a steep slope, looking for them. The search didn't take long, and when they found the first, they were nearly on top of it. The cover was so thick that Dale could see only patches of it, but there was no mistaking that it was big. He aimed through an opening in the scrub, and when he had what he felt was an acceptable shot at the chest, he took it. Quickly, he followed up with two more from the .416, but those were at tumbling, rolling fur as the angry bear thrashed around in the brush. Then the big animal disappeared, and everything went quiet. The bear, which had made quite a commotion at the shots, was now silent and out of sight. Was it dead? Or was it waiting for them quietly?

After a minute or two of nearly unbearable tension, with still no sound from the beast, Dale and Boris began the dangerous task of tracking a wounded bear in thick bush. Wisely they circled uphill, putting themselves at an advantage. During this part of the hunt, the only sounds Dale heard were the beating of his heart and the occasional snap of twigs underfoot, which was unavoidable on the snow-covered ground. There was no sign of the bear. They had hoped to catch a glimpse of it, dead or alive, at a distance. Now they had no choice but to descend into the thick alders to the spot where the last sounds had originated. They would have to come upon it at close range.

A Bullet Well Placed

Boris throws together a quick dinner at fly camp on the beach.

As they negotiated the alders, a grunt suddenly bellowed up from below, and the bear charged from thirty yards. Even charging uphill, the big animal was knocking down brush the way a bulldozer knocks down trees, snapping big limbs with the crack of several rifle reports, snorting, growling, mad as hell, and ready to tear them apart. Despite its size, the big bear was moving blindingly fast. It would be on them in less than a second. But for Dale time had slowed, and the whole episode took on the feel of an instant replay, as if he had all the time in the world to mount his gun and put the bullets where he wanted them. It was a sensation he had experienced several times before, in Africa, when at the receiving end of a charge by dangerous game. So if the feeling was not new, neither were the expectations. He knew that if he did this wrong—that if he failed in his attempt or if his gun misfired—the outcome would be grim. There was a good chance he would leave behind four fatherless kids. This was a game that he was playing for keeps, and it was winner take all.

Despite the possibly grim outcome, despite the sight of a snarling and charging beast, Dale felt surprisingly calm as he mounted the gun to his shoulder, took aim at the angry, furry freight train, and squeezed the trigger. At his ease, Dale fired three times, emptying his rifle, and Boris fired twice before the big bear fell dead at ten paces. The sight

174

of a charging brown bear had to be something, but it was the sounds it made that left the biggest impression on Dale.

"Johnny," he said, "as long as I live I'll never forget the snarling, snorting, and growling that bear made as it came for us."

But the excitement was not over. The two men had no sooner dropped the charging bear at their feet when the second bear arrived on the scene and refused to leave. Incredibly, this one began to paw and chew on the dead animal, claiming it for its own. It made quite a sight, because this second bear was so enormous that it actually dwarfed Dale's very large trophy. Not about to give up an easy meal, the big bear growled at the men and even made a few mock charges. At this point Dale could easily have shot it and had two bears in the bag. In fact he would have liked nothing better than to collect this bigger trophy and was even planning whether to aim for the head or the chest on its next charge. But with the problems we'd had in PK trying to cash traveler's checks, we had only enough money between us for one extra bear. Since we hadn't decided who would shoot a second, Dale held off taking this monster, though he naturally yearned for it. (Now that's a good friend, and the kind of fellow you want to accompany you on a hunt!) A shot or two over its head persuaded the giant to saunter off. Skinning was then performed as quickly as possible, with Dale standing guard should the big bear return.

Before falling asleep Dale relayed an earlier bit of excitement in their day, when their boat had broken down while in the middle of the sea. The outboard quit and wouldn't start, and, if that wasn't bad enough, the boat had picked that exact time to spring a leak. Boris hastily dismantled the engine, the parts rolling here and there on the stern rail and threatening at any minute to pitch into the sea, which would have put them in a real fix. As they drifted ever farther out to sea, Boris tweaked and fiddled, cleaned and poked, his expert hands working in a blur. After much work he threw the engine together, then yanked and yanked the starter rope—but to no avail. While Boris busied himself with the motor, Dale, who had been unable to determine the source of the leak, began to bail the water that was rapidly filling the boat. The only thing Dale knew for certain was that the water was coming in faster than he could bail it out. It was ankle deep by the time Boris finally brought the small outboard to life and coaxed the boat back on plane.

The next day the sea was quite rough, with three-foot waves crashing onto the beach. It was a challenge dragging the boat from the shelf where it had been stored into the oncoming waves and trying to board it without getting knocked down by the waves and completely soaked. The sea had only worsened by the time we—Nicholai, Vassily, and I—left in the afternoon, heading south. In fact, the waves grew quickly into four-footers, and the small boat crashed from one to the next, taking a real beating and threatening to capsize. Waves bashed the bottom of the boat like concrete bashing steel, jarring every bone in my body, and I thought, *Surely we can't continue at this pace. The boat won't take it. Something is going to give.* Even holding on as tightly as I could, I flew from my seat with the impact of each wave, as if bouncing on a trampoline. But it was my gun that got the worst of it. Despite my efforts to hold it safe, the riflescope repeatedly smacked the dashboard when we hit the larger waves, and I prayed that the blows hadn't knocked it off zero.

Finally, as we rounded a rock outcropping, a small cove appeared on the left, and Nicholai hastily beached the boat. I was more than a little glad to be back on firm ground. Right then and there I swore off any future boat rides—other than the boat ride back to camp.

Once the boat was anchored in the shallows, we set off south on foot along the beach. Around the next crag, which jutted out into the sea and required negotiating a stretch of jumbled, wave-splashed rock, we came upon a huge, sweeping bay many miles across. The land sloped sharply up from a sandy beach in the form of steep dirt cliffs, leveled to a tundra knoll on top, then climbed to snowy peaks in the distance. With its access to the beach, this was perfect habitat for bears—a good spot to hunt.

Sure enough, we hadn't gone far when we spotted a bear on the tundra knoll above us, then another on the beach. The one on the beach gave us the slip, so we started the miserable climb up the ridge. It was difficult work in the loose, dark soil—where for every two steps up I slid one step down—and the slope was full of alders and brush and thick banks of snow. Because of the steepness of the slope and the need to use both hands in the ascent, I was forced to hang my rifle crosswise on my chest, and the alders kept tangling with my gun and throwing me off balance. Nor did the hip boots give the best traction in this loose dirt, and near the top I sank to the thigh in snow, having to grasp at nearby branches to pull myself up and out. It was like getting out of quicksand, and soon I had worked up a sweat. Finally we reached the top of the cliff, where the rolling tundra began, but now that we were there we could not locate the bear. It had moved off.

The easy trek on the tundra was a welcome change, though, and after a short search we quickly sighted the bear, now busy digging at the mossy ground. Using hand signals we planned our approach, which mostly involved keeping the wind in our favor. To do so, however, required a fight through a patch of head-high alders buried in a thick bed of snow. The lovely choice was either to sink into the snow and twist an ankle on unseen branches and roots, then trip and pitch headfirst into the snow, or to try to balance on the slick alder limbs above the snow (which was a bit like walking a tightrope), then trip and pitch headfirst into the snow. I tried both ways. Silently I cursed my clumsiness while the guides, of course, glided effortlessly ahead.

Once we had negotiated the patch of alders, we found ourselves in a stand of short pines, also trapped in snow. I slipped several times in the slick snow and struggled in frustration to extricate myself, meanwhile forming a strong resolve never again to hunt snow country!

Eventually, however, we reached the edge of the pines and crept into position. Our approach, despite the difficulty, had been perfect. The bear was now fifty yards away, digging at the snow and tundra. Nicholai glassed the bear and gave me an immediate thumbs up. It was such a close shot that normally I would have fired offhand, but I was huffing from my struggles in the snow and the excitement of the hunt and so decided I had best sit or kneel. That was a bad idea. When I tried to squat for a better rest, my butt sank into the soft snow and I rolled onto my back. Then I wallowed around like a beached whale, trying to right myself, trying my best to be quiet, and

Dale with his terrific bear.

simultaneously working up a string of silent curses that would have shamed a sailor. Fortunately my antics were lost on the bear, and when I regained my footing and looked up it was still digging at roots. I was relieved, of course, but I was more relieved by the fact that none of my little snow ballet had been captured on video. It would have been rather an embarrassment. It was also fortunate that the bear wasn't charging. If so, it would be the one writing the story.

Now kneeling in the snow, I rested my rifle on an alder branch, tried to hold my rushing breath, and squeezed the trigger. I continued to squeeze, but nothing happened. I had forgotten the safety. I guess I was a bit flustered by this time.

Snapping off the safety I tried again, trying to keep the rifle steady and squeeze—not jerk—the trigger, a hard thing to do when winded and excited. So I summoned my resolve to make the shot count, knowing that the totality of body and spirit is needed to shoot a gun accurately, especially in a tense situation, that not giving my all could mean the difference between a perfect shot and a catastrophe, and that the first shot is the most important. The last thing you want to do when hunting dangerous game is wound your quarry. That's when people get hurt.

The bear was facing us now, head down. It was not the ideal broadside shot I had hoped for, but if anything it was a good second choice. I aimed at the center of the bear, above its blocky brown head, at the neck, figuring I had a chance for both spine and heart. The gun erupted in my hands, and the bear dropped like a rock. I reloaded, but Nicholai motioned not to shoot again. When the bear started to rise, though, I hammered it once more. I think my guide was concerned I might hit the gallbladder, but I was more concerned about the prospect of a wounded bear on our hands. That was not an outcome I was willing to risk.

The bear collapsed a second time, and I reloaded with my third and final cartridge, ready to give it one more if it showed any sign of rising. It didn't.

Approaching the bear, however, we were in for quite a disappointment. First, the bear turned out to be a female. Second, it was a small bear, maybe seven feet. We had been told to expect a nine-to ten-footer, thus the reason for my broken expectations. Even Nicholai said, *"Malinki"*—small—in disgust. The Russian method of judging a trophy was now clear: First they shoot a bear, and then they see exactly what size it is. Admittedly, a bear is a difficult trophy to judge, but that is why a hunter needs a guide who can. But there was more at stake here than simple hunter satisfaction: It was the success or failure of their whole hunting operation. In a successful program, it is imperative that guides be able to distinguish between the young and the old. Only by harvesting older bears, letting the young ones grow old, would the Russians be successful in a hunting management plan.

Nevertheless I thanked my guides, neither of whom could speak a word of English, and they set to work skinning the small animal. I was done and glad to be done; it had been a challenging hunt. It was now near midnight, and I was tired and ready to head back to camp. The ocean below had settled and smoothed noticeably as night had neared, and I did not want a repeat of the thrashing waves. I was also in the process of making a pact with God. *God, just get me down those steep cliffs alive, just get me back to camp without drowning, and I am done hunting for this trip.*

On our way down the dirt cliffs, we spotted a bear on the beach; it was ambling in our direction. We saw two more bears snoozing in the alders on our descent. I was a little annoyed when the guides stopped and wasted time trying to judge them. Night was at hand, and I was ready to get to camp; clearly, I did not want a second bear. Furthermore, the sleeping pair had to be a sow and cub, as the boars travel alone at this time of year. Sows and cubs stay together, and it is the mama's job to keep the cubs away from a hungry papa bear, which will readily kill and eat them if given the chance. The biggest threat to a young bear's life, in fact, is none other than papa. Of course, they don't show you that in a Disney film.

We got back to the bay only to find the tide way out. Our boat was stranded some seventy-five yards from the water, mired on the sandy beach. We were stuck for the night and had to wait for whatever the ocean might bring the next morning. The three of us retrieved our gear from the boat and readied for a night on the beach.

As we began the task of collecting firewood, mostly bone-white driftwood, a boat came buzzing into sight around the bend. It was Boris. Alexander was on board and so was an American named Don from Ohio, who had arrived by helicopter while we were out. Before it departed, the helicopter had been put to good use. Boris's boat had been loaded inside and flown many miles south, sparing them one leg of the journey. They had been on their return to camp when they had seen our beached craft. It was now night and too dark for them to continue on, so they joined us on the shore.

We built a fire below the vertical rock face of a cliff, and dinner was quickly set. We tore off chunks of bread, meat, and cheese with

Boris carting one hundred pounds of wet bear skin to camp.

our hands or sliced the food with a hunting knife, and a bottle of vodka was poured into a community tin cup and passed around. Vassily, sitting close to the fire, unwrapped his feet from the bandagelike wrappings that served as socks; they had soaked with the beaching of the boat. He held them up in his hands, tending the garments with great care, and dried them in the heat of the flames. Going to bed with wet feet is a wilderness sin.

In the dark, everyone huddled around the warmth of the fire, the Russians conversing in their own language, Don and I in ours. He and I swapped hunting stories, and it was a pleasure to get to speak English. The camaraderie and the fire cheered me from the gloom I had felt after shooting the small bear, and I was soon back to my old self. I was also quite comfortable, for the first time that day. My legs and arms had that good, heavy, worn-out feeling that comes from physical exertion, and I was warm inside and out. I was warm inside from the hot tea and vodka, and I was warm outside from the fire and the caribou-skin pullover that Nicholai the cook had lent me. It was an amazing piece of clothing. Worn with the hair "in," this native garment is remarkably quiet while hunting, allowing one to slip past branches noiselessly. Even more remarkable was the fact that the natural material "breathes" so as not to collect moisture on the inside. It works the way the high-tech jobbies are supposed to.

After some more hot tea and a final shot of vodka, we took to our sleeping bags on the sand and spent the night spread out about the beach. I fell to sleep as the fire crackled and the wind whispered its nightly song, thinking back on the adventures of the hunt. It was light by 4:00 A.M., and I tossed and turned for the rest of the early morning.

Around 6:00 I crawled out of my bag to relieve myself. My stirrings woke one of the guides, who looked up to see a big bear on the slope above us. The camp came instantly to life, and Don was hustled awake to go after it. They had their work cut out for them, for the steep bank, even in the best spots, was more cliff than bank. After a little perseverance, though, they reached the top. Don caught sight of the bear within range, but when he tried to fire he discovered that his gun was unloaded. That one chance was all he got. They never saw the big bruin again.

While Don and his guides were off on the chase, my group broke camp, rolling our sleeping bags and collecting our gear. We then splashed out to the boat in the shallow water that had returned to lift it afloat. The sea remained calm up to the first bend, but then we had a bit of a rodeo ride until we neared the home stretch and the water mellowed again. When we arrived at camp in midmorning, I told Dale my tale and that I was through.

"No more boats!" I said. "And no more guides who can't judge an immature bear from an adult!"

Then Dale shared his story of how he was both happy and sad to see me. He was happy because when we had left camp yesterday it was just to do a little scouting down south. That, of course, had turned into an unexpected overnight. Figuring that we had met with some disaster and I was dead, Dale had been trying to work out how he was going to tell my wife. So he was happy to see me.

He was sad to see me because we had missed the helicopter yesterday that had dropped off Don and three other hunters. When Nicholai had mentioned it would be possible for us to take that helicopter back to Korf, Dale had hurried to our tent, hastily packed all our belongings (no small feat), and dragged our bags out to the chopper. Through Nicholai he had told the pilots that I would be arriving any minute. Could they please wait? Well, maybe ten minutes, they had said. When the tenth minute neared, Dale invited the pilots in to eat, stalling them, hoping that I would show with a bear and we could be off. After their meal the pilots insisted they had to leave, and Dale watched them lift into the sky with tears streaming down his cheeks (or so he claimed). This sealed our fate to another week in camp, as the only other charter expected was the one we were booked on, six days later. There was no radio in camp and no phone—no way to call and arrange an earlier flight.

Back in the tent, the three of us had a good laugh when Dale and Nicholai relayed a story about the older of the two Germans to arrive in camp, a fellow named Martin, and how he had commandeered little Anatoli, the tent boy, to chop a trail to his own personal latrine. (Apparently he didn't like the idea of sharing the single outhouse tent.) He would point and yell in German, and Anatoli would chop, chop, chop at the alder bushes. Then the German would yell and point some more. Little Anatoli, who was a little slow in the head, had no idea what he was being asked to do. At first he had thought the German wanted a road built to town!

Besides being demanding, the Germans also turned out to be picky eaters who had brought along their own food and drinks. They rudely pushed aside whatever Nicholai the cook placed in front of them, pulling out sausages and foil-wrapped cheeses and beef bouillon cubes to melt in cups of hot water. But there was no need for that, because the food in camp was excellent. The meat was mostly moose meat, and Nicholai the cook served up moose steak, moose burgers, moose Stroganoff, moose stew, and moose sandwiches. There were no complaints, because old Nicholai knew what he was about when it came to moose—his hearty creations were as tender and tasty as those of any fancy restaurant. The food, in fact, had been the biggest surprise of the trip. We had expected it to be poor, or nonexistent, and that was why we ourselves had brought along some freeze-dried fare, which happily had gone unused.

With the wood stove crackling, we huddled in the warmth of the tent and joked about the personal toilet, and whatever else the German might think up for little Anatoli to build. For even now, outside, we could hear the German ordering him about. It was certainly no way to act in another man's country and an embarrassment to us as fellow hunters. Old Martin didn't think much of us, either, upon discovering we were Americans. He glanced our way to mutter that American soldiers had forced him to sit in handcuffs when he was captured during the war. Then he turned stiffly back and never spoke to us again. Considering what went on during that war, sitting in handcuffs did not seem cruel and unusual treatment. In fact, I wouldn't have minded putting him in a pair myself.

After the previous night's short sleep and a heavy dinner of moose steaks, I was ready to turn in early. At 8:30 I announced to Dale that

I was heading to the dining tent for a vodka nightcap, and he agreed to join me. Neither he nor I regularly drink hard liquor, but after the first shot had gone down so smoothly, the suggestion was made that we have one more. Next thing I knew it was past midnight, and we were deep in discussion of one of our favorite subjects—charges by dangerous game. The heated debate continued over which beast was most likely to cause a collection on the life insurance, and which we particularly wanted to hunt next. Alexander and Nicholai the cook joined us at the table, and I'm convinced we were speaking fluent Russian. They understood everything we said and we understood everything they said, and we all laughed and hooted and recounted tales of various hunts. We were one big band of brothers! Vodka was the great unifier, translator, pacifier—all wrapped into one. If only the United Nations were required to bring a few bottles of the magic liquid to its meetings, I truly believe that the world's disputes could be solved and World War III perpetually avoided. Yes, we were one tight, happy bunch.

Much later I looked up in surprise to find that Dale and I were the only ones left. The next surprise came when I rose to find myself incredibly unsteady on my feet. In fact, I could hardly walk. The tundra was pitching about like an angry sea, the tent was moving around in the dark, and the ground had sprouted more ankle-twisting holes than when I had last walked it. Dale was staggering just as badly, and we bumped into each other like a couple of dizzy clowns on rubber legs.

When I crawled into my sleeping bag the world was still spinning, and I knew that the morning was going to be rough. I sat up and munched a Cliff bar, hoping it would absorb some of the alcohol, as sleep was clearly impossible. Indeed I was groggy in the morning but saved from a horrible hangover by that Cliff bar.

We took a day of rest and read and slept and talked. Those are some of the finest days on a hunt, when muscles are sore, you have been pushing hard, and sleep has been neglected. I challenged Nicholai to one chess game after another, winning only one—and that only because he was distracted by playing the German interpreter, Maxine, at the same time.

Dale decided that he was content with his bear, so any further hunting was up to me. But I was just as content, having resolved to remain in camp for the rest of the trip until the helicopter came for us on Friday. I didn't think that the guides, with the exception of Boris, could judge bear size. Nor did I want to pay a second license fee only to end up with a second small bear. I decided that I would rather take the one I'd gotten and call it quits.

And last but not least, there was that little matter of my pact with God.

Around 5:00 P.M., while Dale and I sat under cloudy skies on a large drift log at the edge of the beach, braving the cold and stout wind so I could savor a victory cigar, Nicholai approached with what he called a "gift." He explained that Vassily wanted to take me on foot to try for another bear. I just smiled and shook my head, but Nicholai continued to press his point. When he saw I wasn't going to budge, he got dirty and hit below the belt, making me an offer I couldn't refuse: Hunt a bear, but pay for it only if I was happy with its size. Who says there isn't a Russian Mafia?

Dale shook his head and smirked. "You and your pact with God."

"OK, so I'm weak. But even God must understand an offer like that. In fact, he'd probably send me straight to hell for turning it down."

In late afternoon, with no improvement in the weather—overcast sky and pounding winds—Vassily, Sergei, and I headed south along the beach. An hour later we climbed a steep ridge to glass the terrain above. I say "climbed." The guides climbed. I fought and stumbled and tripped my way up the side of the blasted mountain. I sank in the snow, tripped on the alder branches, and slipped on icy conifer bushes. I admit that I have never been overly coordinated, but this was downright humiliating. I felt like an eighty-year-old grandmother, and I was truly embarrassed by my performance. By the time we reached the top, a half-hour later, I was thinking: *I'm paying big money for this, and I'm not enjoying it. Bear or no bear, I don't care to repeat this poor display.*

Then in response, I reminded myself: *But isn't that often how it is on a big game hunt? You struggle daily against seemingly insurmountable odds, but you suck it up and persevere and get your animal. Once you get home and time passes, you remember the excitement and the adventure, forget the pain and the exhaustion. Months or years later, you start to think what a great idea it would be to go on a similar hunt again. This hunt is no different.*

When my other half didn't respond, I abandoned the conversation and continued to trudge onward, feet sinking in the deep snow, huffing to pull them out, the soles of my boots slipping on icy-slick alders buried underneath.

A short while later, with me losing interest fast, we spotted a bear at least a mile away. It was down an alder slope and up the side of a mountain. Vassily went ahead to find its tracks and examine the paw size. While he was gone, I glimpsed a small bear that appeared to be favoring a front paw as it meandered in the snow. I wondered if it was the one the younger German, Michael, had shot at and could not find.

Staring across the expanse of alders and snow, knowing what it would take to cross it, I came to the conclusion that I did not want to fight my way any farther inland. I was ready to head back. Minutes earlier I had fallen flat on my face—not once, but three times—and had realized how easy it would be to snap a leg tangled amid the roots and branches buried under the snow. Then how would I get out? The simple truth was that this Texas lad was just no good on this terrain. It was miserable stuff, and as much as I hated to admit it, it had me beat. It was time to throw up the white flag, and I did.

When Vassily returned with news that the tracks were small, I motioned to Sergei that I was ready to return to camp. Without any argument he nodded his understanding, and we turned around and began the difficult descent. We had to fight our way back down the mountain, through the thigh-deep snow and head-high alders, but with every step I had the satisfaction of knowing that I was at least one step closer to camp. The weather remained ugly, the wind sharp and stinging the exposed skin of my face. It pushed at us constantly, and the slippery

This is my bear.

branches continued to trip me up—but I could see the finish line up ahead, so to speak, and felt better for it. On tired feet, I made it to camp around midnight.

Before turning in, Dale filled me in on his day in camp and shared an insight into why our guides were eager to shoot any bear with four legs (and a gallbladder). When Martin, who had yet to set foot out of camp, being too busy with building personal toilets and whatnot, finally got around to hunting, he had announced in a firm voice to Boris, "Vee go not far from camp. Shoot zee first bear vee see." And they did. And it was a cub. I'm not stretching it when I say that bear could be picked up with one hand. Martin, nevertheless, was pleased as punch.

Further confirmation came the next day, when we witnessed the conduct of Michael, who yesterday afternoon shot four times at a bear several hours from camp but couldn't find it. A couple of the guides went after it today, leaving Michael in camp. The funny thing was that they were gone only about an hour when they returned with "a" bear. Dale and I exchanged knowing glances. In any event, the German was ecstatic. He promptly got rip-roaring drunk and kept repeating, "I'm so happy! I'm so happy!" Michael was happy to have a bear, any bear. The guides, it turned out, had expected the same of us.

At lunch, Nicholai announced that I would hunt with Boris. OK, OK, I know there was a certain promise made that I would not set foot back in one of those flimsy tin boats and that I was through with hunting for this trip. But now the Russians were offering me their best guide, a fellow who had killed some seventy bears in his career and clearly understood trophy quality. Surely, God would understand that! I knew I did.

So, late in the afternoon, Boris, Sergei, and I loaded into the battered boat and headed south, only to run into a pitching, choppy sea as we rounded a couple of rocky points. The small boat took a real bashing from the waves, and we were quickly soaked with spray. At one point, when the bashing became particularly treacherous, I was ready to tell Boris that I had three young children and really wanted to live to see them again. Only I didn't want to distract him from his task of steering, though it wasn't so much steering as trying to keep the bow from stuffing into an oncoming wave and capsizing us. We battled the nasty chop for another half-hour, then landed in the huge bay where Nicholai and I had shot my bear. The rough water had slowed our progress substantially, and it was now too late to hunt. After beaching the boat we made camp beside the huge trunk of a tree that had washed ashore (who knew from where, as there were no trees around here that big), then settled in for the night.

Once he had gotten the fire going—no easy task in the high wind—Boris, in broken English, told me that in high school he had read Jack London. Building fires, camping, and hunting had looked very "romantic." Now (he mimed shoveling) it was really just hard work. We laughed. We discussed children, and Boris gestured one child and he shoveled; then two children and he shoveled faster; then three children and he shoveled frantically. I laughed and understood completely. Some things cross all borders and cultures. It is times like these, mingling up close and personal with the locals of foreign lands, that you realize that despite all the colors and religions and cultures the world over, we are all just people—people with the same wants and needs and desires. Sometimes we forget that.

After a quick dinner of bread, meat, and cheese, Boris fashioned a cot in the sand beside the tree from flat planks of driftwood. With a sleeping pad under me, I was quite comfortable in the sleeping bag. It was now 10:30 and very windy, but there was a clear sky overhead. On the beach where we were sleeping there were fresh paw prints, one set being 16 cm wide (a big bear, according to Boris), so we knew this was a good area. Our campsite was right at the end of the drainage that the big bear had followed to visit the beach, and Boris was certain it would return again. Admittedly, there was some reflection on my part as to the possible timing of the bear's return and who exactly the bait was. Upon further deliberation, I had to wonder the correct course of action should the bear pop its head over the log at me in the middle of the night. In retrospect, I realized that I had been remiss in my planning for this outing. I should have packed a spare pair of underwear.

Boris and Sergei glassed the beach and hills until 1:00 A.M. or so, then turned in until perhaps 4:00. I awoke around 2:00, covered in ash and wrapped in smoke from the fire, which had been kept going all night. Stripping back part of the lean-to tarp that had been fashioned around me helped considerably to redirect the smoke.

Morning dawned clear and windy. The sun had set to the north, then poked up in the northeast—it really did just about circle the whole horizon on its daily journey this time of year. The tide, which had gone out some two hundred yards at night, was now nearly back in, lifting our previously stranded boat against its moorings in the shallow, lapping water. Although we were up early and glassing the vast terrain, we saw no bears on the slopes or on the beach. That was disappointing,

Departure day. Blessed with lovely weather—and the helicopter even arrived on time.

as I had hoped that the big boy whose prints were on the beach would show. Boris motioned that, with the biting wind, few bears would be out and that we should return to camp.

On the way to camp, however, we spotted two bears tucked into alders high on the side of a mountain. We beached the boat and hiked up to where they had been, but we never saw them again. In all honesty, I was hoping we didn't see them, because all of a sudden—maybe it was the short night's sleep, maybe it was my repeated pacts with God— I was at peace. I had decided that I'd had a good hunt and that I would rather take home my money than a second bear. This hunt was over for me, and, luckily, we saw no more bears on the rest of the ride to complicate my decision.

Despite a rough chop we made it back to camp, but we couldn't land because the surf was pounding and no one was there to help haul in the boat. Racing the motor, we sped up and down the shore hoping someone would hear us. When that failed Sergei fired his rifle into the air, but the blast was lost on the wind—that's how windy it was. Finally Boris got as close as he dared to shore and the breaking waves that promised to swamp us, and Sergei jumped off the bow, landing chest deep in the freezing water.

When help arrived, we began the chore of beaching the boat in the merciless waves. Jumping overboard, we all plunged into the roaring surf, now waist deep, and the icy water filled our hip waders. For sheer awakening power, I will guarantee you that the frigid water had both an alarm clock and a pot of coffee beat. But there was no avoiding it, and we were forced to wrestle the boat onto shore against the crashing waves that alternately tried to swamp the craft and pull it back out to sea. What was most surprising was how quickly my feet and lower legs went numb in the cold water. A minute later, winning the battle, we dragged the boat up the pebbly shore to the shelf, where it was safe from the advancing tide. Once on shore I anxiously pulled my waders off and drained them of the icy water; then I went to the tent to change out of soaked pants and shirt, long johns, and socks.

Once again I had promised God, while riding the chop back to camp, that if he would just get me back alive I would be done hunting this trip. Well, I was. I cleaned my gun for the final time (the salt spray and volcanic ash had made a mess of it) and changed into travel clothes. I told Nicholai that I had had a very good hunt but that I was done. Dale just rolled his eyes, justifiably doubtful. But this time I kept to my word.

The next afternoon was spent sorting through gear, trying to decide what to take home and what to leave behind for the camp staff. Besides its being a customary gesture of thanks (in addition to a tip), we were afraid of getting socked on overweight charges with the heavy bear hides in tow, and so we gave away any heavy or bulky gear we could spare: shirts, socks and hats, freeze-dried food, sleeping pads, water bottles, and the like.

The surf continued to pound all day and was quite strong when Boris took Don out for an evening hunt. As I watched the boat toss in the waves, I must admit I was glad not to be the one venturing out. Dale commented that even Boris did not seem enthusiastic about taking his boat into such rough water. But they were fortunate, and the water soon calmed. The hunting gods smiled on them for their persistence, and Don shot a great bear, almost as large as Dale's.

The following afternoon we experienced exceptionally good weather—clear skies and still. It was the first time on the trip that the wind had called a truce. The snow around camp melted, but although I enjoyed the warm sun, it made me a little nervous about the weather for our departure the next day. If it were bad and the helicopter couldn't fly, we would miss our PK flight and be stranded for another week. And here were two Dallas boys ready to get home! Dale was especially ready. He had gotten his bear seven days earlier and had been passing time in camp ever since. He had read every book we had, and it was fair to say that he had become the world champion in electronic solitaire.

Fortunately, the weather held and the helicopter arrived on time, its distant hum a welcome sound. A tremendous amount of gear went aboard, then all of us hunters. In Korf we had a long wait for our flight, which was scheduled to arrive "whenever it gets here" and to depart "whenever it does." We stood in a dirty corner of the dilapidated building until Nicholai commandeered a VIP room. He brought in lemon cookies and a bottle of vodka, which improved the mood substantially. Everyone had a couple of shots, and Michael, the German, proceeded to polish off the bottle. Now in a jolly, pink-cheeked mood, Michael disappeared twice to return with beer for everyone.

By the time the plane finally arrived and it was time to board we were all feeling pretty good, but the German was snockered—so looped, in fact, that he literally had to be handed up and loaded through the baggage portal, laughing and hooting all the while. The rest of us used the stairs.

Once in Petropavlovsk, our first order of business was a long, hot shower, scrubbing away a week and half's worth of sweat, grime, and crud. A lot of credit goes to the creators of high-tech gadgetry for making our lives less complicated and more enjoyable, but it is my belief that whoever invented soap and shampoo was a genius. Next to clothes, those two items come the closest to making a person feel human. Then came a soak in the steaming waters of the natural hot springs, a tourist attraction at the small inn. It made me feel like a million bucks. Even as we floated in the heavenly waters, drinking German beer and talking over the adventures of the hunt, I could tell that Dale was already thinking up our next quest.

Australia
June 1999

Never had I received so many warnings on a hunt as when I arrived in the dark of night at Smith Point banteng camp in Arnhem Land, northern Australia.

"Don't go *near* the ocean's edge because of the crocs."

"Don't go *in* the water because of the sharks, stonefish, and marine stingers (jellyfish)."

"Don't wander about camp without a flashlight."

"Don't reach into dark places."

"Keep your tent zipped at all times because of the deadly snakes."

No wonder I had an overwhelming feeling of doom as I settled into my tent in the dark. Standing there in the stifling heat, the sweat pouring off me, undressing for bed, I thought, *What have I gotten myself into? One step on a snake and it will all be over. What a foolish risk to be taking when I've got a family to consider.* But as I lay there in bed confidence soon returned, and I felt better as my thoughts shifted to the banteng we would hunt the next morning. I wondered if the wild ox was as aggressive as I had been led to believe. Dale had been charged by his banteng at close quarters, forced to roll his scoped gun so as to aim down the barrel at it, dropping the beast only a few paces away. Everyone else I knew who had shot one had a similar story. I had to laugh when I realized how such thoughts of dangerous game were actually *calming* to me. But to a big-game hunter, dangerous game is a known quantity. Sharks, stonefish, and deadly sea creatures were not part of my expertise. Eager to begin the hunt, I tossed and turned most of the night until the early wakeup call at 4:30 A.M.

In the dark of early morning, all the guides and clients gathered in the dining tent on a short sand dune overlooking the ocean shore, the water of which I had yet to see in the light of day. But I could hear the soft waves, and the damp air carried the familiar smell of salt. My guide was Tom Condon, an affable fellow who is always quick with a well-timed joke or bit of wit. The sheared stubble of golden hair and beard and the encompassing freckles on his plain, smiling face made me guess Irish, but he is from New Zealand—a

"Kiwi," as he jokingly refers to himself. He is also the clear ringleader of any conversation in camp.

Leaving in the Land Cruiser at 5:30, we reached the hunting area an hour later, at which point we set out on foot. In the dim light I found myself watching the dark, leafy ground for snakes. It is a fact that Australia is home to several of the most poisonous snakes on the planet. Getting bitten by one would of course not be without irony for me, having written a short story entitled *A Mamba by Any Other Name* about an African hunter who suffered that exact fate. But as we marched along in the swampy woodlands, the sun dawned, and its early rays filtered around us, I put the thought out of mind and concentrated on the task at hand. We were soon hiking at a good clip. There is a natural calm that comes from the striding pace, especially in the wilds, and I was now in the groove of placing one foot in front of the other, trying to be quiet but trying also to keep up with Tom, who wanted to cover a good deal of country in a short period of time.

An hour later we were forced to traverse a mangrove swamp, sinking up to our calves in stagnant, stinking black muck; there was no way around it. Soon we came to a little clearing where a former client of Tom's had taken a banteng and the pigs had made a banquet of what was left. Bones and bits of hide were strewn about, and there were pig tracks everywhere. We then entered a mangrove thicket where visibility was no more than two or three feet. At times I had to brace my gun in front of me and push through the stuff as if through a reluctant revolving door, the stout branches slapping me in the face and the stubby roots tripping my feet. It was miserable. If you were to break an ankle in there, no one would ever find you. You would end your days as pig food. The sudden thought of having to track a wounded banteng there was sobering, as the odds were beyond calculation in the banteng's favor. No one in his right mind would bet on the hunter. The thick stuff only increased my resolve to make the first shot count when a banteng eventually filled my sights.

Luckily, we spent only one long hour in the nightmare thicket before emerging into more open terrain. We were no better off that I could see for having gone in, nor for the scratches.

Picking up the pace we then circled back into the woodlands, where we soon found dung and tracks of the wild ox—an encouraging find. Around 9:00 A.M., Tom suddenly stopped. Some forty yards in front of us was a mature bull, feeding. It was quite a sight. Tom asked if I would like it, if it was a suitable trophy, and thinking of never having to enter a mangrove thicket again, I liked it very much. The bull was light gray—almost white—and its horns were dark, pointed, and curled up like a bison's or a big Brahma bull's. It wasn't muscled like the big bulls you see in a rodeo, but it had my complete respect. If anything, the slimmer build made it quicker and more nimble on its feet; it was as dangerous as any animal you would ever want to hunt.

I sneaked to a near tree to use as a rest, but as luck would have it the bull did not offer a clear shot. There were trees and scrub in the way. When I tried to sneak to another position, the gray bull spied my movement and became instantly alert. At that same moment, Tom happened to be a step in front of me, fingers in his ears, ready for me to shoot. But I wasn't about to shoot from behind him. Taking a quick step forward, I put the cross hairs on the bull's shoulder and started to squeeze the trigger, but all the activity had been too much. The bull abruptly snorted and whirled before I could get off the shot.

We tried to find it again, tracking it on the soggy ground, but had no luck. The search continued for any shootable bull. After another hour or so of trekking through the marshy woods, and without sighting any banteng, we made our way back to the truck and got to camp around lunchtime. The weather wasn't so much hot as extremely humid, and the sweat had really flowed that morning. I was pleased with my gear: polyester pants, underwear, and socks, and a nylon fishing shirt. Unlike cotton, everything had remained light and dried quickly, despite the soaking it had been put through. Tom and I changed out of wet boots, placing them in the sun to dry, and put sandals on our damp, wrinkly feet. That is a daily ritual while hunting this swampy area—otherwise you risk foot rot and crippling blisters.

In the afternoon we went out for a short hunt. The temperature had seemingly dropped a few degrees since morning (or maybe it was just less humid), and there were no mangrove thickets to contend with in this particular area. Apart from the stagnant smell, I didn't mind the shallow swamps—it was the dense thickets that were no fun to negotiate. The afternoon's hike was a more pleasurable experience, and we covered a good bit of ground—though we encountered no banteng.

During the drive back, a nice black bull appeared in the thick stuff along the side of the road, but it was in the park area, where hunting is not allowed at this time of year. So we stopped just to glass it and for me to get a better look at what I was hunting: the banteng, an animal that had been the culprit in several tourist fatalities. It seems that park tourists, unfamiliar with banteng, had

The dining tent in banteng camp overlooks a magnificent but unusable beach.

tried to approach the animals for photos or had otherwise surprised them in the bush. Unfortunately, it was the tourists who got the surprise—receiving the sharp end of one or both horns. The government, in response, was apparently discussing plans to eradicate the banteng. That would be a real shame, as a little education might go a long way to solve the problem.

The next morning we left camp at 5:00 A.M., reaching just at dawn a grassy plain, the remnants of an abandoned airstrip and an area where Tom suspected we might catch a bull feeding early. We drove the length of the grassy strip with me standing in the back of the truck scouting, optimistic that we would find a bull in the hidden, covelike openings that led off the sides of the strip. But despite our early arrival at what was prime hunting time, and despite our optimism, not a single banteng put in an appearance.

Still, it had the look of perfect habitat. When the drive-by didn't work, we parked the truck and started out on foot. There was plenty of sign, which confirmed my habitat assessment, and we passed through several different ecosystems on that hike: woodlands (mostly), grassy strips (few), swamps (several), and fern–rain forest (mosquito country!). After we had negotiated the swamps my feet grew sore, my toes cramped in the tip of the boot from the socks having swelled with water.

Other than painful feet, though, the morning's march was quite pleasant and peaceful, with the hooting and cooing of the birds in the background. The ground around the marshy area, or "soak" as it is called, was littered with a thick carpet of eucalyptus leaves—big, banana-shaped leaves—and I could smell the soothing, medicinal quality of the eucalyptus in the damp air. Later some white birds looking like egrets flew over, making the most awful screeching—like crows with sore throats, retching. Tom turned around. "Not a very nice sound, is it?"

During this foray we scared up two bulls, each of which came bursting out of a bush not twenty-five yards distant. Both times the effect was immediate, about like getting hit with a pair of those electric paddles the ER folks use to start a patient's heart. The first time it was a dark black bull that, running, never offered a shot. I could have fired, but it's generally a bad idea to shoot at running game. Especially running dangerous game. A moment later another banteng bull pulled the same stunt, though we never got a good look at it. Having the bulls burst out of the brush like that was reminiscent of hunting quail, only here the flushing bulls sounded like grenades going off. And, unlike quail, these big-horned animals had the possibility of ruining your day. But it certainly made for the most exciting part of the hunt.

Around 11:00, on the return, we stopped in the woods to strategize. Looking past Tom through the trees, I saw a sudden movement 150 yards away. It was either a bird flying up or . . . a long tail swishing. I threw my binocular up and, sure enough, it was a tail, though I could not yet see the banteng that it was attached to. Tom confirmed it, and we dropped to a crouch, testing the wind and working out our approach.

Sneaking from tree to tree, we soon found two bulls. As we neared, we discovered there were actually five in total. They were feeding on the move, mingling in and out and making it hard to tell one from the other and to keep any particular bull in view. After some glassing Tom decided that a nice ginger one was the best of the lot, and I stepped forward to brace the gun against a tree. But now that I was well set up and steady, I could see only part of the bull, and it wasn't in an ideal position: A tree blocked the head and the front half of the shoulder, and it was quartering away. What with the thickness of the forest and the fickle wind, however, Tom decided that was the best shot we could hope for, and he gave the go-ahead.

I held a fair margin behind the bull's shoulder, not wanting to hit the tree, but also following protocol in trying to angle the bullet toward the far front leg, and quickly fired the .375. If the bull had any reaction to being hit, I never saw it, as my view was blocked momentarily by recoil. When I looked up, the bull was running to the right at full speed. I worked the bolt and fired a second time through the trees at its running form, which brought it to a stop forty yards from its original position. On the third shot it disappeared from sight. Whether it ran off or went down in the undergrowth, we couldn't tell. All was suddenly still. I quickly reloaded.

Up to this point, all our attention had been on the bull I was shooting. Now I looked up to see three bulls charging directly at us! I simply couldn't believe it. I thought, *These must be the most aggressive animals on earth! There are three of them and I have exactly three cartridges in the gun. Each one's gotta count!* Tom stepped directly behind me; he had no gun. It was all up to me. Despite the intimidating sight I was calm, and I knew what I had to do. Whether I could get all three before they got to us was a question, but I would do my best. That's all one can do.

I threw the gun up and drew down on the lead bull, put my finger on the trigger, and—but just then it veered. It must have been our movement, because all the bulls suddenly flared and ran wide of us. They weren't charging! They just hadn't seen us! We breathed a

Guide Tom Condon takes a break from the morning's hike.

sigh of relief as the big animals trundled past in the forest. (I don't know where the fourth bull went, but we never saw it again.) It's not that I wasn't up to the task of shooting three charging bulls with three cartridges, it's just that I was about half-certain that I wouldn't be needing my return airline ticket—unless it was for use in the luggage compartment.

With the other bulls out of the way, we were left to sort out the banteng I had shot, which was still nowhere in sight or sound. We gave it a minute, then started a slow circle up to where it had last been seen, on a slight rise. Most unsettling of all was that the old bull had been too quiet. I figured that it was either stone dead or five hundred yards away. The third option, of course, was that it was right there, in the brush, waiting silently for us.

We picked our way deliberately through the forest, pausing now and then to listen and glass ahead with our binoculars. Creeping forward, we soon found the ginger bull lying on its side, completely still—the first shot had done its work. Despite the reassuring pose, I gave an insurance shot in the shoulder as we approached. As they say in Africa, "It's the dead one that gets you."

We clasped hands at our success and marveled at the banteng at our feet, a beautiful ginger-colored bull with fine horns. Mature males come in ginger, black, or gray, with the ginger ones being the rarest. Its body condition was excellent, though it had little fat, even coming out of the wet season. The bullets we recovered in its hide had mushroomed perfectly—the Nosler Partitions had done their job.

After a quick skinning job, Tom loaded the heavy head and cape onto his shoulders and we started the long return hike to the car. Although we made the trip with the glowing satisfaction of the kill and the success of the hunt, it was also made with the burden of an eighty-pound load, so that the return seemed a whole lot farther than the way in. It was not the pleasurable hike that the morning had been. Knowing what a burden it was to carry, I took a couple of turns carting the awkward bundle. It was difficult holding onto the greasy, wet hide, and now and then the whole load would slip from my shoulders and tumble to the ground, the porter watching closely where the sharp horns went. I managed each stint until I was huffing and could go no farther, then gave the unwieldy load back to Tom. He looked at me in surprise.

"That's the first time a client has helped carry a banteng."

When we arrived at the car, about 1:00 P.M., we were both fairly covered in blood and stench. We were also in for some bad news. Tom reached into his pocket, then reached again, and I saw that look.

The forest is comprised of exotic trees, including eucalyptus, which cover the ground in banana-shaped leaves that fill the damp air with their distinctive, menthol aroma.

"No, don't tell me," I said.

"Damn! I must have lost them when I stopped to do my business this morning. They obviously fell out."

It would take several hours to retrace our steps, through the swamps and thick stuff, and to locate the exact spot where he had done his deed. It was miles away, and it would be dark by then. It was either that, wait to be rescued, or find another way to start the car. Lucky for me, Tom is a resourceful fellow. He set about taking the ignition apart, methodically removing the barriers that had been set in place by the manufacturer to prevent him doing exactly what he was doing. After an hour of jiggling this wire and that, and with the help of a screwdriver for a key, he got the motor started. I was glad, because I wasn't looking forward to spending the night there, not with all the mosquitoes about.

After a much-needed shower, I took a chair from the mess tent and sat out in the sun, wriggling my toes in the warm, white sand at my feet and enjoying a couple of beers and a celebratory cigar that I had purchased in Port Douglas. Alicia (Tom's wife) and Peggy the cook brought out a plate of appetizers: olives, pickles, crackers, and cheese. What a life! I had about twenty olives. I guess I was salt deprived from all the sweating I'd done. I sat there indulging and looking out over the most beautiful shoreline imaginable, with the bluest water and the whitest sand you ever saw, thinking what a shame it was not to be able to use this beach because of all the vicious critters. It was completely uninhabitable by humans, at least the sun-baking tourist variety, and probably a blessing for it. The poisonous menaces were nature's insurance against human development.

Then came a real treat. Peggy is also a masseuse, and she treated me to a twenty-minute back massage.

"It's going to be hard to convince folks back home that I was roughing it," I told them. "Ice cream for dessert and a back massage at night!"

We had dinner and still there was no sign of Greg Gibson, a friend from Shikar Safari Club, and his guide, Chris. They finally got in at 9:00 P.M., having gotten lost in the mangrove swamp at dark. They had wandered helplessly in the thick mangroves, and I felt for them. I knew firsthand that fighting your way through the stiff branches and stumbling over the knotty roots were tough enough during the day, let alone lost and in the dark. After stumbling into an opening, they had come to the same creek we had crossed, but it was deep. Suddenly the water swirled and fish started to jump into the air. Greg reckoned it was a croc and suggested they search for a shallower (safer) crossing. Their only light was from a small headlamp that Chris wore, and when they came upon a large snake lying in their path that refused to get out of their way, Greg realized that traipsing this country in the dark could be a fatal mistake. He also wondered how long the small batteries would last. Fortunately, they eventually found their way to the car.

Clayton and Modesta Williams, more friends from Shikar, were the other two hunters in camp. Clayton is well known for his oil and gas endeavors and his run for governor of Texas a few years back, but he is a rancher at heart. I enjoyed chatting with him on the subject and was amazed at his operations, which went way beyond the traditional raising of cattle and wildlife. The man is quite involved in the frontier of genetics research and other marvels of modern science, such as transplanting embryos from endangered sheep into domestic sheep. Theoretically, by using domestic sheep as surrogate mothers, a single pair of endangered sheep could produce hundreds of offspring.

Modesta arrived back in camp with a nice banteng as well. The woman is trim, petite, and pretty as any model. She always looks and dresses as if she had just stepped out of a New York fashion boutique, and on first impression you would think how terribly misplaced she must be in a backwoods hunting camp. Only you would be wrong. The lady is as tough as they come in her hunting pursuits, having collected the twelve sheep of the world, most of which are on terrain and in conditions that make this hunt look like a trip to the rifle range. Accordingly, she had my utmost admiration.

I slept in the next morning and took the day easy, getting caught up in my journal and chatting with Tom and the other guides. Later Greg arrived with a big smile and the best banteng of all. In the evening, Greg, Modesta, and I went fishing near the ranger station on a wooden pier that extended way out into the surf. We cut up pieces of shark for bait and placed them on big hooks. Greg caught a tiny, ugly fish that resembled the deadly stonefish. No one was brave enough to pull the hook out, so we cut the line and the fish scooted off the pier. Suddenly guide John's line sailed out as if it were tied to a bottle rocket. It kept going and going until finally I had to ask, "How much line do you have on that thing?" Not two seconds later there was a loud *pop* as the line ran out and snapped. It was a big fish, whatever it was.

A short while later my line zinged out, but just for a few seconds before it went still. John guessed it had been a shark. "Bit the line. Took the hook and all with him."

An Asian transplant, the banteng is a nimble ox with an aggressive, no-nonsense attitude. Given the chance it will ruin your day with a close-up charge.

Back in camp, Greg and I learned that we would fly out the following day, one day ahead of schedule, for buffalo camp. So after a celebration for the three banteng taken, everyone turned in for the night.

Our bush plane landed on the Dhuruputjpi camp airstrip about noon, and there we met Steven Joll (son of Gary Joll of Lillybank Lodge in New Zealand) and Noel Bleakley, who had guided both my dad and Dale Bilhartz in the past. Noel seemed glad to meet me.

"I know your dad," he said. "Your dad helped me follow up a wounded buffalo that another client had shot. Got a charge out of that one, we did." Noel is a skinny runt of a fellow with a hook nose and a quick wit. You might not think much of him at first sight, but Noel is the guy you want beside you when the buffalo charges. I had heard of Dale's adventures from a couple of years back, the story of how he and Noel were forced to stand back-to-back in the swamp, in water up to their waists, the buffalo surrounding them and approaching on all sides, chuffing at them and promising to charge. They were hunting a remote area where the buffalo had never seen man, and the animals' curiosity brought them to within a few close yards before they lost interest and wandered off.

The third guide was Gary Harvey. Jamie, a young burly chap with a shaved head, was the cook. Jack Beal, Bob Powell, and Jim Cummings from Shikar were in camp with us, and all had got buffalo. They were spending their last day fishing and drinking rum— mostly drinking rum. Jamie pulled me aside later that night in disbelief and said, "I don't know how they are still standing. They've polished off a bottle and a half of rum, a bottle of brandy, and who knows how much vodka!" Being a brash army man in his early twenties, Jamie was no stranger to heavy drinking. But my friends did not appear drunk. Sitting around the dining table, they were all smiling and just as pleasant and coherent as could be, eager to relate the adventures of their hunts. Jack, a giant of a man with a deep rumble in his voice that vibrates your chest, joked about his clean thirteen-shot kill. They were a pleasure to have in camp. Since we were a bit crowded, I shared a tent with Bob that night, who proceeded to snore like the buffalo he had spent a week hunting.

Steven and I set out after lunch in the Land Cruiser. The area reminded me of the *miombo* forests of Tanzania, without the occasional open pans. Here the forest was endless, and the termite mounds were more frequent and constructed in a different shape. Instead of being round the tall mounds were long and narrow, standing like misplaced doors in the forest and running north to south, an ingenious design that derives maximum heat from the sun's daily travel from east to west. The termite mounds are mostly beige, like the sand, but where the earth is black they too are black. Driving along, you can be fooled into thinking that a buffalo is standing in the distance. I was deceived a couple of times and cried, "Buffalo!" only to stop and glass and find that it was a termite mound I was looking at. Instead of *miombo* the trees are paperbark trees, which shed their thin skins so that all of the forest looks like it is molting. We saw no buffalo, but we did run into a small group of feral pigs. We followed after them on foot, and I spotted a solid black one running in the grass. It came to a stop forty yards away, and I rolled it with a well-placed shoulder shot.

We continued on, covering a fair amount of country, and I was quite surprised not to see a single buffalo. In fact, I had expected to witness great herds throughout the day, wherever we went. I'd been told that the beasts were plentiful and that it was not a matter of getting one but of looking the vast herds over and stalking the one you liked best.

"It's the monsoon," Steven explained. "It's got the buffalo scattered all to hell. This is quite unusual." Before my arrival, the area had received a phenomenal eighty inches of rain. The camp had flooded— in fact, it had to be abandoned. (The cook showed me the watermark on the wall of the dining tent, some three feet above the ground!) Things had dried out some since, but, as Steven said, the monsoon had scattered the buffalo and left us with some tricky bogs to negotiate. Hunting is generally easier in dry weather, as the animals are forced to seek and congregate at the remaining water holes. Because it was wet, the buffalo might be anywhere, which probably meant they would be in the thickest, nastiest stuff they could find. So it appeared we had our work cut out for us. It wasn't going to be easy to find them, but at least we had five full days in which to do it.

That evening dinner came and went, and once again poor Greg did not show.

"They are lost or broken down," Noel said, pacing back and forth in the dining tent. At 9:00 P.M., Noel and Steven left to find them. What had happened was this: Greg had shot a nice bull just before sundown. The bull ran off, leaving an impressive blood trail and leading them to believe that they would find it any minute. But the blood trail continued for several hundred yards, and they ended up following it until the brush grew thick and the light dim. At last, they jumped the bull at close range. Each fired a shot, and the bull thundered off into the thick stuff. But by that point it was too dark to see their way after the bull. It was also too dark to see their way back to the car, and neither had a flashlight. After four hours of stumbling around in the dark, they finally had to admit that they were lost, and they simply sat down and surrendered to the mosquitoes. The wicked bloodsuckers were merciless in their triumph.

Around 11:00 P.M., our lost companions spotted Noel's headlights and fired a shot into the air. As it turned out, they had been only 150 yards from their car.

They all got into camp a little after 1:00 A.M. Greg was not too happy, having got lost twice on one trip. Wandering in the outback dark like that is a great way to step on a snake, twist an ankle, or get permanently lost. When hunting such immense and featureless country as this—where getting lost is about as easy as stepping out of your vehicle—it pays to keep essential gear on your person at all times. In the excitement of the chase, however, Gary had left everything at the truck—GPS, flashlights, matches, everything.

In the morning, it was decided that the four of us would go together to track down Greg's wounded buffalo, which in practice turned out to be every bit as exciting as it sounded. The dangers of tracking a wounded African Cape buffalo are legendary, but many folks are not familiar with the Australian water buffalo, an animal of the same size and weight and equally capable of ruining your health. The guides had an interesting

The long, sweaty journey back to the vehicle.

explanation for that: "The only reason people think the African buffalo is more dangerous is that the Africans are better story tellers."

The drive, however, was slow and tedious. The monsoon had made a mess of the dirt tracks, requiring us to winch our way past several gooey bogs and to pull ourselves from one tree to the next when negotiating the longer stretches of muck. There were also a few creeks we had to cross, demanding the same assistance of the winch.

As it was, we did not reach the spot where the buffalo had been shot until nearly 11:00 A.M. Once armed and ready, it was easy to see why our comrades had been encouraged to believe the buffalo was close at hand. Blood marked the ground like the yellow painted lines on a highway, and it was equally easy to follow. It was no lie that the buffalo had bled profusely and continuously. The trail led for nearly half a mile (per GPS) to a bloodstain the size of a bathtub where the bull had lain in wait on the inside edge of a thicket and where they had jumped it, firing their final shots. After that, the blood trail suddenly stopped.

Well, the wounded buffalo was either in the thicket or it wasn't, and there was only one way we were going to find out. Fanning out four abreast, we started into the thicket in the direction the bull had last been heard crashing away. We were looking for more blood, broken limbs, or a dead buffalo—but not necessarily in that order. Looking for a live, wounded, and angry buffalo was our first priority. It would be an understatement to say that this search got our blood pumping: easing through the thicket, peering into the shadows, wondering when the buffalo would charge, how fast it would come, and how well I would perform. Like a quarterback envisioning his next touchdown pass, I practiced mounting the gun in my mind, shooting the charging bull between its angry black eyes, and seeing it fall in a spray of dirt at my feet. I debated removing the detachable scope and going with open sights, but in the end I opted for the lowest setting of 1½X. The hardest part of the search, however, was not in keeping an eye out for the bull.

The hardest part was in trying to keep track of each other's whereabouts in the thicket so no one ended up in the line of fire, for we were all out of sight of one another and had only the sounds of pushing back bush and the occasional voice to go by. It was a slow and deliberate process, and I kept expecting one of us to come upon the wounded animal at any moment. At length, however, we had combed every foot of the thicket and seen nothing of the wounded bull.

Arriving at the other end of the thicket, we found neither blood nor tracks. Clearly the wounded bull had left the thicket, and the search had to be carried on in the surrounding open country. I differed with Gary on how to go about it. Gary chose to pursue a straight course through the wooded forest. At three hundred yards or so, I suggested we return to the thicket and begin ever-widening circles, looking for blood. Stubbornly, Gary shook his head and continued the march to a thousand yards. In my opinion, after two hundred yards we were wasting our time, but he was the boss. The odds of our being on the bull's exact path at a thousand yards, with no tracks or blood to go by, were about twenty to one against us. On the way back Steven and I jumped a bull at some distance, and our guns went up quickly, but it wasn't ours. Fortunately we didn't fire. The only thing worse than having a wounded buffalo on your hands is having two wounded buffaloes on your hands. Gary and Greg got separated on the long trek (my opinion of Gary quickly dropping—you're not supposed to lose track of your client), and we soon found Greg marching solo. We encountered one more buffalo on the way back, but it wasn't the wounded one either. Although the nearly four-hour search had been in vain, I was glad for the chance to have participated. Following up a wounded buffalo, whether mine or someone else's, is much more exciting than hunting a new bull from scratch.

It was past 2:30 when we arrived at the vehicles and broke out lunch. At 3:30, Gary mentioned that he and Greg were going to carry

Guide Gary Harvey and Greg Gibson back at the Jeep after an intense search for a wounded buffalo.

on *away* from camp. Good thing I was sitting down when he said it, or I would have fallen down.

"It's three hours till sundown," I said, "and it's two hours from here to camp. That doesn't leave much time, does it?" I hated to sound arrogant, but he had already lost Greg one night. Why push for two in a row? The man wasn't thinking. Steven chimed in his agreement, then pointed out that Gary's winch was not reliable, as it had frozen up the day before. After some reflection Gary soon agreed, and we all headed back. We saw a few cows and calves but no bulls. Everyone applauded Gary when he arrived in camp a few minutes after we did.

The whole of the following day we saw only a couple of cows and calves. But it was not for lack of trying. We covered miles and miles of country. Then, right before dark, we spotted two small herds emerging from a thicket, and we got out and stalked the closer bunch. When the first herd proved to be only cows and calves, I suggested we try the second: We still had a little light left.

"No," Steven said, "let's wait to see if a bull will show."

Sure enough, a bull stepped out a minute later, but it was not quite what we were looking for. That was really too bad, because crouched there on the ground, with my rifle at the ready, I had it dead to rights. It would have been the perfect ambush, too, assuming that I had made the perfect shot—for the bull had to take but a single step to disappear into the thickest scrub imaginable, and it was now close to dark. Even if it wasn't a shooter, the stalk up on the herd had been exciting, and getting in place undetected and having the jump on it like that was 90 percent of the fun. It was what the Indians of old must have experienced when taking coup—touching or tapping an enemy and leaving him unharmed but with the knowledge that you could have killed him if you had wanted to.

When we finally rose to depart, the buffalo all whirled to face us. Like its African cousin, the Australia buffalo looks down its nose at you, trying to get a sniff of what you are. The Australia buffalo is a big animal, and it had earned every bit of my respect. Under the current conditions they were not traveling in large herds, seeming to prefer bands of two, three, four, or sometimes ten. As I said, I had expected to see herds of several hundred. They were also proving harder to hunt than I had imagined. The banteng hunt was the one that I had expected to be most difficult. In fact, I had assumed only a 50 percent success rate going into it.

We didn't see much the next morning, but a real treat came while afield at noon. We had just eaten lunch and were sitting at the edge of

Steven Joll poses beside a large termite mound.

a swamp chatting when I heard something splish-splashing in the water. A moment later a couple of dingoes emerged from the swamp. Quickly retrieving my gun, I stepped forward and rested the stock against a tree but did not have a clear shot before they trotted out of sight. I tried to stalk them but was unsuccessful. I was just standing there, listening and watching, trying to decide which way the red, coyote-sized dogs had gone, when one of them appeared in the corner of my eye. The wily critter had circled back on me. At thirty-five yards I took it offhand as it trotted past. I considered the dingo a rare trophy and was glad to have gotten one, but I didn't take the head because it was just too doglike for a trophy room. This pooch was emaciated, too—either sick or starving. It had barely hit the ground before its lank face was covered in meat ants. Its death was their gain. Mother Nature wastes nothing.

Steven relayed a funny story about the local Aborigines, who live in a small village near camp. When the buffalo camp was abandoned after the April floods, an Aborigine bloke decided to "borrow" their boat, which was in keeping with their custom that each has a right to any property owned by another. (Gary claims that Aborigines are the "original communists." As soon as one gets any money or property it is taken—"shared"—by the others. Thus an accumulation of wealth or a higher standard of living is impossible.) However, when the wife of the fellow who had "borrowed" the boat wanted to use it, the fellow apparently was strongly disinclined, as he proceeded to chop several holes in the bottom with an ax. Retrieving the craft, Jamie was able to patch the holes, but the boat still leaked when used to fish the wide river that ran beside camp.

A tiger snake went under my tent that day while I was out hunting. It was three feet long, dark black, and, of course, deadly. Jamie saw it duck under and enlisted Gary's assistance to kill it. "Sweeping" the floor of the tent, Gary flushed it out with a broom, and Jamie dispatched it with .22 ratshot.

That was the second snake in camp during my stay. In Africa the campground is raked free of all grass, weeds, and shrubs in order to make seeing snakes easier. Here that was not done. Of course the Australians don't have the readily available labor pool to accomplish the task, though that needn't be the case. The Aborigines, who get paid by the government simply for being Aborigines, are not interested, and there is a minimum wage of ten dollars an hour for hiring these native people. Consequently no one can afford to hire them, and the natives remain on the dole. The upshot is that the

Here I am with my last-minute buffalo.

natives learn no modern skills or trade, and the country misses out on the fruits of their labor.

Out early the next morning we spotted a couple of herds and stalked them, but whereas the buffalo had been fairly calm and uninterested in us the first couple of days, today they were skittish and cautious. Maybe it was our body language, and they were reading us the way a zebra reads a crouching lion. Somehow they knew that we were nearing the end of the hunt and that we meant business. Because their sixth sense was in high gear, we couldn't get close enough even to see if there were any good bulls. Each time we approached they either sighted us or winded us and stormed off. Then by 9:30 we stopped seeing buffalo altogether. It seemed that this buffalo hunting was really going to prove a challenge.

Outsmarted as we had been thus far by our quarry, Steven decided that we needed to take a different approach. At midday, abandoning the vehicle and the few passable roads that we had been forced to travel, we loaded our guns and ventured on a long hike through the swamp and surrounding woodlands. The water was knee-deep in places and the mud beneath it as adhesive as freshly poured cement, but I truly enjoyed making new tracks through unexplored country. There is something of the explorer in all of us, and it is good for the heart to see new country. Despite my love of wilderness wandering, however, I am often the first person to get lost, so I made a conscious effort to pay particular attention during our ramblings through the swamp and woods. That was no easy task, with no landmarks of any kind in sight. Making it even more difficult was the fact that everything looked the same—every tree, every bush, every feature. I'm sure that even the buffaloes would have looked the same had we seen any. We didn't see a single ox. Nonetheless, it was worth the try and enjoyable just the same.

When it came time to return to the car, Steven headed south.

"Wait a minute. I thought the car was that way, west."

Steven switched on the GPS, and damned if the truck wasn't west, as I had said. That was a first—my outguessing the guide on the direction back! Without the GPS, who knows how long we might have been out there? And we weren't in any shape for an aimless trek through the bush. Our feet were soaked and our legs tired from plodding through the sucking mud and water.

When we got back to the truck, I could tell that poor Steven was getting discouraged. He was trying as hard as he possibly could, but a hunter can do only so much. In order to achieve success, the quarry must cooperate, to a certain degree.

We spent the remainder of the afternoon driving the high ground, staring into the shadows of the swamps and mud wallows, willing a buffalo bull into existence. It had been a good hunt, and whether we met with success or not I was proud of how it had started. On our first afternoon out, Steven had asked me what kind of bull I was looking for. Did I want a "sweeper" (wide horns that go almost straight out) or a "lunar" (moon-shaped)? The former was probably more to my liking, but since I had never shot a water buffalo, I indicated that either would be fine. Did I require a certain score? When I shook my head and laughed as if at a joke, he stopped me and said he was serious. He went on to tell me that he'd had clients actually arrive with a photocopy of the record book, their friends' names highlighted, and stating that they had to shoot a bigger bull than so-and-so. I don't know what you call that, but it ain't hunting.

"Today there are too many people hunting with a gun in one hand and a record book in the other," I told him. "They have completely missed the point." Perhaps it is a symptom of our overly competitive society. Whatever the reason, too many Americans bring their hard-driving work personality to the hunting camp, where it is unwelcome and out of place. Once there, they continually prod and push their guides, making everyone miserable in the process. Shaking my head again and sighing, I ended with, "Tell you what, let's just go have some fun and hunt buffalo!" An ear-to-ear smile had filled Steven's young face. I knew he felt the same.

So, still enjoying myself, I had now reached the last hour of the last day of the hunt, and we were on our way slowly back to camp. It didn't look like a buffalo was in my future—not on this hunt, anyway. But that was hunting, and I'd known that going into it. I'd had a great time and a wonderful experience, which was what hunting was all about. So we just drove along and stared out opposite sides of the car, the sun dropping closer and closer to the horizon. Not much was said: We had discussed every movie, song, and joke we knew. All our favorite hunting stories had been told and retold. Spending hours a day in close quarters with your guide, you get to know each other pretty well.

Then we came around a corner, and there, suddenly in front of us, was a big buffalo bull. I saw it first and said, "Buffalo—can I shoot it?"

"Quickly," was all Steven said.

I stepped out, and the instant the cross hairs touched its shoulders I pulled the trigger. The old, solitary bull staggered, and I fired again at the shoulder. It started to run, now facing straight away, and I shot it in the hip with a solid that had been intentionally placed at the bottom of the magazine and that couldn't have been planned better. The bull veered to the left, and I knew that it had been well hit for I could see the blood pumping out its side with each breath. Hastily I reloaded and fired a fourth shot, this one quartering to the far shoulder. With the blow the bull turned back to the right and fell to its knees. Immediately I put a fifth bullet into the right shoulder. The buffalo rolled onto its side, and an insurance shot in the brisket ended the chase.

That was one tough animal, and we were two happy hunters. Needless to say, we had worked hard for it, and we both felt the victory was well earned—the best feeling to have with a trophy at your feet. Then came the chore of butchering and caping—the last completed in the beam of the headlights—and loading it all into the back of the truck.

"It was a clean six-shot kill," I joked in camp.

"You were down to the last hour of the last day," Gary remarked.

"Well, I always like to get my money's worth. No sense in shooting one the first day."

"I can appreciate that," Gary said. "I appreciate a hunter who likes to get full value out of his hunt, expecting to hunt until the very last minute. Of course, Steven cheated you out of forty-five minutes of

My last-minute fish: a purplish-scaled, 6-pound saratoga.

your hunt, and you should lodge a complaint! In fact, you should talk to the outfitter about a refund!" Everyone had a good laugh.

In the morning I went with Jamie to fish the river by camp. As we loaded into the boat, the young cook joked that he was trying to make up for the forty-five minutes of missed hunting. We poled our way across the dark shallows of the connecting swamp, between trees and over bulging roots, until we reached the river itself, which was wide, dark, and flowing gently, like what you would expect of the Amazon, with a canopy of huge-rooted trees overhead. Armed with bait-casting reels and large, colorful lures, we tried for barramundi, but nothing bit. Here in the deep water a small outboard whisked us along, and we stopped now and then to check the yabbi traps secured with thin rope from low overhanging limbs. We found a total of three yabbies—a dark, freshwater crustacean somewhere in size between a shrimp and a lobster.

In keeping to form for this trip, in the last two minutes of fishing I caught a six-pound saratoga. It is a good-looking fish with pink-rimmed scales on its long, sleek body, and it put up quite a fight. After lunch we went to the airstrip to await the bush plane from Darwin. Then came a delightful dinner on the wharf with the Williamses and a phone call home to check on the troops. Once I had heard those precious words, "Everybody is OK," I could relax for the long flight back. "No worries," as they say in Australia. The flight home was on my birthday, and I could drag the celebration out to thirty-nine hours or so with the time change back to Dallas.

One last word of advice. When in Australia, don't touch it and don't pet it. Chances are it's venomous.

Mongolia
September 2000

It is no easy feat to reach the High Altai Mountains of Mongolia. There are four days of travel involved, including six airplane jaunts and eight hours of rough riding in a 4x4. You arrive in the capital city of Ulan Bator on day three, and chances are it is cold and windy. Ulan Bator is nothing special as a city, and you spend the night in the Chinggis Khan Hotel, which is nothing special as a hotel, except for its twelfth-century namesake (known as Ghengis Khan at home), who is synonymous with adventure. So perhaps that was what did it for me.

Every hunt has a starting place—a place where the hunt seems to come to life, where you can taste the excitement in the air, sense the quarry at hand, or feel the adventure sweeping you along, and for me this hotel was the place. So on night three (or what would have been night three had we not stopped for some sightseeing in Beijing), Dale Bilhartz and I found ourselves in the Chinggis hotel bar drinking Chinggis beers. In no time we were reliving past hunts and adventures and fantasizing over the high-climbing ibex we would soon be hunting. I was glad I had packed warm clothes. Camp would be twice the current altitude of 4,500 feet, and much colder.

On the morning of the fourth day, two fellows from Mongol Safaris collected us: Geleg, a big, beefy fellow, the epitome of what you would picture a big Mongolian to look like, and his son Uzee, nearly as big, who would serve as our interpreter. Geleg, at first glance, was a little frightening. Apart from his great bulk, the right half of his face is deformed—through injury or defect—so that it is quite swollen and presses outward, making him speak out of the left side of his face. But his true personality showed through when we stepped outside to the awaiting car and I asked Dale to take a picture of us—Geleg on one side of me and Uzee on the other. He said, "You can tell them back home that we are your bodyguards. We are here to protect you from beautiful Mongolian women." Although cursed with a misshapen face, he showed his heart by his laugh. I liked the giant instantly.

Inside, the airline terminal was chaos. The people at the ticket counter were yelling and waving at the ticket agents like frenzied

Dale and I are inside the Forbidden City, off limits to locals, much less tourists, for centuries. It features 9,999 rooms, one less than God's house, the number deemed fit for an emperor.

traders on the floor of a stock exchange. Uzee flung himself into the crowd, persevered, and got us checked on. The airplane was an ancient Russian model with twin props that rode surprisingly well during the two-hour journey to Tosontsen-Gel, in the Zarkhan province, where we stopped for fuel and to let everyone, including the pilots, have a smoke in the shade of the wing as it was being filled with fuel. Dale and I took a few steps back—way back. Then it was another hour-plus flight to the small town of Khovd. There we were met by our driver, Jagar, who was well dressed in slacks and tweed golf hat. He is a tall thin fellow with jet-black hair, high cheekbones, and the deep creases at the temples that come from squinting against a lifetime of strong winds. Jagar secured all the bags, and we left in a Russian 4x4 outfitted in Persian rug seat covers.

After a quick lunch we started our lengthy drive across the Mongol steppe, on dirt roads that spoked off in all directions from town. How Jagar knew which ones to take was beyond me until I realized that driving across the steppe was probably more a matter of keeping to a certain direction than it was picking a particular road. In the middle of nowhere, several herds of double-humped camels plodded across the barren terrain, headed to Blackwater Lake in the distance for a drink. Grass was nonexistent—there were just rocky rubble, sand,

and dirt in any direction you looked. There was not a patch of green anywhere in sight, except along the perimeter of the dark lake. It appeared that the drought had been as severe as we had been told. The wildlife had to be living off fat reserves and a prayer, for there was nothing for it to eat. My hope was that the ibex, high in the mountains, were better off. Surely, the altitude had brought them wetter weather.

The roads grew rough and bumpy as the elevation increased and we entered the roller coaster terrain of the Altai Mountains. Once the dark of night came it was difficult to stay awake, but it was also impossible to sleep with my head bouncing like a basketball from the rough ride. It was near midnight when we finally arrived in camp. Half comatose and stumbling from the 4x4, I shook quick hands with the smiling staff that came out to greet us, went promptly into our *ger* (Russian for "yurt"), too tired to notice whether I had adhered to custom and entered to the left for men or to the right for women, pulled out my sleeping bag, kicked off my shoes, climbed in, and fell into a deep sleep. Before I drifted off one of the lady cooks arrived with plates of food, but I just said, *"Bayarla"*—thank you. I was too sleepy to eat.

Chinese houseboat.

The Great Wall, one of man's greatest, lasting architectural achievements, right up there with the Great Pyramids of Egypt.

Although camp, per GPS, was only 149 miles as the crow flies from Khovd, the actual mileage, twisting and turning, up and down the mountains, was much more. I was eager to test the nifty gadget, as this would be my first hunt with it. With a price tag of less than $150 at Wal-Mart, I consider the GPS as important a tool in the modern-day checklist of camping essentials as a first-aid kit and a water bottle—maybe even more so. But, like any tool, its use requires practice, and no tool can ever replace common sense. I had been warned not to expect to pull it new from the box at camp and feel comfortable with it. So I had taken mine on hikes around the neighborhood, learning its quirks, and used it driving in the car on family vacations.

Because of our late arrival, the Mongols let us sleep until 7:00 A.M. I was awake by 5:00 but remained snug in my bag, as the temperature was in the twenties. So I lay there in the dark thinking about the hunt ahead until it got light enough to take in the accommodations, which had failed to make an impression on last night's unconscious mind. The *ger* was surprisingly spacious and comfortable in its furnishings. With a diameter of nineteen or twenty feet and a high, teepeelike ceiling, it had room for three beds, a table and chairs, and a box stove in the center. The stove was fueled by dried yak dung, though camel, pony, and goat dung were used as well. It put out a great deal of heat but only for a short time without refueling. After a quick breakfast of sausage and omelets, we piled—and I mean "piled"—into the Russian 4x4. We headed south into the mountains with Jagar and Dale in front; me, my guide Erka, Dale's guide Dashka, and sumo-sized Uzee in the back.

Here I should say something of the mountains in which we were hunting. The Altai is an ancient mountain range whose peaks have eroded with the eons of time. What were once sheer slopes and pointy summits have weathered and crumbled, and the valleys have filled with the resulting rubble and debris. Thus over time the mountains have dropped and the valleys risen, straining to meet in the middle. As a result the mountains are "rounded" on top and roll from one to another, giving the impression of a prairie but on a grander scale. Although most are of the rounded, rolling variety, allowing you to drive right up onto the flattened peaks, there still remain a few steep mountains with craggy rocks at the tops or in the bowls.

We drove high into the saddle of two mountains, got out, and hiked the last few hundred yards to the top. I was huffing and puffing in the thin air—although it was not really that high, as mountain hunts go, maybe twelve thousand feet. Once we got on top we were greeted with a tremendous view. We could see the mountain range and the plains below extending out in every direction—a beautiful sight.

Although it was beautiful, it was also dangerously dry and empty. Looking over this barren expanse of land, it was not difficult to imagine what Ghengis Khan had faced during similar droughts and the effects that disastrous weather had had on his nomadic people. With nothing for their starving herds to eat, they had to go somewhere, so they went south to China. Apparently it was a pattern that had been repeated over and again, for the Chinese began construction on the Great Wall in an effort to keep the raiding barbarians out centuries before the great Mongol conqueror was even born. At one point the emperor of China conscripted a million peasants (one-fifth of the population!) for ten years of service to erect the wall.

I was glad we had taken time in Beijing to see this incredible structure, for it is one thing to read about the Great Wall and quite another to stand there and actually experience it. It is an impressive sight, to say the least. This barrier, which winds up and over and about the mountains like an unending serpent for as far as the eye can see, is strategically built on the steepest and most inaccessible terrain. The Great Wall was constructed so as to make it nearly impossible to assault, and it also had to be the most difficult construction for the men who built it. Standing on the Great Wall, I could feel history beneath my feet.

Now slipping down and around the side of this twin peak, we arrived at an outcrop of rock that offered an unhindered view in several directions. Soon we spotted four male ibex resting in a craggy bowl half a mile away. Erka used my spotting scope to confirm that one was *tom*—large. Excitedly, we skittered down the mountain to the 4x4, drove quickly over to the neighboring mountain, and then ascended on foot, trying to minimize the crunch of rock we made with each step near the top. Although we glassed and glassed, however, we never caught sight of those four ibex again. They had smelled us or heard us and moved off to parts unknown—which was probably just as well. It would have been a little too easy to shoot one right out of the box like that. It was a good example of the fine balance that exists in big-game hunting, the eternal quandary in which the big-game hunter finds himself: wanting to find and shoot his quarry immediately, yet wanting his quarry to remain difficult to find and to shoot. That fine balance is what makes for great hunting.

Deciding that they could move much faster and more quietly without us lowland city folks slowing them down, Erka and Dashka then made a long pilgrimage out on their own. Later I spotted Erka on

A Mongolian tot with a melon bought from a street vendor.

A double-humped camel on the incredibly desolate steppe leading up to the Altai Mountains.

another ridge, an incredible distance away. Secretly, I wished I could have kept up with him, but I also knew it would take a couple of days to acclimate to the altitude. He was gone about two hours but saw nothing. We returned to the car and continued in another direction, then stopped for a short lunch of mutton sandwiches. The guides didn't eat much. They had a small tin of tuna each and our leftover sandwiches. I ate only about half of mine, as the meat had a greasy taste I did not care for.

After lunch, the procedure changed. We began to drive some of the valleys and ravines, stopping now and then to let Erka, Dashka, and Jagar scamper up the rocks to scout. It was a little embarrassing that we appeared in such poor shape, but if there was any consolation it was that young Uzee was huffing even more loudly than Dale and I. The rest of the group were middle-aged: Dashka, the only one who doesn't smoke, was the oldest but looked the youngest of the three. There is nothing more frustrating than hunting high country, gasping for each breath, only to find your guide with a cigarette in his mouth and progressing with ease.

Around 3:00 P.M. the wind whipped up and dark clouds moved in. We even got a light sprinkle of rain. In one saddle the wind was blowing so hard that the car rocked as if driving down a bumpy road—only it was parked at the time. When Dale stepped out his hat blew off like a kite, and he had to chase it down into the bottom of a ravine, where the wind finally brought it to rest. Then, about four o'clock, with the clouds and strong wind showing no sign of letting up, the guides decided we were wasting our time, that we should head for camp and try again in the morning. Although we saw no sign of living animals, driving the bottoms of the ravines we found two argali sheep heads and a total of fourteen ibex skulls. My first thoughts ran to meat poachers or wolves. Dale's explanation, though, made sense: Over time everything tumbles into the ravine, making it a final graveyard of sorts for the wildlife in the area.

We got into camp for dinner, which featured vegetable soup (with enough salt to float a brick), baked chicken (good), a shredded salad of sorts (heavy on the vinegar), and sliced carrots and pickles. The *coup de grâce* arrived in the form of an after-dinner bowl of harmless-looking yogurt. Yak yogurt. One bite was enough to knock you down. I admit I'm not a big fan of yogurt, but this stuff was like dynamite. For a moment, we were at a loss what to do. There was no way we could eat it, but we hated to leave it and appear rude.

"What if we pour it out at the side of the *ger*?" I suggested.

This yurt (ger) will be home for the next week.

Complete with a table and chairs, dung-burning stove, and cots, the ger *was quite comfortable.*

"Well, she'll probably figure we loved it and show up with an even bigger bowl tomorrow!"

In the end we left it untouched, unwilling to face the worse fate.

Before turning in for the night, it was time for something I had been looking forward to all day. On a chair outside the *ger*, I set up the satellite phone in the dark and called home. Five-year-old Lauren was awake and mad at me for leaving town. I told her I would not do it again for a long time, and she said, "That's what you always say!" How is that to make you feel guilty? I spoke to everyone, and it was wonderful to hear their voices—like a great weight off my chest. Deeply content, I turned to the night sky and stared up at the plentiful bright stars, shrugged against the cold breeze chilling my neck, and smiled to myself while Dale anxiously made his own phone call home.

It was then I realized that my homesickness on the hunt was not unique. It occurred to me that hunters everywhere and across all times have had to contend with it. Although eager for the meat and hides the hunt would bring, even cavemen, I'm sure, had dealt with the same conflicting emotions that we do—of wanting to be on the hunt yet also wanting to be home with mate and kids.

But there is another factor, which is the benefit that comes from being away. Although it is perhaps hard on young kids, time away is actually *good* for a marriage, because everyone needs time alone. You need a break from anyone you have been around for days on end. My parents once commented how few couples in the Dallas Safari Club were divorced. That is particularly ironic, because many of those fellows catch a tremendous amount of grief over the long hunting trips they take, often kidded that their wives will get fed up and leave them. But just the opposite is true. The wives relish the time apart. I know my mom is happy for the chance to dawdle and get "house things" done while Dad is gone. And I'm sure Alexandra is glad to have my sour puss out of the house for a while. The old saying, Absence makes the heart grow fonder, is aptly applied here. So go on a long hunting trip and save your marriage. You owe it to your spouse!

At 2:30 A.M. I awoke in the dark of the *ger* and couldn't fall back to sleep, so I simply lay in my warm bag thinking over the first half of our adventure and what was ahead of us. I had a feeling that one of us might get lucky today, and I wondered how high and how far and how difficult of a shot it might be. I fantasized how the shot would look in the scope.

Erka came to wake us at 5:00, and soon the cook arrived with our breakfast of sardines and crackers, which was a bit unusual for breakfast but an immense improvement over anything from a yak. In long johns, wool pants, insulated boots, and a thick coat, I was sitting at the table shivering when I noticed that the heavyset lady appeared comfortable in nothing warmer than a T-shirt and sweat pants. Not a single goose bump showed on her fleshy arms, and it made me feel like a real wimp. I guess her tolerance to the cold was to be expected (as was my susceptibility to it, having just left the Texas August heat). When you live in a country where the thermometer regularly plunges to minus 40 degrees Fahrenheit in winter, 20 above must feel like springtime. The Mongols are used to the cold the way the Kalahari Bushmen are used to the heat. If they were to trade places, I wouldn't be surprised if both races abruptly perished from exposure.

We got off in the dark around 5:30 A.M. Fortunately, it was my turn to sit up front and Dale's turn to be crunched in the back. At daybreak, we passed some likely looking mountains on the left that to me had "ibex" written all over them. I wondered aloud if we should try for ibex here, and not a minute later we turned off toward the tall peaks. I don't know if it was my question or their original plan, but that was where we headed.

Jagar brought the car to a stop at the base of the mountains near the opening of a large ravine, and once our gear and guns were situated we started the long hike upward. Right off the bat we glimpsed several

A young Mongolian shepherd astride his pony. These small but hearty horses permitted Ghengis Khan and his men to travel great distances.

females—an encouraging sight. They trotted quickly out of view, and we continued our way up the long, steady slope, craning our necks to glimpse the high terrain on either side. An hour later, as our group made slow but steady progress in the increasing altitude, four male ibex appeared on the slope of a great bowl above us. They were feeding and hadn't yet eyed us. Quickly we dropped below a ridge near the bottom of the ravine and glassed them in turns, so that no more than one of our heads was poking up at a time. After some further glassing and discussion, the guides decided that the horns on the best billy would go forty-one inches; the others they thought were much smaller.

A good ibex is forty-two inches, a great one forty-five. Without any hesitation, Dale and I agreed that we would be happy with this male. But who was going to be the one to hunt it? This hunt had been billed as a one-on-one, meaning one hunter with one guide, and normally such a question wouldn't come up: Dale and his guide would go one way, my guide and I another. But our guides worked well together and seemed reluctant to separate. Admittedly there was only one interpreter, but that was a minor concern. You can do amazing things with hand signals. I know; I have done it many times.

But now that a choice had to be made, it was time to flip a coin. Since no one had a coin to flip, young Uzee hid a stone in one hand, placed his hands behind his back, and then brought his fists out crossed one over the other. Dale said, "You pick." I chose the right hand, and Uzee opened his fist to reveal the stone.

Now that we had the shooter question settled, the next question was how best to reach the ibex, some four hundred yards away. To Dale and me it seemed a simple matter. To our right was a small hill at the base of the bowl; it would serve as perfect cover. After a short climb to the top I would peep over the rounded crest for an easy two hundred-yard shot. In twenty minutes it would all be over, and everyone would be shaking hands. It was going to be a piece of cake. I was already planning where the mounted head would hang on the wall at home. But Uzee smiled and shook his head, then pointed up the mountain toward the high peaks, enveloped in white, misty clouds.

"What we will do," he interpreted, "is climb to the top of the mountain."

"*What?*"

I had to ask again, because I was certain I had heard wrong. I hadn't.

The Mongols' plan was to circle to the left of the bowl, getting out of sight of the ibex, and to climb the backside of the mountain to the very tip-top. And when they said the top of the mountain, they meant *the top of the mountain*. It took a good two hours and a lot of sweating and huffing (and even a good bit of cursing) to reach the summit, some 12,000 feet in elevation. But we made it to the top, high above the bowl that held the ibex. Or *had held the ibex*, if you were thinking negatively, for I seriously doubted we would ever see those four animals again. We had climbed some two thousand feet above them, and though we had tried our best to be quiet, there was no denying that a number of kicked and sliding rocks had rattled our ears like cannon going off, announcing our presence to all the mountain's inhabitants.

Once at the summit we hunkered just below the rocky peak, where we were literally in the clouds, the great white wisps embracing us like a low-lying fog. Because of the clouds we could see nothing below us, neither on our side of the mountain nor on the bowl side, and there was nothing to do but to wait the weather out. Squatting there in the jumble of boulders, I was light-headed from the altitude and the heart-pounding climb, not to mention the excitement of the hunt, all of which only served to enhance the surreal feeling created by the sight of the swirling, enveloping clouds, which shielded everything from view except for the crouching fellow next to me and the boulders within arm's reach. I felt as if we were all floating in the sky, and we looked like ghosts. It was one of those weirdly mystical feelings that come only a few times in a person's life. Maybe it's what a first-time pilot feels.

When the sky finally cleared, Erka peeked over the craggy ridge and to my utter amazement happily reported that the four ibex were bedded below. I couldn't believe it! I had figured that the noise of us clambering up the mountain had scared them away, or that enough time had elapsed for the billies to wander off. Consequently, during the climb I had half believed we were on a wild goose chase, and I didn't take it as seriously as I should have. As it turned out, the Mongols' plan had been nothing short of brilliant. It had taken the wind and the animals' daily habits into consideration. As our guides knew their prey would, the ibex had fed up the mountain, up the bowl, with the wind at their tails. They were now high above where we had first seen them. Had we followed our instincts, Dale and I would have peeked over our little hill to find the ibex on the move and far out of range, or worse, not there at all. The scent carried by the wind at our backs would likely have spooked them to kingdom come. It was a good lesson in ibex hunting and a reminder why a good guide is worth every bit you pay him.

Dashka shows off a marmot taken by a local. This will be either lunch or dinner.

Our nightly ritual—calling home on the satellite phone.

The plan now, detailed in hushed voices, was for Erka and me to venture out alone and sneak down to our quarry. I left my daypack— something I am loath to do, forsaking my survival gear—taking only my coat and rifle. That is usually the time you end up needing it. "We aren't going far, just over there" are famous last words.

A rocky ridge ran down the side of the bowl separating an adjacent but narrower bowl. Using this ridge for cover, we began our descent out of sight of the ibex in the narrow bowl, which was filled with a slide of rocks, all covered with lichen the dark-orange color of a stale tangerine. The lichen gave the top half of the bowl that new-rust color that comes from metal left accidentally overnight in the rain. The hardest part of the descent was trying to be quiet and not slide on the loose stones or trip over any to go crashing downward. Accordingly we took it slow, choosing our footholds, with Erka stopping now and then to peek below. But for all his searching Erka could not locate the ibex, and I worried they had moved off. Finally we got to an opening in the crags of the ridge that offered a better view, and he spotted the ibex bedded below us—four in a row.

Moving slowly and deliberately, we crept forward and huddled at the base of the opening in the rocks. Erka studied them again with his binocular, but there was no need. Even with the naked eye I could tell which was the biggest. Erka then held up four fingers of his left hand, very careful to make sure that I understood which ibex to shoot, that it was number two from the left, number three from the right. Evidently there had been a mistake or two made in the past, and he had learned from it. My guide removed his coat and motioned for me to do the same. He laid our rolled-up coats on a flat rock for a rest, and I peered through the scope at the recumbent billies some 150 yards away.

Just as I got set to shoot, Erka noticed a rock in the field of fire. He had me lean to my right to avoid it, and now I was not quite as steady as before—but there was more going on than just the awkward angle. Erka noticed and coached me to take a couple of deep breaths. I did. I guess I was breathing even more heavily than I thought. Then pushing in close to me, he offered his shoulder as a rest for my right elbow, showing good judgment on his part and an understanding of shooting fundamentals that many locals lack. The ibex was lying broadside with the legs tucked under its body, facing to the right, so that I could see only the top half of its body—the rest was hidden behind the rocks. It wasn't the best setup for a shot and I hesitated, but short of waiting for them to stand there wasn't much choice. We might have made a noise and spooked them into standing, but that was just as likely to scare them into a mad dash.

I placed the cross hairs above the intervening rocks, on the slim margin of hair, squeezed the trigger, and—*pow!* All four rams jumped to their feet, alert, and stood there bewildered and looking for the source of the threat. But none of them were more bewildered than I, because I had missed entirely! My bullet had apparently gone high, which in hindsight was not surprising given the downhill grade, something I had forgotten to compensate for. As I chambered another round the ibex ran to the right and Erka gestured number one, but I couldn't find it in the scope. The magnification was too high. I dropped it to 3½, the lowest setting, and now easily picked up the ibex and fired as it went running up the far slope. I missed, but fortunately the shot turned them back toward us and down the slope, and I fired again. They finally came to a stop in the exact spot where they had earlier bedded, unaware where the shots were coming from and casting their sharp eyes about. But before I could get my gun reloaded the four ibex trotted to the left, disappearing over the ridge we had used for cover.

At this point the hunt should have been over. Either the ibex should have been mine or it should be gone. Erka and I hustled down the steep ridge, with me cursing my poor shooting, until we came to a gap that allowed us to view the other side. Luckily the billies had turned and run up the mountain, not down. If they had run down they would have quickly gotten out of range. Likewise, if they had continued their course to the next bowl, they would have been safe and away. But luck was on our side. I threw my rifle over a rock for a rest, and as the ibex came by us it suddenly stopped broadside, one hundred yards away—you couldn't have asked for a better presentation.

I put the cross hairs on its shoulder, determined not to make a mess of this "gift." Collapsing at the shot, the ibex kicked a couple of times, then slid forty or fifty yards in the loose, tangerine-colored rocks and was still. The other three ibex ran on up toward the top of the mountain where the rest of our party were waiting. Despite some disappointment because of my earlier shooting, I was elated. I was also glad not to have botched it, dragging Dale to the top of the mountain for naught. Unbeknownst to me Dale and the others had watched the first three shots from above, but they couldn't see over the ridge to where the battle had ended with shot number four.

Glancing skyward, Erka and I thanked the ibex gods and shouted out in exuberance, in triumph at our accomplishment. We shook hands again and again and slapped each other on the shoulders and marveled at the trophy lying at our feet. It hadn't taken many days to find it, but I certainly felt we had earned it. Our comrades came scuttling down the slope, eager to see the ibex. Its salt-and-pepper hide was colored to blend with the grays and browns and blacks of its home, and it had a tuft of hair at the end of its chin like its relative the goat. The legs of the ibex are short but powerful, its trunk the size of a mule deer's. The dark, ribbed horns sweep back in an impressive arc and are generous in length, appearing too big for the body. It is as if they were made for an animal much larger, as if God had made a mistake, shortchanging another critter like the nilgai of its due. We posed the heavyset billy on a flat boulder and took plenty of pictures. I even marked the spot on my GPS for posterity.

After caping the head and taking both hams for meat, Erka did something that I had never witnessed in the field dressing of an animal—even in Africa, where every part of the animal is used. Erka borrowed my empty water bottle to collect the blood from the chest cavity—for what I had no clue, though Uzee claimed it was to be used as medicine. Ingeniously, Erka then cut a strip of the stout leather hide and tied each end to a ham so that the heavy load could be carried slung over the shoulder or around the neck. Jagar proceeded to load

Jagar overlooking the valley below as the clouds begin to descend upon us.

up everything—the hams, ibex head and cape, and the bottle of blood—refusing to let me help, and we said our good-byes to Dale and the rest, wishing them luck.

On the way down the mountain we happened upon a young Mongol riding his pony up the valley to check on his herd of sheep. Jagar enlisted his help and slung the hams over the pony's saddle. We followed the pony down to the parked car at the base of the mountain. I had no wallet with me or anything else of value to give him for his helpful assistance, though he had certainly neither asked nor appeared to expect payment of any kind. But after help like that I felt in his debt, so Jagar gave him a cigarette and I a pack of Juicy Fruit gum.

About 5:00 P.M. we caught sight of Dale and his crew descending a ravine at the base of the mountain, and we drove over to collect them. It turned out that he'd had quite a day. During their hike across a steep slope, a red fox had jumped up in front of them, at which point Erka and Dashka began yelling, "Chute! Chute!" Dale plunked down his fanny, threw his gun up, and shot at the running blur of a fox, which was dashing here and there in the rocks, two hundred yards away. The gods must have been smiling on my good friend, for he killed the fox dead with a shot to the head. The guides were ecstatic, suddenly jumping up and down, and they began punching Dale on the arm and yelling at him. At first he thought he had dome something wrong, that he had shot the wrong animal, so hard were the punches to his arm and the forcefulness of their shouts, but it turned out to be the Mongol way of expressing praise.

"In Mongolia," Uzee explained, "to see a fox while on a hunt is bad luck. Very bad luck. Unless you kill it. You are a hero, Dale. These guides will do anything for you now. You have saved the hunt!"

Later, after miles of hiking up and down the peaks, they came upon a monster ibex high on the slopes above them, some six hundred yards in the distance. But the ibex had seen them and was soon climbing away. Normally you would pass at a shot that far, but the billy was so big that the guides encouraged Dale to try. He took a couple of Hail Mary shots but did not hit it. They continued the hunt on other slopes and bowls, up and down mountains, running out of water in the process, and were really beat when we picked them up. It's easy to dehydrate fast in this dry air, and they now chugged at the extra water bottles in the 4x4. Their plan was to return tomorrow to look for that same fellow but with double the water supply.

Dawn brought our coldest morning yet, and the wind was blowing hard. Lucky for me, I got to stay and indulge my journal while Dale

This rocky ridge, separating one bowl from the next, provided excellent cover for the stalk.

A couple of proud hunters: Erka and me.

was destined to pound the mountains and valleys. I rose to a leisurely breakfast, then took a walk around the area, later bringing a chair outside and taking advantage of the sun, which poked out in midday. With a long wooden pole one of the lady cooks peeled back the dual cloth flaps at the teepee top of our *ger,* allowing fresh air to circulate.

One of the most surprising things to me is that there was not a single tree, living or dead, in the whole region. In fact, there was not a bush higher than your shinbone anywhere. There was no grass in the valleys—the flocks of goats, sheep, and yaks had grazed it bare. High in the mountains, where the domestic stock can't reach, there is short, thin-stemmed grass in fair abundance, but it was dead and brown, and less nutritious than in its green state. The growing season there must be quite short, not more than a couple of months, I suspect. Surprisingly, the land, in topography, resembles the area around Iliamna, Alaska, except that Alaska is cold and wet and here it is cold and dry. One has muskeg and tundra, the other sand and rocks, but given a change in rainfall they could swap places.

The location of the camp was determined, I'm sure, by the location of the stove fuel—yak and sheep dung. There is absolutely nothing else to burn for miles in any direction. The herdsmen collect the dried, disk-shaped yak dung and stack it in tall piles beside their *gers* the way we at home stack firewood. Thus we are camped in the middle of a valley surrounded by three or four *gers* that house Mongol families which subsist solely on their herds of yak, sheep, and goats, plus the few marmots they shoot in the hills with the *.22* rifles they are allowed to own. A shallow stream provides the other necessity.

On foot the Mongol children drive the noisy herds up into the hills at dawn to feed. I was still snuggled in my warm goose-down bag when the yaks passed through camp early this morning. The shaggy-coated animals do not *moo* like cattle. The deep guttural grunts they make reminded me of the grunts you hear at night or upon waking in Africa, the grunts that come from a nearby pond full of hippos. The two sounds are remarkably similar, and with eyes closed and ignoring the temperature you could easily be confused about which country you were waking in.

Lunch was a real treat: ibex steaks, sliced in thin, quarter-inch medallions, and topped with light brown gravy. It was marvelous, very tender and tasty. I could eat it every day, whereas the domestic meat here was truly awful. The Mongols enjoy mutton the way we enjoy beef. It was ironic that the wild game meat was tender and tasty, while the domestic mutton had a musky, gamy taste. I had already lost weight, unwilling to choke down the rank, greasy meat. But it gave me a great idea for the next weight loss fad at home: the Mutton Diet—eat as much as you want, whenever you want.

As I sat in front of my *ger*, soaking up the rare sun, I noticed that one of the four local families was in the process of dismantling their *ger* for a move to lower, warmer country in preparation for winter. While Mom and Dad were busy sorting and packing the contents of the dismantled *ger*, a small child of five was given charge of several camels. The stubborn animals would not stay put for him, and the little child, who was absolutely dwarfed in size by the huge beasts—his head did not even reach their stomachs—went running and yelling after them, trying to herd them back. When a small switch failed to produce results, he picked up stones to throw at them. The camels continued to plod along, while the child was having to run all out just to keep up, his little legs a blur. But if anything the tot was persistent, and finally, after much yelling, stone throwing, and switching, the large animals submitted to his coaxing. It was hard to believe, but the young Mongol had mastered the giant beasts. Perhaps I was looking at a direct descendant of the great Khan.

As encouraging as this young boy's skills were, the sight made me wonder at the infant mortality rate here. The locals had two or three children each, not the ten or twelve you might expect of a nomadic, agrarian people. In farming communities children are workers, especially when there are no schools to distract them. More children equals more workers, their only cost being food and shelter. Even now, I can arrive at no other explanation than high mortality.

Speaking of kids, while sorting out my gear I found two more hidden notes written by my daughter Lauren, and they made my day. One read: "I love you. You're the best Dad." The other: "Love you, Dad, Lauren." Both were in her handwriting, and pretty good for a five-year-old.

It was after 6:00 P.M. and nearly dark when Dale got in. As the car neared I could see him in the passenger seat resting his head on his hand and looking as though depressed or in pain. As he climbed slowly out, I said, "What's wrong? Did you get hurt?"

"No, I'm just bushed and beat," he answered. "We must have hiked twenty miles!" Then he told me that he had run into Dick Cabela, who with his brother has created a little piece of heaven for hunters and fisherman in the form of the best sporting goods company in the world. Dick and his wife are members with Dale and me of a small, fifty-year-old hunting club, so Dale and I knew Dick, but it was surprising running into somebody we knew out in the middle of nowhere. And we were out in the middle of nowhere. You couldn't get more out in the middle of nowhere if you tried.

"So, you didn't get an ibex?" I asked.

"No," he replied. "I didn't get an ibex." There was silence. Even the guides just stood there staring blankly. It made me wonder if there was something he wasn't telling me, some bit of misfortune too bad to speak of, something that had driven an unbridgeable wedge between them. Then Dale broke into a great big grin and blurted out, "I got two!" The whole group exploded into laughter and celebration. And what fine ibex they were, at 43 and 45 inches, and done with three shots in total!

Once in our *ger*, however, Dale's face went a sickly gray. He flopped down on his bunk, grabbed his stomach, and began to moan.

"What the hell's happened to you?" I asked.

He groaned some more before the reason came out.

"It was awful, Johnny. Not the hunt—" he had read my face—"the hunt was great. It was all the celebrating afterward. We must have stopped at twenty different *gers* to celebrate." Apparently, all the celebrations were the same. Each consisted of consuming yak milk, yak cheese, and copious amounts of vodka. In each *ger* the same custom was followed: men entered to the left, women to the right. As the guest of honor, Dale was given the largest stool at the center of the small table. Bowls of steaming yak milk were passed around the circle, chunks of dried yak cheese were handed out, and lastly a bowl of vodka made the circuit. The tradition before drinking the vodka is to hold the bowl in your left hand, dip the tip of the right ring finger into the clear spirits, fling a drop to the sky, then one to the left and right, then lastly to dot your forehead. It symbolizes the sky, the wind, the earth, and the mind. If, like Jagar, you do not drink alcohol, instead of touching your forehead you touch your heart and pass the bowl to the next.

"If you think the yak yogurt is bad—you haven't tried anything until you try the yak cheese. Honest to God, Johnny, it was the worst thing I ever tasted in my life!"

It was now clear to us why yaks are exclusive to this part of the world and why they do not exist in ours: the milk tastes rancid, the yogurt disgusting, and the cheese hideous—a small nibble is enough to bring on a gag reflex. Yaks exist here only because they can withstand extreme cold that our cattle could not. Dale was feeling sick from slurping yak milk and nibbling yak cheese, all of which had churned

The whole crew pose: Uzee, Dashka, Erka, Jagar, and me.

unpleasantly with the vodka in his stomach. He lay there and continued to rub his belly.

After a half-hour or so Dale felt somewhat better, and we joined in the big celebration in camp. An invitation had been made to join the guides in their *ger* for dinner. There a bottle of the vodka we had brought for just such an occasion was joyfully passed around, and the volume of the voices went up a few decibels in the enclosed space. Nothing melds the spirits of people from vastly different cultures like the taking of a difficult trophy and the consumption of large quantities of alcohol. In doing so, you become buddies for life. Comrades forever. At least until the next morning, when the alcohol wears off. Dashka hugged Dale. I hugged Erka. They spoke no English. We spoke no Mongolian. We were blood brothers.

Dale went to bed early, his stomach churning. I remained a while to watch the guides and cooks play a lively card game called *Moshik*, not quite ever understanding the rules. A local nomad participated in the game, and they were all quite passionate about winning or losing, slapping cards down and bantering loudly back and forth. It seemed less a card game than a shouting match in which the loudest player won.

Despite our late celebration the hunt continued first thing the next morning, though not at the crack of dawn. After a late breakfast, we departed for the Gobi Desert so Dale could try for a blacktail gazelle. Per GPS, our farthest point from camp, as the crow flies, was only forty-five miles. The elevation dropped significantly, though, as we left the rolling mountains for the flat pan of the desert floor, and there was not a single blade of grass or other vegetation in sight. The ground was mostly sand with dark pebbly rocks coating the surface. Now and then a cluster of small sand dunes, no more than hip high, rose to break the level surface, and in the distance the surrounding mountains were an ugly black, creating a desolate feeling. The place was a wasteland, and it was a marvel that any life form could survive.

For several reasons, I had declined to hunt the gazelle. The first reason was the method. The gazelle is chased in a car until it stops from exhaustion, at which point you jump out and shoot it. Second, my dad had hunted one that way years before and, experiencing regrets, told me he wouldn't do it again, and that he would pass on it if he were I. Third, in high school I had read about the fleet-footed gazelle, how they could reach sixty miles per hour and sustain that speed for some time. The Mongolian gazelle is the long-distance runner of the animal world. In track, my best friend and I used to joke that we were

A couple of happy ibex hunters show off their trophies.

Mongolian gazelles when running together. They were our mascot, so to speak. I couldn't bring myself to hunt them.

Dale was interested in the gazelle solely as a species collection. He did not condone the method any more than I did, but he accepted it in the spirit of "When in Rome . . ." In the open, flat country, there was no other way to approach them.

We covered a lot of country, country that allowed you to see for miles in any direction. During our journey we saw seventeen females but only one small male. That was all. So Dale did not get a chance to collect a gazelle.

On the return to camp, as we neared the outer edge of the Gobi, we stopped at the *ger* where Erka's mother and father lived. We were immediately invited inside, stooping through the squat wooden door, the men entering to the left and taking seats inside the humble shelter. The floor of the *ger* was covered in rough mats, and pictures of family, Mongolian trinkets, and religious emblems hung on the cloth-wrapped walls. Erka's mother shuffled about to make her guests welcome in their tiny home, where bedroom, living room, and kitchen were all one. The old woman looked ancient. She was missing most of her teeth and had more wrinkles in her face than her age could have warranted. Dressed in the pants and baggy shirt of a nomad, she was stooped sharply at the waist and limped badly on widely bowed legs. There was no doubt that every step for her was the source of pain, but her ailments didn't slow her down in attending to her guests with bowls of warm yak milk. Her bowed legs reminded me of my grandmother Irene's legs before she got knee replacements. It is a hard life the Mongols live.

Finally we made our escape, not from the people but from their foodstuffs, happy that the yellow slabs of yak cheese aging on the sloped roof had remained forgotten. We climbed into the car. The family reunion tour continued, however, with a stop at Erka's brother's *ger*, also on the edge of the Gobi. This time we remained in the car, fearful of more yak products—but also with an eye on the big, barking dog out front. It was the same intimidating kind of dog that every Mongol family owns for protection. The dogs are similar to a chow in build, with the same thick fur, but they are larger in body. When approaching a *ger*, the custom is to say, "Please hold your vicious dog." As Dashka made that statement, four tiny children, the eldest no more than four, fell all over the big, black dog. The big dog could easily have dragged the four keepers with it, but it stayed put and neither growled nor showed any aggression toward the toddlers now clasping its fur, ears, and neck—the mark of a good dog. I had only one piece of gum left, so I tore it into four equal pieces and gave one morsel to each child. One tot, apparently suffering from a bad cold, had snot running down his face, chin, and neck, but no one bothered to wipe it away.

We arrived late in camp, tired from the long, dusty drive. The next morning I figured it was my turn to take fire detail, since Dale had done it previously. So at first light I crawled out of my warm bag and into the cold of my clothes, only to find that our fuel box was empty of dung. While stepping out to brush my teeth, I flagged down the lady cook to tell her of our predicament. Apparently the hand signals worked, for not a minute later she brought in a nice big box full and soon got the fire going and the *ger* toasty.

We were soon packing our gear for the return to Khovd, leaving as much behind as possible—old hats, power bars, batteries, and so forth, to cut down on weight for the trip home. We also worked out what the tips should be for the guides and staff, though we would not give them out until the morning of our departure.

At lunch the staff set up a table outside—taking advantage of the mild, sunny weather—and laid out a big feast. The main course was a big bowl of boiled mutton. (Secretly I had hoped for some more grilled ibex, but that was not to be.) Mixed into the greasy mess were hot black stones that everyone fished out and juggled in their hands, as was the custom. Once your hands were warm (and suitably coated with mutton grease), you dropped the smooth stone to the ground, its purpose having been served. Then the mutton itself was plucked out and gnawed off the bone. Not enjoying the handful of grease, I quietly disappeared to the *ger* to wash. I couldn't recall having had mutton in the States, but one whiff of the stuff was enough for me. I stuck to the other dishes, such as potato salad and bread.

A local nomad and his wife joined in the feast, and through Uzee we questioned each other on our respective ways of life, each of us nodding our heads as if we understood the life of the other completely but knowing deep down we had not a clue. I'm sure that each of us felt with total conviction that he had the best of all lives in this world, and that the other must be miserable in his, so different were our worlds. I could not imagine a world without modern medicine and technology, and the nomads I'm sure could not imagine a developed, paved-over world without their camels. When we expressed curiosity about the latter, the nomads offered to let us ride the large, interesting beasts.

An outdoor picnic was in order for this mild, sunny day. Joining us is a Mongol nomad couple outfitted in their finest.

243

Dale shows off his equestrian skills.

Mounting a camel, I found out, is a lot different from mounting a horse. For one thing, a camel is mounted with the animal lying on the ground. Additionally, it is a four-part maneuver for the camel to stand erect, a procedure that is done awkwardly but methodically. Here is what I learned: When you go to mount a camel you had best hold tight to the thick wool of its hump, because its ass end is the first to rise. It will tip you out of the saddle and onto the ground if you aren't careful. Then the forelegs come up and lift the camel to its knees, which tilts you back. Then the rear legs press to full extension, with another precarious toss forward. And finally the front legs come up and level you out. But if the mounting is awkward and unusual, the ride is a pleasant surprise. Once traveling, the camel's gate is unbelievably smooth—unlike the rough chop of a horse—and the large beast positively flows over the sand and rocks. The camel is turned like a horse, except that instead of reins there is a single rope tied to a peg through a sensitive part of the camel's nose. The double humps make for a natural saddle, holding you in place and providing a solid backrest for the lazy traveler. Unlike a horse, however, the camel is haughty in demeanor, in full belief that it is your better in every way. That is evident from your first meeting with the beast, the way the camel looks down its nose at you like an arrogant butler answering the mansion door and finding a tramp.

The next morning we began the long trek home—four days in total. It was quite a haul, but when I thought back to how folks had to travel one, two, or three hundred years ago, I realized how spoiled I was. There was nothing to do but to wait out the flights, one by one, to get home.

In Beijing we arrived to quite a hustle and bustle, with everyone getting ready for the 1 October national holiday and celebration. Tiananmen Square, with Mao Tse-Tung's famous smiling portrait overlooking it, was decorated in a halo of red flags. The capital city itself had surprised me: Although not overly prosperous, it was not the downtrodden third world city I had expected. Unlike eastern Russia, where there had not been a new building or a single crane constructing one in sight, Beijing had many new buildings in progress and old ones under renovation. There were certainly lots of people. At 1.2 billion, they flowed like ants. Getting through cross-streets was a combination of "might makes right," in which the smaller traveler gives way to the larger, and the game of chicken.

Dale wanted to walk around the square, I wanted to find fur hats for my children, and we both wanted to eat—anything American. We decided to do all three, and wandering around the city we soon found in the distance . . . a McDonald's. Perhaps we weren't as far from home as we had thought.